POST-GUPTA DYNASTIES

Encyclopaedic History of India Series

POST-GUPTA DYNASTIES

Dr. Mahesh Vikram Singh
Professor, Deptt. of History
Mahatma Gandhi Kashi Vidyapeeth
Varanasi (UP)

Dr. Brij Bhushan Shrivastava
Head of Deptt., Ancient History, Archeology & Culture
SMMTPG College, Ballia (UP)

CENTRUM PRESS
NEW DELHI-110002 (INDIA)

CENTRUM PRESS
H.O.: 4360/4, Ansari Road, Daryaganj,
New Delhi-110002 (India)
Tel: 23278000, 23261597, 23255577, 23286875
B.O.: No. 1015, Ist Main Road, BSK IIIrd Stage,
IIIrd Phase, IIIrd Block, Bangalore-560085 (INDIA)
Tel: 080-41723429
Email: centrumpress@gmail.com
Visit us at: www.centrumpress.com

Post-Gupta Dynasties

First Edition, 2011

ISBN 978-93-80836-63-8

PRINTED IN INDIA

Printed at Mehra Offset Press, Delhi

प्रो. विपिन चंद्रा
अध्यक्ष
Prof. Bipan Chandra
Chairman

नेशनल बुक ट्रस्ट, इंडिया
नेहरू भवन
5 इंस्टीट्यूशनल एरिया, फेज़-II, वसंत कुंज, नई दिल्ली-110 070
फोन/ Phone: 011-26121880 फैक्स/ Fax: 011-26121883

NATIONAL BOOK TRUST, INDIA
Nehru Bhawan
5 Institutional Area, Phase II, Vasant Kunj, New Delhi-110 070
ई-मेल / E-mail: chairman@nbtindia.org.in
वेबसाइट / Website: www.nbtindia.org.in

FOREWORD

The term 'history' is derived from the Greek word 'historia' that means knowledge acquired through investigation. Obviously, this knowledge can be correct if the method of investigation is objective and not vitiated by any kind of bias. In other words, if the study of human past is comprehensive and obtained through scientific inquiry, it can provide perspective on the present day problems and help one plan for the future.

A true historian has to identify the sources that can be most useful in a given context. Documents, coins, archaeology, anthropology, geography, travel accounts, oral traditions, mythology and so on can be useful but they can be used only after their veracity is tested and they are critically examined. They should be checked and counter-checked.

Over the centuries, one finds the study and writing of history vitiated by biases. There are numerous instances in which historical data have been distorted to support or oppose certain preconceived ideas and purposes. Strictly speaking such history is just like fiction to accord with preconceived notions and serve some ulterior purposes.

The study of the past has never been static. Conclusions go on changing because of the discovery of new materials and tools of investigation. To give a concrete example, the carbon 14 or radiocarbon dating test has revolutionized the study of civilizations and settlements, especially of prehistoric times, for which written documents, coins, etc. are seldom available. This method has enabled historians to determine more accurately than before the time period of a particular civilization or settlement. This method was discovered only 70 years ago by American scientists.

In our country, excavations brought to light the Indus Valley Civilization and its various features, hitherto unknown. Similarly, no complete text of Kautilya's Arthashastra was available before it was discovered by Shamasastry, the chief of the Mysore Government Oriental Library in the first decade of the last century. Likewise, people's knowledge of the history of the Buddhist period got extended after excavations at Sarnath and the ruins of the Asokan period at Patna. In the future, if the Harappan inscriptions are deciphered, our knowledge of the Indus Valley Civilization will increase enormously. All these instances underline the fact that our knowledge of history is never static and its frontiers go on extending.

In the light of what has been said above the encyclopedic history is going to be of great help to students interested in Indian history. It is comprehensive and as far as possible free from biases. It includes the latest materials, and objective conclusions.

Prof . Bipan Chandra
Professor Emeritus, JNU
Chairman, National Book Trust, India

Contents

Preface

The people of India have had a continuous civilization since 2500 B.C., when the inhabitants of the Indus River valley developed an urban culture based on commerce and sustained by agricultural trade. This civilization declined around 1500 B.C., probably due to ecological changes. During the second millennium B.C., pastoral, Aryan-speaking tribes migrated from the northwest into the subcontinent. As they settled in the middle Ganges River valley, they adapted to antecedent cultures.

The political map of ancient and medieval India was made up of myriad kingdoms with fluctuating boundaries. In the 4th and 5th centuries A.D., northern India was unified under the Gupta Dynasty. During this period, known as India's Golden Age, Hindu culture and political administration reached new heights. Islam spread across the Indian subcontinent over a period of 500 years. In the 10th and 11th centuries, Turks and Afghans invaded India and established sultanates in Delhi. In the early 16th century, descendants of Genghis Khan swept across the Khyber Pass and established the Mughal (Mogul) Dynasty, which lasted for 200 years. From the 11th to the 15th centuries, southern India was dominated by Hindu Chola and Vijayanagar Dynasties. During this time, the two systems—the prevailing Hindu and Muslim—mingled, leaving lasting cultural influences on each other.

The first British outpost in South Asia was established in 1619 at Surat on the northwestern coast. Later in the century, the East India Company opened permanent trading stations at Madras, Bombay, and Calcutta, each under the protection of native rulers. The British expanded their influence from these footholds until, by the 1850s, they controlled most of present-day India, Pakistan, and Bangladesh. In 1857, a rebellion in north India led by mutinous Indian soldiers caused the British Parliament to transfer all political power from the East India Company to the Crown. Great Britain began administering most of India directly while controlling the rest through treaties with local rulers.

In the late 1800s, the first steps were taken toward self-government in British India with the appointment of Indian councillors to advise the British viceroy and the establishment of provincial councils with Indian members; the British subsequently widened participation in legislative councils. Beginning in 1920, Indian leader Mohandas K. Gandhi transformed the Indian National Congress political party into a mass movement to campaign against British colonial rule.

—Authors

1

Post-Gupta Kingdoms in North India

In the sixth century A.D. the disintegration of the Gupta empire gradually paved way for the growth of many smaller kingdoms. In certain regions new kingdoms emerged and in other areas the dynasties which had earlier accepted Gupta suzerainty now declared their independence. For example, kings like Yasodharman and political powers like the Maukharis, the Hunas and the later Magadhan Guptas were the new powers. Besides these the Pushyabhutis, the Gaudas, the Varmans and the Maitrakas also grew in importance. This Is an attempt to give a brief sketch of the political history of these kingdoms. It also takes into account certain other aspects like the nature of the administrative system under Harshavardhana of the Pushyabhuti family, political patronage to Buddhism, etc.

The Regional Powers

In the absence of a strong power there emerged quite a number of regional powers in different regions. These powers, representing different dynasties, established their kingdoms and were often at war with each other. Here we briefly mention some of these powers:

Yasodharman

During the reign of Kumaragupta-I his feudatory Bandhuvarman ruled over Mandasor as it was a major Centre of western Malwa. He belonged to the Aulikara family which perhaps ruled there up to the beginning of the sixth century A.D. Two stone pillar inscriptions from I Mandasor in Madhya Pradesh, one of which is dated in 532 A.D., refer to a powerful king Yasodharman. One of these inscriptions reports the victories of Yasodharman. The inscription describes him as the victor of all those lands which had not been subdued even

by the Guptas. But the names of the defeated powers have not been mentioned except that *of* Mihirkula. It appears that Yasodharman rose to power in about 528 A.D. and continued to rule till 532 A.D., (the date of Mandasor inscription) but by 543 A.D. his power must have been eclipsed.

The Maukharis

The Maukharis were an old family as we find references to them in Patanjali's work and in other early documents.

The Maukharis must have started gaining political power towards the end of 5th century A.D. as the Harsha inscription of 554 A.D. mentions the rise of Yajnavarman from Gaya during this period

We also get the names of three Maukhari kings mentioned in the Barabar and Nagarjuni inscriptions who ruled in Gaya, about 150 years earlier then their successors at Kanauj. The tirst three Maukhari kings are Yagnavarman, Sardulavarman and Anantavarman. Some of these kings held simply the title of Samanta which indicates that they were acting as kings under the over-lordship of the Guptas.

From the Asirgarh Copper seal we get the names of (1) Harivarman, (2) Adityavarman, (3) Isvaravarman, (4) Isanavarman, (5) Sarvavarman, who had ruled over Kanauj in U.P. The first three kings had the title of Maharaja whereas Isanavarman is called Maharajadhiraja.

It was perhaps Isanavarman who set up an independent kingdom. The early Maukhari kings had established family ties with the later Guptas. However. Isanavannan's declaration of his independence must have spoilt the relations between the later Guptas and the Maukharis for the Apshad inscription tells us of the victory of Kumaragupta the fourth king of the Later Gupta family of Magdha, over Isanavannan. But the dynasty seems to have continued its rule.

Sarvavarman, the second son of Isanavannan, was successful in retrieving the lost prestige of the Maukharis by defeating

Damodaragupta of the Later Gupta dynasty. The last of the Maukhari kings was Grahavannan who was married to Rajyasri. the daughter of Prabhakaravardhan of Thaneshwar and sister of the famous ruler Hạrshavardhana. The Malava king Devagupta attacked Kanauj and killed Grahvarman bringing the Maukhari kingdom to an end. The Maukharis held sway over modem U.P. and parts of Magadha. However, the innumerable wars which they lost and won kept changing their ḅoundaries.

The Later Guptas

From around the middle of sixth century A.D. till about 675 A.D. the kings who ruled Magadha were known as Magadha Guptas or Later Guptas. However, it is not clear what connection they had with the Imperial Guptas of the earlier period.

The Aphsad inscription from Gaya gives the names of 8 Gupta Monarchs:

(1) Krishnagupta
(2) Harshagupta
(3) Jivitagupta
(4) Kumaragupta
(5) Damodaragupta
(6) Mahasenagupta,
(7) Madhavagupta and
(8) Adityasena.

The Later Guptas entered into matrimonial alliances with other contemporary ruling families. For example. Harshagupta married his sister to a Maukhari king. Throughout this period the Later Giiptas remained engaged in battle with one enemy or the other. For esample, Harshagupta had to fight the tlunas; his son Jivitagupta tought against Lichchhavis of Nepal and Gaudas of Bengal: and Jivitlgupta's wccessor king Kumaragupta defeated Maukhari King Isanarvarman.

The next king Damodaragupta, son of Kumaragupta, was defeated and killed by Maukhari king Sarvavarman and lost a portion of Magadha. For some time the successors of Damodaragupta retreated to Malwa because of the Maukharis but they again established their supremacy in Magadha. Their most powerful ruler was Adityasena, who ruled in Magadha in 672 A.D., a date which seems to occur in one of his inscriptions. The Later Gupta power survived the empire of Harshavardhana and Adityasena signalised his accession to power by the performance of a horse sacrifice. According to the Aphsad inscription, his empire included Magadha, Anga and Bengal. It is just possible that his kingdom included a portion of eastern Uttar Pradesh.

He was a Parama-Bhagavata and got a temple of Vishnu constructed. The Later Gupta line came to an end with the expansion of the power of the Gaudas of Bengal westward. But the Gaudas themselves were subdued by Yasovarman of Kanauj. Besides the abovementioned dynastic powers the other important states that emerged in the post-Gupta period were those of the:

- Maitras of Valabhi in Gujarat
- Gurjaras in Rajputana and Gujarat
- Gaudas in Bengal
- Varmans in Kamrup (Assam)
- Mana and Sailodbhava families in Orissa.

The Maitraka kings of Valabhi had initially been under the overlordship of the Imperial Guptas and they gradually established their own supremacy. The founder of the Gurjara kingdom was Harichandra whose three successors ruled till about 640 A..D. Gauda. the region of north and north-west of Bengal was ruled by Sasanka, a contemporary and arch-rival of Harshavardhana, as an independent kingdom in the early seventh century A.D.

The Prayagaprasasti recording the achievements of the Gupta ruler Samudragupta refers to two kingdoms in Assam : Kamarupa and Davaka. Kamarupa became an important political region in north-eastern India from the middle of the fourth century A.D. Pushyavarman probably founded, around this date, the first historical royal family of Assam. This family ruled for twelve generations till the time of Bhaskaravarman who was a contemporary and an ally of Harshavardhana of Kanauj and ruled in the first half of the seventh century A.D. Although there is evidence that some local rulers of Orissa owed allegiance to Imperial Gupta rulers towards the end of Gupta rule, two autonomous kingdoms emerged in Orissa in the second half of the sixth century A.D. One was the Mana kingdom which extended from Balasore to Puri district and the other was the kingdom of the Sailodbhavas of Kongoda, which extended from ~h'ilka lake to Mahendragiri mountains in Ganjam district. Both kingdoms suffered setbacks because of the rise of Sasanka of Bengal and Harshavardhana of Kanauj.

The Pushyabhutis of Thaneshwar and Kanauj

A variety of sources inform us about the rise of the family of Pushyabhutis which first ruled from Thaneshwar in Haryana and later from Kanauj in Uttar Pradesh. These sources include the text Harshacharita of Banabhatta, accounts of Hiuen-tsang and some inscriptions and coins etc. Banabhatta informs us that the founder king of this dynasty at Thaneshwar was Pushyabhuti and that the family was known as Pushyabhuti vamsa. However, the inscriptions of Harsha make no reference to him. The Banskhera and Madhuvan plates and royal seals mention five earlier rulers among whom the first three are given the title of Maharaja. This may indicate that they were not sovereign monarchs. The fourth king Prabhakarvardhana has been described as a Maharajadhiraja which makes us infer that he was an independent monarch and had established matrimonial relations with the Maukharis by marrying his daughter Rajyasri with Grahavarman.

Thaneshwar, during this time (about 604 A.D.) was threatened by the Hunas from the western side. Banabhatta has described Prabhakarvardhana as "a lion to the Huna deer". According to him an army under Rajyavardhana was sent to defeat the Hunas but due to the sudden illness of his father he had to come back. With Prabhakarvardhana's death the family had to face troubled times for a while. The Malava king killed Gra!avarman and took, Rajyasri prisoner. It appears that the Malava and the Gauda kings entered into alliance and even Thaneshwar was threatened. Rajyavardhana defeated the Malavas but was killed through treachery by Sasanka, the Gauda king. Now it was Harsha's responsibility to seek revenge and in due course he was able to establish a strong empire.

Vardhan Dynasty (550-647)

After the downfall of the Gupta Empire in the middle of the sixth century CE, North India was split into several independent kingdoms. The Huns had established their supremacy over the

Punjab and parts of central India. The northern and western regions of India passed into the hands of a dozen or more feudatory states.

Prabhakar Vardhan

Prabhakar Vardhan, the ruler of Thanesar, who belonged to the Bains or Virk family, extended his control over all other feudatories. Prabhakar Vardhan had two sons-Rajya Vardhan and Harshavardhan and one daughter-Rajyasri.

Prabhakar Vardhan was the first king of the Bains or Virk clan with his capital at Thanesar. Thanesar is now a small town in the vicinity of Kurukshetra in the state of Haryana near Delhi.

[Note: As per Bana's harshacharita and Harsha's inscriptional records we have the founder as Pushpabhuti followed by Naravardhana= wife Vajrinidevi, Rajyavardhana-I=wife Apsarodevi, Adityavardhana= wife Mahasenaguptadevi, Prabhakaravardhana=wife Yashomatidevi, Rajyavardhana-IIand Harshavardhana.

There is no question of calling any of these kings as Virk. Even their Malava connection is unproved. The Pushpabhutis appear to have ruled as feudataries of the Guptas to begin with. They must have had to work under the Hunas for some time and must have filled the gap in the Thanesar region to begin with on the decline of the gupta supremacy and demise of the Huna rule.

Rajya Vardhan

After Prabhakar Vardhan's death in 606 AD, his eldest son, Rajya Vardhan, ascended the throne. Harsha Vardhana was Rajyavardhan's younger brother.On getting the news that Devagupta, the king of Malawa, combining with the Gauda king Shashanka had attacked and killed the Maukhari ruler Grahavarman, the husband of her sister, Rajyashri Rajyavardhana immediately left thanesar for Kannauj.

In a war with the above enemies he defeated Devagupta. But by a combined statagem of the two he was invited to their camp for an agrement and was instead put to sword unaware. The above incident related by Banabhatta in his Harshacharita is testified by the Banskheda and Madhuban Copper Plate Inscriptions of Harshavardhana. Rajyavardhana is described as paramsaugata in the above inscriptions.

Harsha-Vardhan (606-647)

Harsha or Harshavardhana or "Harsha vardhan" (590–647) was an Indian (Hindu in earlier life, became a Buddhist later) emperor who ruled Northern India for forty one years. He was the son of Prabhakar Vardhan and younger brother of Rajyavardhan, a king of Thanesar. At the height of his power his kingdom spanned the Punjab, Gujarat, Bengal, Orissa and the entire Indo-Gangetic plain North of the Narmada River. After the downfall of the Gupta Empire in the middle of the sixth century C.E., North India reverted to small republics and small monarchical states. Harsha united the small republics from Punjab to Central India, and they, at an assembly, crowned Harsha king in April 606 AD when he was merely 16 years old.

Harshavardhana's Ancestors

The origin of Harsha's ancestors is obscure and little is known about them. For a detailed analysis of Harsha's Virk origins, an excellent argument is provided by Bhim Singh Dahiya-an excerpt is available online. According to Banabhatta's *Harshaæárita* they were descended from a certain *Pushpabhuti* who founded and ruled the kingdom of *Sthanvisvara* or modern Thanesar, an ancient Hindu pilgrimage centre and one of the 51 Shaktipeeth's, now a small town in the vicinity of the newly created Kurukshetra in the state of Haryana north of Delhi. The name Pushpabhuti is the key to Harsha's origins and the relevant reference point is an inscription dated 181 AD and found at Gunda in the state of Gujarat. That inscription mentions a general of Rudrasimha I or Rudrasingh by the name Rudrabhuti. Rudradaman I, an ancestor of Rudrasimha I had conquered the Yaudheya, who were the original masters of Haryana.

The famous Chinese Buddhist pilgrim monk, Xuanzang, states that Harsha was a 'T, *feishe* or of the Vaishya caste but makes no comment about his family's origins.

According to Alexander Cunningham, in 1871 Xuanzang must have mistaken the *Vaisa* for Bais Rajput. Thomas Watters has pointed out this is most unlikely as Xuanzang, "had ample opportunities for learning the antecedents of the royal family, and he must have had some ground for his assertion." However, Banabhatta clarifies that the *Bais Rajput* descent must have been correct considering the *Harshacarita* the author Bana never stated his background to be strangely non Kshatriya. Harsha's Royal descent being known (rulers of Sthanvisvara, modern Thanesar) and his sister being married into prominent Kshatriya families of Maukharis. (a highly contentious occurrence, had Harsha's family not been of royal or Kshatriya descent).

Moreover, upon his formal coronation ceremony, Harsha took the title *Rajputra.*

Pre Harsha Vardhan Rule

After the downfall of the Gupta Empire in the middle of the sixth century CE, North India was split into several independent kingdoms. The Huns had established their supremacy over the Punjab and parts of central India. The northern and western regions of India passed into the hands of a dozen or more feudatory states.

Prabhakar Vardhan, the ruler of Sthanvisvara, who belonged to the Pushyabhuti family, extended his control over neighbouring states. Prabhakar Vardhan was the first king of the Vardhana dynasty with his capital at Thaneswar.

After Prabhakar Vardhan's death in 606 CE, his eldest son, Rajya Vardhan, ascended the throne. Harsha Vardhana was Rajya Vardhan's younger brother.

This period of kings from the same line has been referred to as the Vardhan dynasty for distinction purposes in some publications, though the dynasty was not necessarily known as the Vardhan dynasty in its era.

Harsha's Ascension

Rajya Vardhan's and Harsha's sister Rajyasri had been married to the Maukhari king, Grahavarman. This king, some years later, had been defeated and killed by king Deva Gupta of Malwa and after his death Rajyasri had been cast into prison by the victor. Harsha's brother, Rajya Vardhan, then the king at Thanesar, could not stand this affront on his family, marched against Deva Gupta and defeated him. But it so happened at this moment that Sasanka, king of Gauda in Eastern Bengal, entered Magadha as a friend of Rajya Vardhana, but in secret alliance with the Malwa king. Accordingly, Sasanka treacherously murdered Rajya Vardhan.

On hearing about the murder of his brother, Harsha resolved at once to march against the treacherous king of Gauda and killed Deva Gupta in a battle. Harsha ascended the throne at the age of 16.

Harsha ascended the throne of Thaneshwar around 606 A.D. and immediately marched against the Gaudas. He also entered into an alliance with Bhaskarvarman-the king of Pragjyaotisha (Assam) as both had a common enemy in Sasanka, the king of Gauda (Bengal). We have no information whether Harsha entered into battle with Sasanka but he was able to save his sister Rajyasri and the kingdoms of Thaneshwar and Kanauj were combined with Harsha now ruling from Kanauj. In fact Hiuen-tsang's account mentions him and his predecessors as rulers of Kanauj. Both Bana and Hiuen-tsang refer to Harsha's vow of defeating other kings. Subsequently, he fought the rulers of Valabhi and Gurjaras in the west; Chalukyas in the Deccan; and Magadha and Gauda in the east:

The Maitrakas of Valabhi had emerged as a strong power in the Saurashm region of Gujarat. Valabhi is generally identified with Wala, 18 miles from Bhavnagar in Kathiawar. We find the names of five Valabhi kings who were contemporaries of Harsha. Hiuen-tsang has mentioned the Valabhi king Dhruvasena I1 Baladitya as Harsha's son-in-law who also attended the religious assembly called by Harsha at Prayaga. This indicates that Harsha's hostilities with Valabhis ended through a matrimonial alliance: However, through the inscriptions of Gurjara kings we know that their king Dadda 11, had supported the Valabhis. The Valabhis remained a strong power during the reign of Harsha.

From Bana's account we know that the Gurjaras were hostile to the Vardhanas. A family of Gurjara rulers was ruling at Nandipuri in the Broach region of Gujarat in this

period. This might have continued during the period of Harsha. It appears that the Gurjaras accepted the suzerainty of Chalukyas of Badami in Karnataka as a safeguard against Harsha, for the Aihole inscription mentions Lata, Malava and Gurjara as feudatories of Pulakasin 11, the Chalukya ruler.

An eulogy or prasasti of Pulakasin 11, placed on a temple wall at Aihole, also mentions Pulakesin's military success against Harshavardhana. Hiuen-tsang's account mentions that inspite of his victories over many kingdoms he was not able to defeat Pulakasin 11, the Chalukya ruler of Badami in Karnataka. We have no details of the battle and where it was fought but this is clear that Harsha could not achieve success against Pulakesin.

Harsha was successful in his eastern campaigns. A Chinese account mentions him as the king of Magadha in 641 A.D., we have already mentioned his alliance with Bhaskaravarman the king of Assam and it is possible that they jointly conducted campaigns in Bengal and other parts of eastern India.

Harsha had diplomatic relations with the Chinese for his contemporary T'ang emperor sent three embassies to his court. The last of these, under Wang-hiuen-tse, arrived in India in 647 A.D. when Harsha was no longer alive. Harsha himself had sent a brahmana envoy to China in 64 1 A.D. Harsha ruled for a period of 41 years and is said to have died about 647 A.D. The administrative set-up under Harsha was in some ways a continuation of the system prevalent under the Guptas. Hiuen-tsang mentions that Harsha used to take up tours throughout his kingdom.

The king remained the supreme authority, assisted by his ministers and other officials of different categories. For example, the Madhuban copper plate mentions the names of various officials like uparika (provincial governor), Senapati (Army chief), Dutaka (informer), etc. However, his inscriptions, Bana's Harshacharita and Hiuen-tsang's account leave no doubt that the stability of the administration and of the empire had come to depend much on the support of allies and feudatories (samantas and mahasamantas). The officials, it appears, were not paid salaries in cash. Instead, they were given land as payment for their services. The law and order situation seems to have slackened during this period as Hiuen-tsang himself had to face plunder by dacoits.

The Banskhera, Nalanda and Sonepat Inscriptions of Harsha describe him as a worshipper of Siva. However, later on he became a Buddhist and convened a conference at Kanauj. Here the docmnes of Mahayana were propagated with utmost precision. This assembly, according to Hiuen-tsang, was attended by eithteen kings and three thousand monks and continued for eighteen days. Another such event during Harsha's reign was the Quinquennial distribution ceremony at Prayaga. Harsha performed five such ceremonies in his last thirty years. He used to distribute all the treasures accumulated during the last five years in these ceremonies.

Learning and education got royal patronage during this period. Nalanda university had more than ten thousand students. Harsha had given hundred villages in donation to this University.

Shashank and his Conflict with Harsha

Shashanka, the first important king of ancient Bengal, occupies a prominent place in history of the region. It is generally believed that he ruled approximately between 600 CE and 625 CE, and two dated inscriptions, issued in his 8th and 10th regnal years from Midnapore, and another undated inscription from Egra near Kharagpur have been discovered. The copper plate (dated 619 CE) from Shashanka's subordinate king of Ganjam (Orissa) Madhavavarma, Harshavardhana's Banskhera and Madhuvan copper plates and the Nidhanpur copper plate of the Kamarupa king Bhaskaravarman contain information about Shashanka. Shashanka also issued gold and silver coins. A number of independent rulers flourished in Bengal in the intervening period between the decline of Guptas and the rise of Shashanka, and their existence is known from a few inscriptions and gold coins. The seal-matrix of Shri Mahasamanta Shashanka from Rohtasgarh, the contemporary literary accounts of Banabhatta and the Chinese pilgrim Xuanzang (also known as Hiuen Tsang) as well as the Buddhist text Aryamanjushrimulakalpa are important sources of information on him.

Shashanka has been described both in the inscriptions and literary accounts as the ruler of Gauda. In the narrower sense Gauda is the territory between the river Padma and Bardhaman region, however in course of time it embraced much wider area. In the Satpanchasaddeshavibhaga (Seventh Patala of Book III, Shaktisangama Tantra) Gauda is said to have extended from the Vanga up to Bhuvanesha (modern Bhubaneshwar in Orissa). It is not unlikely that the author had described the extension of Shashanka's Gauda kingdom, which also encompassed parts of Orissa.

Early Life

Very little information about the early life of Shashanka is known. It appears that he ruled for sometime as a chieftain (mahasamanta) of Rohtasgarh under the Gauda king of Karnasuvarna, who possibly belonged to the family of the

Maukharis. According to the Vappa Ghoshavata grant of Jayanaga, Karnasubarna served as the administrative capital for a king named Jayanaga (prior to the reign of Shashanka). In fact, Karnasuvarna was the capital of Shashanka and the famous metropolis was situated near modern Chiruti railway station close to Rajbadidanga (the site of Raktamrttika-mahavihara or modern Rangamati) in the Murshidabad district, West Bengal.

The decline and fall of the Gupta Empire coincided with considerable progress in the outlying regions. Many obscure areas, which were possibly ruled by tribal chiefs and were thinly settled, came into historical limelight. This applied to the red soil areas of West Bengal, north Orissa and the adjoining areas of Madhya Pradesh which formed part of the Chhotonagpur plateau and were difficult to cultivate and settle.

From this perspective Shashanka attempted to extend his political influence in different parts of India. His first task was the recapture of Magadha from the Maukharis. With his ally Devagupta, the king of Malava, Shashanka waged war against the Maukhari king Grahavarman (the son-in-law of the Pusyabhuti king Prabhakaravardhana), during which time Grahavarman was killed by Devagupta. At this point Rajyavardhana, a Buddhist, and the eldest son of Prabhakarvardhana (who had become king of Sthaneshwer) proceeded against Devagupta and defeated and killed him. However Rajyavardhana himself was killed in an encounter with Shashanka.

Conflicts with Harshavardhana

Most of the authorities admit the result of the encounter with Shashanka, but passes the blame of the murder of Rajyavardhana on the shoulders of Shashanka. According to Banabhatta, Rajyavardhana, though routed the Malava army with ridiculous ease, had been 'allured to confidence by false civilities on the part of the king of Gauda, and then weaponless, confiding and alone, despatched to his own quarters'. The Xuanzang also relates the same story. However, fair criticism of Shashanka's conduct is impossible in the absence of detailed information relating to the actual circumstances that led to his enemy's death. Both Banabhatta, whose feelings were deeply shaken at the death of his patron's brother and Xuanzhang, whose pro-Buddhist predilections and personal regard for Harshavardhana are well known, may have found it difficult to restrain their emotions in stating their opinions concerning the affair.

In the opinion of some scholars it is likely that Rajyavardhana was prepared to enter into negotiation for peace with Shashanka, and for this purpose accepted an invitation in the enemy's camp. Shankara, a 14th century commentator of the Harshacharita, states that the Gauda king invited Rajyavardhana in connection with a proposal of marriage between himself and the daughter of the king of Sthaneshwer. The truth of this statement is difficult to verify, as the source of his information is not disclosed. The information about Rajyavardhana's death, furnished by the Banshkhera copper plate inscription of Harsavardhana, is meagre, but the negative impressions created by the accounts of Banabhatta and Xuanzang are considerably mitigated when it is related in the inscription that Rajyavardhana lost his life in keeping with the truth (satyanurodhena) in the abode of his enemy (although the name of the enemy is not given). It appears that Rajyavardhana's death was a result to the unfinished peace-talk, but Shashanka's personal responsibility for this matter cannot be determined with certainty.

After these events the younger brother, Harshavardhana, ascended the throne of Sthaneshwer and gathered a huge army before proceeding to punish Shashanka. Harshavardhana had also formed an alliance with Bhaskaravarman (Kumara of Bana), king of Kamarupa and the eastern neighbour of Shashanka. According to Banabhatta, Harsha entrusted Bhandi to lead the army, while he engaged himself in searching for his widowed sister Rajyashri in the Vindhya forest. It is mentioned in the Harsacharita (8th ucchavasa) that Harsha reunited with the advancing army after rescuing his sister. Later, Harsavardhana became the ruler of Kanyakubja (Kanauj) with the consent of his sister Rajyashri. The progress of Bhandi's march is not known for certain, but there can be no doubt that Shashanka continued to rule his empire vigorously, which included northern Orissa and southern deltaic regions of Bengal.

Towards the end of his reign in 640-43 CE Harsa's authority in southeastern Bihar and Orissa was established and during the same time Bhaskarvarman appears to have also conquered the capital Karnasuvarna. These events are likely to have occurred after the demise of Shashanka as nothing more is heard about him, resulting in a decline of Gauda power. The story of the defeat of Shashanka at the battle of Pundravardhana by Harsha and Shashanka's reign for 17 years, as suggested by the Buddhist text Aryamanjushrimulakalpa are not supported by any other contemporary accounts. Rather, Shashanka's newly discovered inscription from Southern Midnapur records the existence of Dandabhukti-Janapada, combining parts of Midnapur and Orissa points to the contrary.

Evaluation

Harsha, a Shaiva in his early years, had gradually become a great patron of Buddhism. As a devout Buddhist he convened a grand assembly at Kannauj to publicise the Mahayana doctrines. It is here that Harsha is said to make a bloody suppression of a revolt by the Brahmanas. After Kannauj, he held a great assembly at Prayaga and both the assemblies were attended by Xuanzang and all the tributary princes, ministers, nobles and other officials. Xuanzang is said to have made a remark that Harsha was born at the behest of the Bodhisattva to punish Shashanka, a hater of Buddhist religion.

He also cited a few instances of Shashanka's anti-Buddhist activities. But it may be mentioned that the flourishing condition of the famed Buddhist University at Nalanda (where Xuanzang himself had studied for some time) and the existence of a number of monasteries in Shashanka's kingdom including the Raktamrttika-Mahavihara near Karnasuvarna, goes against the claims made by Xuanzang.

In other words, it appears that the Chinese pilgrim, who enjoyed the patronage of Harsha, exhibits a strong bias against the adversary of his patron. The vituperative languages used by Banabhatta, court poet to Harsha, against the Gaudadhipa (the name of Shashanka, meaning Shiva, is never mentioned; possibly Banabhatta himself was a devout Shaiva) as Gauda-bhujanga or Gaudadhama etc demonstrates his contempt for Shashanka. While it is true that Shashanka was a strong champion of Brahmanical religion and a devout Shaiva, and had little sympathy for Buddhism which received patronage from the wealthy mercantile classes and from no less than his arch rival, Harshavardhana himself. It is not unlikely that it wounded the sentiments of the Buddhists of his time.

On the contrary, Harshavardhana's pro-Buddhist and anti-Brahmanical attitude (the bloody suppression of a large number of Brahmanas during the Kannauj assembly may be cited here) caused despair among the followers of Brahmanical religion who began to migrate to eastern India in large numbers. Xuanzang mentions of an influx of learned Brahmanas in Kamarupa, where a large number of them were granted lands in Kamarupa by Bhaskaravarman for their settlement. The Kulaji texts also note the influx of Kanauji Brahmanas into Bengal. The story of the migration of Graha-Vipras from the banks of the Sarayu river (in Uttar Pradesh) to Bengal, possibly at the invitation of Shashanka, may be taken notice of in this connection. The impact of this large-scale migration though initially was welcomed both in Bengal and Kamarupa, told upon the socio-economic fabric of the respective countries. The social restrictions in behaviour, attitude and co-mingling among the different classes though not much felt under the rule of Buddhist Palas, became more and more acute under the Senas, who championed the Brahmanical religions, widened the gaps among different classes of people. The emergence of lowly untouchable classes and the antaja classes in the society became more and more pronounced.

Legacy

He was succeded by his son Manava, who ruled for 8 months.

Soon after Shashanka's demise, his kingdom fell apart, and was captured by Harshavardhana and his ally, Bhaskarvarmana. His death marked a state of great political and social unrest in Bengal, with small kings and vassals fighting intermittently to gain power; which is often termed as the era of "Matsyanyay"a, a word that translates as "law of the fish", alluding to the unwritten law of the ocean, where a smaller fish is devoured by a larger fish, only to be devoured by a still larger fish, sooner or later. This era of uncertainty lasted for about two centuries, before the rise of Gopala and the establishment of a new dynasty, the Paia Empire, which unified Bengal once again.

Patron of Buddhism and Literature

Harsha's father, Prabhâkara was, apparently a sun-worshipper and of Bargujar clan, his brother followed Hinayana Buddhism while, according to Bana, Harsha himself was a Mahayana

Buddhist. Harsha was a tolerant ruler and supported all Indic (or Hindu) faiths-Buddhism, Vedism and Jainism. Early in his life, he seems to have been a follower of Sun Worship, becoming a patron of Shaivism and Buddhism later on.

His sister Rajyashri's conversion to Buddhism presumably had a positive effect on his support to the religion. His approach to religion is evident in his celebrated play Nagananda. The play's theme is based on the Jataka tale of the Bodhisattva Jimutavahana, but Harasha introduces the Goddess Gauri, Shiva's consort, as the saviour of Jimutavahana, a feature not found in the Jataka.

According to the Chinese Pilgrim Xuanzang, who visited his kingdom in 636 CE, Harsha built numerous stupas in the name of Buddha. Xuanzang entered a grand competition organized by Harsha and won the theological debate. Harsha also became a patron of art and literature.

He made numerous endowments to the University at Nalanda. Two seals of Harsha have been found in Nalanda in the course of the excavations. All these favours and donations of the great emperor were crowned by the construction of a lofty wall enclosing all the buildings of the university to defend the institution from any other possible attack. In 643 he held a Buddhist convocation at Kanauj which was reputedly attended by 20 kings and thousands of pilgrims.

In 641, following Xuanzang's visit, Harsha sent a mission to China which established the first diplomatic relations between China and India. The Chinese responded by sending an embassy consisting of Li Yibiao and Wang Xuanze, who probably traveled through Tibet and whose journey is commemorated in inscriptions at Rajagriha-modern Rajgir, and Bodhgaya.

Harsha was a noted author on his own merit. He wrote three Sanskrit plays – *Nagananda, Ratnavali* and *Priyadarsika*. His reign is comparatively well documented, thanks to his court poet Bana and Xuanzang. Bana composed an account of Harsha's rise to power in Harsha Charitha, the first historical poetic work in Sanskrit language. Xuanzang wrote a full description of his travels in India.

Nagananda

Nagananda (*Joy of the Serpents*) is a Sanskrit play attributed to king Harsha (606 C.E.-648 C.E.).

Nagananda is one of the best Sanskrit dramas in five acts dealing with the popular story of Jimutavahana's self-sacrifice to save the Nagas. The unique characteristic of this drama is the invocation to lord Buddha in the Nandi verse, which is considered as one of the best examples of the dramatic compositions.

Nagananda is the story of how prince Jimutavahana gives up his own body to stop a sacrifice of serpents to the divine Garuda.

Characters

- Jimutavahana – The Hero and Vidhyadhara Prince
- Jimutaketu – The father of hero
- Vidushaka (Atreya) – The friend of the hero
- Mitravasu – Son of Vishvavasu and brother of the heroine
- Shankachuda – A serpent, intended to be the victim of Garuda
- Garuda – King of birds and enemy of the serpents
- Kanchukin – Superintendent of the harem
  Malayavati – The heroine and daughter of king Vishvavasu
- Devi – The mother of the hero
- Vriddha – The mother of Shankhachuda
- Gauri – The Goddess
- Chaturika – Maid of Malayavati
- Manoharika – Maid of Malayavati
- Navamalika – Maid of Malayavati.

Synopsis

The first act of the play opens in the penance-grove near the temple of Gauri. Jimutavahana with his friend Atreya, the Vidushaka is in search of a suitable place of residence on the Malaya mountain as his old parents have expressed a desire to stay there. He would spend his youth in serving the parents, as he considers such a service far above the enjoyment of the pleasures of kingdom. He had done everything in his power to make his subjects happy and had made the kingdom secure. Moving about, both of them are struck by the grandeur of the mountain and decide to stay there. Here, they happen to hear the ravishing tunes of melodious music. They enter the temple of Gauri but hide themselves to find out who was singing. Through her conversation with her maid they learn that she is a maiden and that Gauri revealed herself to her in a dream and conferred a boon that the Emperor of Vidhyadharas, Jimutavahana will marry her. The two friends reveal themselves only to make Malayavati embarrassed. Malayavati leaves the temple with a hermit without knowing Jamutavahana's true identity. The hero and heroine fall in love with each other, though they are yet strangers to each other.

Source

The story of Jimutavahana is found in the Kathasaritasagara of Somadeva and Brihatkathamanjari of Kshemendra both written in 11th century A.D. The story of Nagananda follows closely the shorter narrations in both these books. Both these books are the Sanskrit versions of the Brihatkatha of Gunadhya in Paishachi language, composed about the 1st century A.D. But neither the Kathasaritsagara nor the Brihatkathamanjari, both composed in 11th century A.D. can be accepted as the source of Nagananda which was composed in 7th century A.D. Sri Harsha has added his own ideas and has deviated from the main story in Brihathkatha in many places. It must be admitted that the treatment of it at Harsha's hands is quite original and that the play on the whole is a very charming and fascinating one.

Ratnavali

Ratnavali is a Sanskrit drama about a beautiful princess named Ratnavali, and a great king named Udayana. It is attributed to the Indian emperor Harsha (606 C.E.-648 C.E.). It is a Natika in four acts. One of the first textual references to the celebration of Holi, the festival of Colours have been found in this text.

The Main Characters

- Udayana (aka Vatsaraja)-The Hero, King of Kaushambi
- Ratnavali (Sagarika)-The Heroine, Daughter of King Vikramabahu
- Vasavadatta-Queen, wife of Udayana
- Susangata-Bosom friend of Sagarika
- Vasanthaka (Vidusaka)-The Hero's companion and Court-wit
- Yaugandharayana-The Chief Minister of Kaushambi Vikramabahu-The King of Simhala

- Vijayaverma-Commander-in-chief of the King
- Babravya-The Chamberlain of the King
- Vasubhuthi-The Minister of Vikramabahu
- Aiyndrajalika-A magician
- Medhavini (Sarika)-A talking bird.

Synopsis

The astute minister Yougandharayana plans Udayana's marriage with Ratnavali, the daughter of Vikramabahu. This plan is motivated by a sage's prediction that the person who would marry her would become a Sarvabhauma (emperor). But Udayana is already married to Vasavadatta, who happens to be Vikramabahu's niece. Naturally, Vikramabahu rejects Yougandharayana's plan for fear of wounding Vasavadatta's feelings.

Yougandharayana then spreads a rumour that Vasavadatta has died in a fire at Lavanaka. After hearing this, Vikramabahu agrees to the marriage of Ratnavali to Udayana. The marriage takes place with great pomp, but because of a custom, the bride and groom do not see each other's face clearly during the marriage, and can only see each other after some traditional rites after they reach Kaushambi. Ergo, after the marriage, the couple are escorted back to Kaushambi in a ship. Unfortunately the ship wrecked on the way. Udayana is rescued and is taken back to Kaushambi. Ratnavali is also rescued, but in a separate path, by a merchant and brought to Kaushambi. Yougandharayana comes to know of her rescue, puts her in Vasavadatta's custody renaming her as Sagarika, without disclosing her identity as the princess.

Once, in the cupid festival, Sagarika sees Udayana, but does not recognize him as her husband. She is wonder-struck by his beauty, and instantly falls in love with him. Sagarika sits in a grove and keeps herself occupied in drawing Udayana's picture and fantasizing about him. Her shrewd friend Susangatha finds her, takes the picture into her hands and draws the picture of Sagarika by the side of the king. Sagarika confesses her love to Susangatha and a bird Sarika hears the conversation. Suddenly, there is a panic in the grove because of an escaped monkey and the maidens run away from there. After a while, the Udayana and his jester enter the grove and hear the bird Sarika reproduce the ladies' conversation. They find the picture Sagarika and Susangatha have drawn, and Udayana finds it alluring. By this time, the two maidens return and overhear the conversation of the king and his jester, and see that Udayana is interested in Sagarika. Susangatha then makes a plan to bring Udayana and Sagarika together, but Vasavadatta (Udayana's first wife) also finds the picture when walking in the grove. Susangatha's plan is destroyed by the angry Vasavadatta and she leaves the grove without accepting Udayana's words of appeasement.

In the third act, the jester and Susangata hatch a plan to make Udayana and Sagarika meet. Sagarika disguises herself as Vasavadatta, and Susangata as her maid. They go to meet Udayana, who has been told of the plan and is expecting Sagarika to come in Vasavadatta's disguise.

But the real Vasavadatta comes to know of this plan and also sets off to meet Udayana. Vasavadatta reaches him first, but Udayana mistakes her for Sagarika and declares that he loves her. Vasavadatta is very angry at Udayana for the second time, and reproacnes him and walks away. Sagarika comes to know that their plan is foiled again, and ties a noose to her neck wanting to commit suicide. Meanwhile, Udayana is frantically searching for the real Vasavadatta, and finds Sagarika about to die. He mistakes her for the real Vasavadatta, and saves her. Afterwards, the two recognize each other and finally they have a chance to declare their love. But at this exact same moment, Vasavadatta, having calmed down, comes back to Udayana ready for appeasement. She is outraged for the third time on seeing Sagarika and Udayana together, and throws Sagarika into prison.

In the fourth act, no one knows where Sagarika is imprisoned by Vasavadatta. Suddenly, there is heard a news of the royal harem catching fire. It turns out that Sagarika is kept there, and Vasavadatta turns remorseful.

She implores Udayana to run to her rescue. Udayana comes out safely from the fire with Sagarika. It is later revealed that the entire fire was a trick by a magician. At this tense moment, Babhravya and Vasubhuti recognize Sagarika to be the Simhala princess. Yaugandharayana enters and reveals himself to be the plotter. Vasavadatta now gladly brings about the marriage of Udayana and Ratnavali, her cousin, relying on the prophecy.

Sources

A Natika should be based on an invented love-story according to Sahityadarpana. But this play, although a natika, does not present to us an entirely original story.

The Udayana legend is found in both Jaina and Bauddha literature besides the Kathasaritsagara, Brihatkathamanjari and Brihatkathalokasangraha. The Jaina legends are not earlier than the 12th century A.D., while the Bauddha ones are of about 4th century A.D.

Many distinguished poets of ancient India, who flourished evn before Sri Harsha, have referred to the love of Udayana and Vasavadatta, and the devotion of Yougandharayana for his master Udayana. This shows how popular the story of Udayana was even in Ancient India.

Kalidasa has referred to Udayana in his Meghaduta. Eudraka refers in his Mricchakatika to the devotion of minister Yaugandharayana to Udayana. Bhasa has dramatized the story in his two plays Pratignayougandharayanam and Swapnavasadattam.

In conclusion, it can be said that it is not unlikely that Sri Harsha took the frame-work of the Udayana story from either the Bauddha literature or some early version of the Brihatkatha and dramatized it in his own way. Although the story is not entirely invented, it must be admitted that the treatment of it at Harsha's hands is quite original and that the play on the whole is a very charming one.

Banabhamma

Banabhamma (7th century) also known as BaGa was a Sanskrit scholar and poet of India. He was the *Asthana Kavi* (Court Poet) in the court of King Harshavardhana, who reigned in the years c. 606-647 CE in north India.

Bana's principal works include a biography of Harsha, the *Harcacarita* and one of the world's earliest novels, *Kadambari* (*Kadambari* is the name of the heroine of the novel). BaGa died before finishing the novel and it was completed by his son BhkcaGabhacca (Pulinda in some manuscripts), which is known as the *Uttarabhaga* of the novel. The other works attributed to him are the CaGikataka and a drama, the Prvatpari Gaya.

Life

A detailed account regarding his ancestry and early life can be reconstructed from the introductory verses attached to the *Kadambari* and the first two *ucchavasas* of the *Harcacarita*, while the circumstances behind the composition of the *Harcacarita* are described in the third *ucchavasa* of the text.

Early Life

Bana was born to Chitrabhanu and Rajadevi in the village of Pritikuta on the banks of the Hira Gyavahu (the present day Son River) in a Maga Brahmin family of Vatsayana gotra. Chitrabhanu expired when he was fourteen, Rajadevi having expired even earlier. After the death of his father, BaGa led a wandering life for some period but later came back to his native village. Here, on a summer day, on receiving a letter from Krishna, a cousin of King Harsha he met the king while he was camping near the town of Manitara. After receiving him with mock signs of anger, the king showed him much favour.

Composition of the Harshacharita

When BaGa returned from the King Harsha's court, his cousins pressed him with a request to write a narrative on the life of King Harsha. But he decided to write only a part of the life of him as he was not sure whether he could do the slightest justice to the remarkable career of the king. From the third to eighth *ucchavasas* of the work, he described the ancestry and the life of king Harsha till the rescue of his sister Rajyashri.

Kadambari

Kadambari is a romantic novel in the Sanskrit language, which Banabhatta wrote in the seventh century.

Synopsis

The king of a race of demigods had a daughter named Kadambari. Mahashweta, the daughter of a celestial nymph, was one of her companions, and met one day a young man named Pundarika, along with a friend of his, Kapinjala, near a lake named Acchoda. Pundarika was the son of a sage named Shwetaketu and the goddess, Lakshmi, and he fell in love with Mahashweta. However, unaware of reciprocation of Mahashweta's love, he died of grief. In a state of grief before dying, he cursed the Moon, who had caused him so much heartache, that the latter would be born on the earth and also suffer pangs of love the way he himself had suffered. The Moon cursed him back that he too would share the sufferings on the earth in his next life on the earth after transmigration of his soul.

A heavenly being carried away dead Pundarika's body to the heavens while Mahashweta heard a voice that she should not end her life since there would be a reunion between her and Pundarika. When Pundarika's body was being carried away, his friend Kapinjala pursued him on a horse. While doing so, he inadvertently ran over a semi-divine being, who then cursed him that he would die and be reborn as a horse on the earth after transmigration of his soul.

The Moon was born on the earth as a son of Tarapida, the king of Ujjayini, and his parents named him Chandrapida. Pundarika was born as a son of Tarapida's minister, Shukanasa, and his parents named him Waishampayana. Kapinjala was born as a horse named Indrayudha, which Chandrapida once subsequently received as a present.

One day Chandrapida and Waisampayana set out with an army on an expedition of conquest over the world. Chandrapida rode on Indrayudha. One day Chandrapida saw a pair of demigods and decided to chase them, riding on his horse, Indrayudha, but the horse carried him away from his companions, and he reached Acchoda lake and met there Mahashweta, who had been waiting for Pundarika. Mahashwveta narrated her life history tc Chandrapida, and took him to the palace of Kadambari's father. Chandrapida saw Kadambari there, and left.

Soon, however, he received a message from Kadambari's father that he should return. By this time he had rejoined the army, so he asked Waishampayana to bring the army and hurried back. He was eager to pay a second visit to the palace where Kadambari was, but he could not do so until Waishampayana had returned. He received next the news that Waishampayana had gone to Acchoda lake. Waishampayana had met Mahashweta there and fallen in love with her, but she could not reciprocate the love since she was in love with Pundarika and was waiting for his return. She did not of course know the identity of Waishampayana and

Pundarika. Waishampayana pursued her "like a parrot", and Mahashwveta angrily cursed him that he would die and become a parrot in his next life. Waishampayana fell down dead, and became a parrot in his next life. Chandrapida went to the lake in search of Waishampayana, heard about the latter's fate, and, unable to bear the sorrow, ended his life.

In his next life, Chandrapida got reborn as King Shoodraka of Vidisha. One day a woman of the hunter community brought a parrot of wonderful abilities to the king. That parrot was of course a reincarnation of Waishampayana, and narrated to the king the events in his prior two lives. They all next went to the hermitage of a sage named Jabali, who, on seeing the parrot, knew all about its previous life as Waishampayana, and affirmed the parrot's story. On the completion of Jabali's narration and affirmation, Shoodraka fell down dead, and rose back as Chandrapida. The parrot too fell dead, and Pundarika, whose body had been preserved in the heavens, came down to the lake as Pundarika himself.

Chandrapida married Kadambari, and Pundarika married Mahashweta. All lived happily thereafter.

Chandrapida spent his time partly in his own home town of Ujjayini, partly at Hemakuta, the home of Kadambari, and partly on the Moon inasmuch as he was an incarnation of the Moon!

2

Administration of Harsha

The administration of Harsha is one inname only. Whatever information we have on it does not speak well of it. And the only relieving feature of this picture is the striking personality of Harsha.

Harsha's interest indirect supervision of administration is one plus point. Hiuen-tsang writes that "If there was any irregularity in the manners of the people in the cities, he went amidst them." Inscriptions reveal that Harsha had stayed in two places during his travels. Harsha travelled ingreat state and his camps looked very impressive because he was surrounded by a number of guests. Hieum-Tsand writes: "The king's day was divided into three periods of which one was given to the affairs of government, and two were devoted to religious work. He was indefatigable, and the day was too short for him." The way in which Harsha worked was recorded by Bana also.

The emperor appointed provincial governors known as Lokapalas who were posted at chosen centres in different quarters. The provinces were known as Bhuktia, districats as Vishayas, sub-divisions of districts as Patakas and Villages as gramas.

Next to the sovereign was the chief minister and the mantriparishad. According to Bhandi, a cousin of Rajayavardhana, Harsha's accession to throne was approved by the parishad. This account is corroborated by the Chinese pilgrim. Avanti was the supreme minister of war and peace, according to Bana. For maintaining law and order, a great number of military and executive officers were employed. At times, some of the high officers were combined in one and the same persons. A few other names also are known: Simhanada was Harsha's senapati. Harsha treated him with great respect as he was a scholarly man. Also, we hear of a handful of officials who themselves were chiefs indicating that in all probability Harsha's sovereignty was of a confederate nature. According to Hiuen-Tsang, both ministers and officials received land grants instead of salaries. One-fourth of eth crown land was set apart for the endowment of great public servants and another one-fourth for the expenses of government and State worship.

The army of Harsha was organized into four traditional divisions. Probably 60,000 elephants and 100,000 horses. However, some of the regions were not free from brigands as is known from the experience of Hiuen-Tsand who was way laid.

Lawlessness was not the order of the day but there were plots against kings including one against Harsha. The offender was punished by imprisonment for life for offance against social morality the punishment was either mutilation of limbs or deportation. Trial by or deal was common. Justice was harsh, but as the Chinese pilgrim maintains, the government was very generous and did not make any large demands either on the liberties or pockets of the people.

In general, the country was not entirely free from brigands who made traveling very risky. Hiuen-Tsand himself twice had narrow escapes from the clutches of bandits, Villagers haunted by the fear plunder often questioned the right of the King to rule according to Bana. However, as Hiuen-Tsand states that since the government was honestly administered, the people lived on good terms and the criminal class was very small.

Regarding administration of provinces and villages very meager information is available. The territory of the empire was called rajya or desa, which was divided into bhuktis, visayas and gramas. The governor of the provinces was, at times, a member of the royal family. The governor appointed his suordinate officials. Probably, the officials mentioned in the Gupta period continued to work in the time of Harsha. Besides the officials of states non-official element was also associated with the local administration. The Madhuban plate of Harsha (grant of an agrahara to some persons) states that the grant was made in the presence of all his chief officers and the resident people who were summoned as witnesses to this transaction. Such orders of the king were, at times, signed by Harsha himself. The Banskhera plate was signed by Harsha and described as one given under his own hand and seal. Often the king's orders were delivered through messagers to local officers, who in turn, grew up necessary charters and handed over the grant to the grantees.

Finally, regarding fiscal administration we get some information from inscriptions. In all probability, land was surveyed measured and divided into holdings with well-defined boundaries. The holdings were of different sizes. At times these were served by common land which in certain cases, had irrigation wells. The names of owners of land were entered in the village records. It appears that record of village census was also kept. It is certain that land revenue was only a modest percentage of total yield. Taxation was light-revenue from crown lands amounted to only one-sixth of the crop, according to traditional standard. The other sources of revenue were trade, and duties at ferries and barrier stations.

The enlightened character of Harsha's administration is shown by the creation of a department of records and archieves. Both good and bad were faithfully recorded in officials annals and state papers while instance of public calamities of good furtuns are set forth indetails. Taxation was light. The land tax was one-sixth of the crop. According to tradition, standard revenue was also derived from trade. Ligth, duties were levied on ferries and barriar stations.

In this manner, we have a very shetchy knowledge of Harsha's administration. Ineed the administration was not well integaretd as Harsha domain itself was so shaky. However, the fat that the knig devoted himself to the welfare of the people by traveling in the country and the generosity with which he gave grants, shows that he was one of the illustrious rulers of Inda the manner of Ashoka and Shaivaji.

Exaggerations of Bana and Hueun-Tsang

Harsha who ruled between 600 and 647 A.D. was viewed till recently as the last great Hindu rulers, but this assessment is no longer tenable. His achievment were exaggerated both by Bana and Hiuen-Tsang.

The chief source for assessing Harsha's achievement in the Harsha Charitra of Bana. His expression in the book is poetic, allusive, and full of punning references. At oneplace sunset stands for bloody wars, buzzing bees, for arrowsn and blooded moon, for the rising power of Gauda King. "Harsha Charitra is as much based on real events as Scott's quantin Durward of Waverley."

The points of dispute in Bana's version and the following First, Bana claims that Harsha installed Bhaskar Varmen on the throne. Secondly many rulers owed their appointments to him. Thirdly, the ruler of Kashmir surrendered the tooth relic of the Buddha to Harsha. Fourthly, the rulef of Sind was stripped of his royal fortune. Fifthly, no mentions made about the defeat of Harsha by Pulakesin. Sixthly, that elephants and horses were not unharnessed for six years by Harsha. Seventhly, description of internal administration is full of panegyrics-no foged documents, no multilation of offenders, no quarrles about revocery of debts, and no occasion to resort to courts of justice. All these remarks of Bana should be taken with a pinch of Salt in view of the facdt that they differematerially with the available information.

In like manner the accounts of Hiuen-Tsand, too, era open to debate. First, his praise of Harsha is an eulogy. "He was indefatigable and the day was to sought for him. His qualification moved heaven and earth, and his sense of justice was admired by the gods and men. His renown spread out everywhere." To describe all his conduct would be to tell again the deeds of Sudhama. He forgot sleep and food in his devotion to good work". Secondly, his statement that Harsha had 60,000 elephants was an exaggeration.

His other statements that after sixth years of struggle and fighting agains the "five Indies" Harsha enjoyed peace for 30 years with out resorting to arms, in sdefinitely false, Thridly, his remark that one-forth of the revenue from the crown lands was earmarked for rewarding scholars or literarymen is an exaggeration. Fourthly his praise of Harsha on account of his predilection for Buddhism is uncalled for because Harsh's affinity to Buddhism is in no way contrary to the tradtion of ancient India. He states, At the ryoyal lodges every day viands wer provided for 1,000 Buddhist monks and also 500 brahmins. The King's day was devided into three periods of which one was given to the affairs of government and the other two were devoted to religios work". Dr. R.C. Majumdar states that his account of Prayag quinquennial conference is ins all likelihood about a perversion of truth. Of course, the information as given by him about the quanquennial assembly on the condition of Kanauj and no the declining nature of Buddhism in the different parts of India, are quite valuable.

Apart from this, the praise of these two contemporaries is not reliable because of the following reasons. The unity maintained by Harsha was superficial. In norther India the Maukhar is ruled independently over the astern protions of their hereditary dominions. Madhava-Gupta and Magadha was a powerful ruler. The Maitrekas of vallabhi and Bhaskar Varman were hardly vassals of the empire. The administrative system not that god as made out by the two contemporaries. Even the Gauda ruler, against whom Harsha took an oath of Vengeance, remained powerful till his death in 637 A.D. and this Gauda rulers was subdued by Bhaskar Varman of Kamarupa, not by Harsha. The Chiecene chroniclers record serious disturbances from 618to 627 A.D. Harsha was defeated by Pulakesinin 637 A.D. A record of the Gurjaras of Broach refues to the defeat of Harsha by prince of Vallabhi. After Harsha's death one of his ministers usurped the throne, All these go wo show that the Picture was not as the rosy as presented by Bana and Hiuen-Tsand.

Indeed, Harsha was undoubtedly a great monarch. At one time the ruler of Kamarupa wasconstrained not to detain a Chinese pilgrim against the will of his mighty ally. The ruller of Kashmir, Sind, Sallabhi and Kamarupa feared and also respected him. Sasanka was forced a withdraw, leaving Kanauj alone. Even after the defeat in the south, Harsha was the only ruler entiled to use music-pace durms. Besides his sense of duty, literacy merits, patronage of scholars and unheard of philanthropy are really remarkable.

And the very fact that the capial of Harsha, Kanauj, became the eynosure of all the neighbours from 647 to 1200 A.D., speaks volumes. Thus, without dyenying to Harsha what undoubtedly is his, we have to be critical of the wo Boswells who exaggerate the greatness of their Johnson.

Events towards the end of Harsha's reign are described in Chinses sources. An embassy was sent by the Tanj emperor of the dayin 643 and agina in 647. It was on the second occasion that the Chinese abassador found that Harsha had recently died and the throne was usurped by an undeserving the King. The Chinese ambassador rushed to Nepal and Assam and raised a force with which he defeated the usurper and he was taken to China as a prisoner. The kingdom of Harsha his death, disintegrated rapidly into small states.

Harshavardhana and his Times

The age of Harsha was a trubulent one. Yet, the general life of people was a prosperous one.

In estimating the social life of people during the Harsha, We have to keep in view the administration of Harsha, for the social life of a people anywhere in olden days, to some extent was influenced by its administrative system. Hiuen-Tsang attributes commendable administrative vigilance to Harsha-made tours of inspection throughout his kingdom, and promoted benevolent activities like construction and maintenance of roads, sarais, hospitals, etc.

Hiuen-Tsang states as the government is generous officials requirements are few. Families are not registered and individuals are not subject to forced labour contributions the king's tenants pay one-sixth of the products as the rent."

But talking of justice, cruel punishment continued. Trial by or deal was common. For offences against social morality, disloyal and inferior conduct, the punishment ws to cut of the nose, ear, hand, foot or to banish the offender to another country or into wilderness.

Hiuen-Tsnad maintains that as the government was honestly administrated and the people lived on good terms the criminal classes was small. But Chinese pilgrim about whom special care may have been taken by the government was robbed of his belongings, although he records that according to the laws of the land severe punishments we inflicted for cirme. Robbery was considered to be a second treason for which the right hand of the robber was amputated. But it seems that under the influence of Buddhism the severity of punishment was mitigated, and criminals were imprisoned for life.

Talking of political life, in most cases kingshop was hereditary although at times a king was nominated by his predecessor or elected by people or nobels. Nandivarman Pallava was raised to the throne by the mula prakritis. At Thaneshwar the crown was offered to Harsha by a council of nobles headed by Bhandi. Secondly the tradition that the welfare of king depends on the welfare of people was still believed in. Fa-Hien, Hiue-Tsang and Suleiman record that rulers did their best to live up to this anciant maxim. Fourthly quite a number of important rulers loved learning and patronized the arts.

Harsha, Mahendra varman, Amoghavarsha I, Bhoja of Dhar somesware III of Kalyan and Ballala Sena of Bengal were writers of no mean repute. Fitthly, the king was all important even though has was assisted by Ministers.

Manu's recommendation of council of seven or eight ministers was normally followed Sixthly the chief source of revenue was land-one-sixth of its produce. A few other taxes were imposed on ports, ferries, etc. Apart from taxation, returns from royal lands, mines etc. and tributes from vassals filled royal coffers. Finally, kingdoms were divided into smaller units for the convenience of administration. And royal armies mostly relied on elephants, infantry and cavalry. From the features delineated above, one can easily deduce that the political structure of the day did impinge upon the lives of people.

Relating to social life, Hiuen-Tsang metions four chief castes and also innumerable sub-castes. But Bana mentions that castes mixed freely. Bana even makes mention of his two brothers born of Shudras.

The Chinese traveler, Hiuen-Tsang, refers to prohibition, widow-remarriage and the costom of sati. Yet, women were not regarded as inferior to men. Som of the royal ladies were skilled in music and dancing. Rajyasri sat along with Harsha and listened to the discourses on Buddhism.

Interestingly, Hiuen-Tsang notes the absence of tailors and shoe-makers; the simplicity of brahmins and kshatriyas; the luxuries of king's nobels and rich men; honesty and morality of the people because of the fear of retribution in life to come: and, suicide of very old men of people afflicted with incurable diseases in the Ganges. Another interesting point mentioned by him is the etiquette of lifting the turban as a mark of greeting is social gatherings. Regarding the temperament of people, the travelers note that they were hasty and inecisve but moral. The people were not deceitful by nature and valued their pledges and promises. The country was prosperous. Vegetables and minerals were abundant. Fish and mutton were consumed occasionally. Onions and garlic were not much used.

The brahmins and kshatriyas are reported to have led a simple life, but the nobles and priests led a luxurious life. Hiuen-Tsang calls the Shudras agriculturists, which is significant. In the earlier texts they are represented as serving the three higher varnes. The Chinese pilgrim takes note of untouchables such as scavengers, executioners, etc. They lived outside the villages and consumed garlic and onion. The untouchables announced their entry into the town by shouting loudly so that people might keep awap from them.

Coming to the cultural life of people, we cannot ignore the contribution of Harsha to it. Probably Harsh wrote the three dramas Ratnavali, Priadarshika and Nagananda in Sanskrit. The Chinese traveller, I-Tsing recorded that Harsh versified the story of Jimutayahana in Nagananda and extremely fond of literature. It is contended that the Banskhera and Madhuban copper-plate inscriptions were probably composed by Harsha himself. The other works attributed to him are the two Sanskrit stotras in praise of the Buddha and a work on grammer. Besides Harsha, Bana was the Chief poet who wrote Hadembari and is also supposed to have written the' Parvati-parinay' and the Chandiskata, A writer Mayura was a master of erotic poetry. A other literary figure was Matanga Divakara.

Apart from royal court, the sylvan ashramas were the centres of intellectual activity. Bana records a detailed account of the ashrama of the Buddhist saga Divakaramitra in the Vindhyas. Hiuen-Tsand credits the people of the middle country with clearness and correctness of speech. According to him children were taught the five subjects of grammer, mechanical arts, medicine, logic and philosophy from the seventh year onwards. He was all praise for the great scholars of the day. Among educational centres the most famous was the Nalanda university. It attained international repute. It was patronized by Kumaragupta I, and also by Hrasha. The famous teachers of the university were Dignaga, Dharmapala and Shilabhara.

The teacher, Dharmapala, originally belonged to the city of Kanchi and wrote books on Buddhist logic and metaphysics. It was during the time of Shilabhadra that Hiuen-Tsang visited

Nalanda. Even though the university was a Mahayana institution, brahminical subjects like the Vadas were included in the curriculum. Those who sought admission in the university were examined by the keepers of the gate.

It is said that not more than 20 per cent of candidates could pass this examination of the gate-keepers. There was no fee for education. Boarding lodging and clothing were free. The university derived its revenues from the villages granted to it by royalty. During the time of Hiuen-Tsang there were about 10,000 student and women were also included in it. I-Tsing says that the discipline was strict at Nalanda. Sanskrit was the medium of instruction. The method of teaching was primarily tutorial even though there were some lectures. Time was regulated by a water-clock. I-Tsing says that there were eight halls and 300 rooms in this university. It possessed an observatory and a laboratory also.

With regard to art, the Guptam style was continued. Hiuen-Tsang refers to a copper statute of the Buddha. The brick temple of Laxmana at Surpur is one of the most beautiful in India, unsurpassed in the richness and refinement of its ornaments.

Talking of religion, it was a remarkable era. In the Gupta period brahminism re-asserted itself. The reading of the Gita was popular with intelligentsia. The leader of Hindu reformation Sankara, in the 8th century, commented on the Gita. By the time of Alberuni it was so popular that Alberuni quotes the text of the Gita.

Nevertheless, Hinduism, of the Gupta age witnessed a set-back some developed the dectrine of mimamsa. The doctrine was quite ancient but it became popular with prabhakara at the end of the sixth century. Another great exponent of it was Kumarila in the 7th century. Another doctrine imprimarily concerned with the technique of thought, that is, it is only concerned with rituals. 'The Mimamsa lives in a world of self-revealed Vedas and is concerned only with correct performance of the rites as laid down".

This doctrine was poles apart from popular puranic religion of people. Also, it contradicts the idea of a popular personal deity which is to be realized either through bhakti or yoga. Luckily this barren ritualism was attacked by Sankara in the 8th century. Here we must also note that Buddhism was on the declire. Hiuen-Tsang notes the dacay of Buddhism even though he was not conscious of it. But Buddhism gained popularity in Kanara, in certain parts of UP and in Bengal.

Thus, there is nothing unique about the life of people during the age of Harsha. The creative urge witnessed in the Gupta period continued. Yet, as the future was to prove, the quiet greatness of this age was only as afterglow.

Political Condition of North India in Post-Harsha Period

The empire built up by Harshavardhana had a very loose structure; after his death even this structure collapsed.

The events immediately following the death of Harsha have been described at Some length by Wang-Hiuen-tse who had been deputed as an ambassador by the Chinese emperor. But as he reached the borders of India, the news of Harsha's death reached him. He tells us that Arjuna (Ti-no-fo-ti) sent an army to check the entry of the Chinese ambassador. Somehow Wang-Hiuen-tse escaped and came back to fight Arjuna with an army of one thousand from Tibet and seven thousand from Nepal. Arjuna and his army were defeated and captured. Later the queen of Arjuna continued the fight but was defeated. wang to Uk Arjuna to China and presented him to his King. However, the authenticity of this account is doubted by certain scholars.

Post-Harsha Dynasties

Among the post-Harsha rulers the Nidhanapur inscription of King Bhaskaravarman mentions about his rule in Karnasuvarna in the Murshidabad district of Bengal and nearby places. Similarly, the Aphsad inscription' mentions Adityasrna's rule over Magadha. In Kashmir Durlabhavardhan established a dynasty known as Karakota. His grandson Chandrapida checked the entry of the Arabs in Kashmir. Another king of this dynasty, Lalitaditya Muktapida, attacked Kanauj and defeated Yasovarman. It appears from Chinese accounts that Muktapida did not annex the kingdom but entered into an alliance with him. After about 75 years of Harsha's death Yasovarman rose to power in Kanauj. He defeated the Gaudas and also won Magadha. Yasovarman, besides being a great wamor, was a great patron of scholars. His court was graced by Vakapati and Bhavabhuti. Vakapati wrote Gaudavaho in Prakrit, while Bhavabhuti wrote Malatimadhava, Mahaviracharita and Uttara-Ramacharita in Sanskrit.

Although the rule of many of these royal families lasted only for a short period, we Should remember that in many regions of the Indian subcontinent this period saw the beginnings of stable state structures.

These were not all-india empires, but they represented the beginnings of regional political structures. We have already referred to the kashmir valley where, inspite of many dynastic changes, we find for the first time the functioning of a local state system. In Bengal, the emergence of Pala power from the middle of the eighth century A.D. and its duration for several centuries marked a new phase in the political history of the region.

Similarly, in Western India, covering both Rajasthan and Gujarat, emerged many new ruling families like the Gurjara Pratiharas, Guhilas, the Chahamanas and others who came to be considered as different clans of the Rajputs who dominated the political scene of western India for centuries. Thus, the decline of Gupta power and the collapse of Harsha's empire did not mean beginnings of political anarchy. After the end of these empires, the regional powers consolidated themselves and played important roles in the history of subsequent periods.

In the post-Gupta period many kingdoms came into existence. These kingdoms were not as large as the Gupta kingdom. The political fortunes of the dynasties which ruled these kingdoms fluctuated with time.

Some of the powerful kings like Harsha managed to bring almost the whole of northern India under their control, but their kingdoms were short-lived. However, simultaneously we find that in many regions new political powers emerged which lasted for many centuries. The beginnings of many regional states can be traced to this period. Although the rule of many of these royal families lasted only for a short period, we should remember that in many regions' of the India subcontinent, this period saw the beginnings of stable state structures.

These were not all-India empires, but they represented the beginnings of regional political structures. We have already referred to the Kashmir valley where, inspite of many dynastic changes, we find for the first time the functioning of a local state system. In Bengal, the emergence of Pala power from the middle of the eighth century and its duration for several centuries marked a new phase in the political history of the region. Similarly, in Western India, covering both Rajasthan and Gujarat, emerged many new ruling families like the Gurjara-Pratiharas, Guhilas, the Chaharnanas and others who came to be considered as different class of the Rajputs who dominated the political scene of Western India for centuries.

Thus, the decline of Gupta power and the collapse of Harsha's empire did not mean beginnings of political anarchy. After the end of these empires, the regional powers consolidated themselves and played important roles in the history of subsequent periods.

3

Vakataka Dynasty

The Puranas recongnise the greatness of the Vakatakas, known as Visdhya Sakti. For over a hundred years the Vakatakas, known as Vindhya Sakti. For over a hundred years the Vakatakas with their capital at Nandi Vardhan ensured peace and tranquility over central India and re-established the orthodox social system which had suffered considerable battering by the inroads of Kushans and Yavanas. In one of Prithivisena's inscriptions the dynasty is described as one whose economic and judicial administration had been perfected for a hundred years, a significant if vain glorious announcement of the greatness of the Vakatakas.

There are four views of the origin of Vakatakas. It is said that the Vakatakas were a northern dynasty since the Puranas maintain this view. But it is held by Jayaswal that they hailed from a place called vakataka. This view is no longer up held. The one evidence is that the Vakatakas never struck and coins in their own names, but utilized those of western Kshatrapas and later of Guptas. No early records of their have been found north of the Narbada. On the other hand there are several indications that they hailed from south. Their Sanskrit and Prakrit inscriptions are similar to those used in early pallav grants. The name Vakataka figures in an inscription of the 3rd century AD on a pillar at Amaravati in Andhra Pradesh.

One school holds the view that the Vakatakas were Brahmins by caste. Vakataka records mention of Vishnuvriddhaas the gotra of the Vakatakas. In the Basim copper plate a Vakataka prince is named Gautamiputra. Both these facts make us believe that the Vakatakas were Brahmins.

The formal establishment of Vakataka empire is placed at about 284 A.D. it is generally held that Vindhyasakti was one of the earliest kings of the dynasty. The Vakataka grants mention their gotra. It is also said that Vindhyasakti extended his king-dom and performed vedic sacrifices which were in abeyance during the rule of the later Satavahanas.

Vindhyasakti succeeded by his son Pravarasena I who was the real founder of the Vakataka empire. He extended his sway further to the north as for as to Narmada. He performed of the seven Soma Sacrifices including Vijapeya and also four Asvamedhas. Pravarasena I assumed imperial titile and his authority was well established all over Hindustan. Pravarasena is attributed a long reign of 60 years, but it is strange that he never struck any coin. There are no visible signs of their supremacy outside Vidharba. At the most south Kosala, which borders on Vidharba might have come under their in fluence. However in the south his kingdow may have extended till the Tungbhadra or a little beyond that.

According to the Puranas, Pravarasena I had four sons. All of them became Kings. It is quite likely that the extensive empire of Pravarasena I was divided among his four sons after his death.

Pravarasena's son Sarvasena established a branch of the dynasty at Bassin which in course of time extended its authority as far south as Karnataka. In fact the Vakatakas in middle India succeed to the empire of the Satavahanas and held their sway north and south of the Vindhyas, and fully earned their title of Vindhya Sakti.

Gautamiputra was the eldest son of Pravarasena. His son rudrasena I succeede Pravarasena I and ruled over the northern parts of Vidharba. Possibly he was the contemporary of the Gupta king, Samudragupta. The Gupta ruler himself never attacked the Vakataka ruler. It might have been that Samudragupta thought that it was wise not to attack a power which occupied a strategic position with respect to the powerful western Kshetrapas whom Samudragupta has not yet subjugated.

Rudrasena I was succeeded by his son Prithvisena I. This king seems to have pursued a peaceful policy which brought happiness and prosperity to his people. Probably he had a long reign which terminated about 400 AD. It was his son's alliance with the daughter of Chandragupta II that brought the Guptas and Vakatakas to gether. Prithvisena was succeeded by a son Rudrasena II, who was a devotee of Vishnu unlike his ancestors who worshipped shiva.

Rudrasena died after short reign leaving two sons who succeeded one after the other. The first son Divakar Sen'a rule was for a short period. He was succeeded by this brother Damodara Sena. More than a dozen grants of this prince have been found in different districts of Vidharbha. Probably he ruled for nearly 35 years ending with the year 455 AD.

Apart from this line, one more line of the Vakatakas was that of Narendar Sena, one of the sons of Pravarasena I. He seems to have followed an aggressive pllicy and made some conquests in the east the north. Probably he married a princess of the Rashtrakuta family. Possibly he had a short reign of about 10 years. Also by the close of his reign the territories were invaded by the Nala kings.

Prithvisena II, the son of Narendrasena, raised the prestige of the family. Tow stone inscriptions of his feudatory clearly prove the extension of the kingdom. He was also a worshipper of Vishnu. He may have been followed by one or two princes, but their names are not known to us. After the death of Prithvisena II, the kingdom was incorporated by one more branch of the Vakatakas called Vatsagluma branch.

Sarvasena was the founder of the Vatasagluma branch and he was the son of Pravarasena I. He was followed by a son Vidhyasena who is named as Vindhyasakti II in one of the inscriptions.

Vindhyasena was followed by his son Devasena. An inscription indicates that Vatasagluma was the capital of his branch of the Vakatakas.

Vindhyasena was succeeded by Devasena. He have a very righteous and capable minister named Hastibhoja. The kingdom was entrusted to his care.

Devasena was succeeded by a son Hari Sena in about 475 A.D. He was the great warrior but unfortunately much is not known about him. His conquests did not lead to permanent annexation of any territories. His minister Varahadeva caused the Ajanta cave 16 to be excavated and decorated with sculpture and picture galleries. In all likelihood the dynasty was overthrown by the Kalachuris in abouth 550 A.D.

The causes that ultimately led to the downfall of the Vakatakas are not clearly known. One of the works of Dandin throws some light. According to this the central power of the Vakataka empire became weak and the feudatories began to show signs of revolt luring the reign of Harisena's misguided successors who led a desolute life. This confusion led to the invasion of the Kadambas. Also the Vakatakas suffered a disastrous defeat and the Vakataka ruler was killed in the battle which was fought on the banks of the Wardha. Talking of their importance the Bharasivas and the Vakatakas cannot be looked upon merely as bridge heads to the imperial Guptas. The glory of Samudragupta and his successors has obscured in a measure the great achievements of their predecessors who not only expelled the foreigners from Indian soil but re-established the imperial tradition which was threatened by Kushan intrusion. Even more it is these dynasties, more than the Guptas, that contributed to the re-establishement of Hinu society and Sanskrit culture over Hindustan as may be seen not merely from the numerous Asvamedhas performed by the kings of these dynasties but the very orthodoxy which they claim for the mselves. The growth of classical Sanskrit literature to its full greatness was also in this period for Harisena's great prasasti of Samudragupta on the Allahabad pillar bears clear evidence to the evolution and perfection of the Kavya style.

It would seem however from the inscription itself that the Vindhya and Maharashtra country the home domains of the Vakatakas, were not attacked or conquered by the Guptas. The continued existence of powerful Vakataka monarchs and their close alliance with the Guptas, under Samudragupta's successor, would seem to indicate that Samudragupta did not challenge the Vindhyan power but satisfied himself with an allience. Chandragupta II's marriage with a Vakataka princess and his own daughter Prabhavati's marriage with a Vakataka monarch are further indications of the fact that the uptas shared their imperial power with the Vindhyan State.

Chandragupta II married a Vakataka princes anmd thus allied himself with the historic imperial tradition. His daughter Prabhavati Gupta married Rudra Sena, the Vakataka king. A lady of remarkable ability she seems to have ruled the Vakataka empire as Regent for her son and in her inscriptions we see reflected the pride both of the Vakatakas and the Guptas. Chandragupta's firm alliance with this great power based on the Vindhyas enabled him to concentrate all his forces against invaders Despite the personal performance of the Vakatakas for Brahmanism, both Buddhism and Jainism flourished in their vst empire with liberal support of ministers and feudatories, Pravarasena performed the seven Vedic sacrifices including Asvamedha, which he performed four times. Serveral Vakataka inscriptions record grants lf land and even whole villages to pious and learned brahmins. Most of the Vakatakas kings were the followers of Shiva, whom they worshiped under the name of Maheshvara and Mahabhairava.

Some of the Vakataka kings were grant patrons of learning and were also authors of Prakrit kavyas. Sarvasena, the founder of the Vatsagulma line was the author ofa Prakrit Kavya harivijaya. This kavya has bee copiously cited by later Sanskrit poets. The capital, Vastugulma, became a great center of learning and culture.

Pravarasena-II of the elder branch of the family was also a reputed author of the Gatba Saptasati and of the famous kavyas Sethubandha composed in Maharashtra Prakrit. Dandin and bana praise the kavya Sethubandha. It is also suggested that Kalidas lived fro some time in the court of Pravarsena II and helped the king in the composition of his kavya. Probably, Kalidas composed his own lyric Meghaduta during this stya there. In the field of architecture, a few shrines came into existence in Vidharaba at Tigowa and Nachna. The pillars in the Tigowa Shrine resemble the Indo-Persepolitan style. Status of the river goddess Ganga and Yamuna guard the entrance of the Sanctum. Regarding painting, it is stated that caves XVI, XVII and XIX belong to the Vakataka age. In the cave XVI we have a huge statue of the Dying Princes.

Vindhysakti

The founder of the dynasty was Vindhyasakti (250-270), whose name is derived from the name of the goddess Vindhya after whom the mountains were named. The dynasty may be originated there. Almost nothing is known about Vindhyasakti, the founder of the Vakatakas. In the Cave XVI inscription of Ajanta he was described as the *banner of the Vakataka family* and a *Dvija* (Brahmin). It is stated in this inscription that he added to his power by fighting great battles and he had a large cavalry. But no regal title is prefixed to his name in this inscription. The Puranas say that he ruled for 96 years. He was placed variously at south Deccan,

Madhya Pradesh and Malwa. K.P. Jayaswal attributes Bagat, a village in the Jhansi district as the home of Vakatakas. But after refuting the theory regarding the northern home of the Vakatakas, V.V. Mirashi points out that the earliest mention of the name Vakataka occurs in an inscription found on a fragment of a pillar at Amaravati which records the gift of a *Grihapati* (householder) Vakataka and his two wives. This Grihapati in all probability was the progenitor of Vidhyashakti. It appears from the Puranas that Vindhyasakti was a ruler of Vidisha (in the present day Madhya Pradesh state) but that is not considered to be correct.

As per Dr Mirashi, who has rejected the identification of Rudra Deva in the Allahabad pillar inscription of Samudra Gupta with Rudra sena I. He has also pointed out there are no coins of Vakataka and there are no inscriptions of them in the north of Vindhyas. Hence, a south home of Vakatakas is correct. However, it is true that they have ruled on some of these places, since the epigraphs were available in MP etc.

Pravarasena I

The next ruler was Pravarasena I. (270-330), who maintained the realm as a great power, he was the first Vakataka ruler, who called himself a *Samrat* (universal ruler) and conducted wars with the Naga kings. He has become an emperor in his own right, perhaps the only emperor in the dynasty, with his kingdom embracing a good portion of North India and whole of Deccan. He carried his arms to the Narmada in the north and annexed the kingdom of Purika which was being ruled by a king named Sisuka. In any case, he certainly ruled from Bundelkhand in the north (though Dr Mirashi does not accept that he has crossed the Narmada) to the present Andhra Pradesh in the south. The puranas assign him a reign of 60 years.

As per V.V. Mirashi, it is unlikely that he made any conquest in Northern Maharashtra, Gujarat or Konkan. But, he may have conquered parts of North Kuntala comprising of Kolhapur, Satara and Sholapur districts of Maharashtra. In the east, he may have carried his arms to Dakshina Kosala, Kalinga and Andhra. He was a follower of Vedic religion and performed several *Yajnas* (sacrifices) which include Agnishtoma, Aptoryama, Ukthya, Shodasin, Atiratra, Vajapeya, Brihaspatisava, Sadyaskra and four Asvamedhas. He heavily donated to the Brahmins during the Vajapeya sacrifice as per the Puranas. He also took up the title of *Dharmamaharaja* in addition to *Samrat*. He called himself as *Haritiputra*. His prime minister Deva was a very pious and learned Brahmin. The Puranas say that Pravarasena I has four sons. He married his son Gautamiputra to a daughter of King Bhavanaga of the powerful Bharashiva family, which might have proved to be helpful. However, Gautamiputra predeceased him and he was succeeded by his grandson Rudrasena I, the son of Gautamiputra. His second son, Sarvasena set up his capital at Vatsagulma (the present day Washim). Nothing is known about the dynasties set up by the other two sons.

Branches of Vakataka Dynasty

It is generally believed that the Vakataka ruling family was divided into four branches after Pravarsena I. Two branches are known and two are unknown. The known branches are the Pravarpura-Nandivardhana branch and the Vatsagulma branch.

Pravarapura-Nandivardhana Branch

The Pravarapura-Nandivardhana branch ruled from various sites like Pravarapura (Paunar) in Wardha district and Mansar and Nandivardhan (Nagardhan) in Nagpur district. This branch maintained matrimonial relations with the Imperial Guptas.

Rudrasena I

Not much is known about Rudrasena I, the son of Gautamiputra, who ruled from Nandivardhana, near Ramtek hill, about 30 km from Nagpur.

There is a mention of Rudradeva in the Allahabad pillar inscription, bundled along with the other rulers of Aryavarta. A number of scholars, like A.S. Altekar do not agree that Rudradeva is Rudrassena I, since if Rudrasena I had been exterminated by Samudragupta, it is extremely unlikely that his son Prthivisena I would accepted a Gupta princess (Prabhavatigupta) as his daughter-in-law. Secondly, no inscription of Rudrasena I has been found north of the Narmada. The only stone inscription of Rudrasena I's reign discovered so far was found at Deotek in the present-day Chandrapur district, so he can not be equated with Rudradeva of the Allahabad pillar inscription, who belonged to the Aryavarta.

Prithvisena I

Rudrasena I was succeeded by his named Prithvisena I (355-380), and Prithvisena I was succeeded by his son named Rudrasena II.

Rudrasena II, Divakarasena and Pravarasena II

Rudrasena II (380-385) is said to have married Prabhavatigupta, the daughter of the Gupta King Chandragupta II (375-413/15). Rudrasena II died fortuitously after a very short reign in 385 C.E., following which Prabhavatigupta (385-405) ruled as a regent on behalf of her two sons, Divakarasena and Damodarasena (Pravarsena II) for 20 years. During this period the Vakataka realm was practically a part of the Gupta Empire. Many historians refer to this period as the Vakataka-Gupta age. While this has been widely accepted more than 30 years ago, this line of argument has no proper evidence. Prabhavati Gupta's inscription mentions about one "Deva Gupta" who is her father and the historians equated him with Chandra Gupta II. However, there is no other source to prove that Deva Gupta is really Chandra Gupta II. This is questionable more since the dating of Vakatakas is more or less established while that of Guptas is sometimes predated to that of Greek invasion of Alexander by the Indeginists.

Pravarasena II composed the *Setubandha* in Prakrit. A few verses of the *Gaha Sattasai* are also attributed to him. He shifted the capital from Nandivardhana to Pravarapura, a new city of founded by him. He built a temple dedicated to Rama in his new capital.

Narendrasena and Prithvisena II

Pravarsena II was succeeded by Narendrasena (440-460), under whom the Vakataka influence spread to some central Indian states. Prithvisena II, the last known king of the line, succeeded his father Narendrasena in c.460. After his death in 480, his kingdom was probably annexed by Harishena of the Vatsagulma branch.

Vatsagulma Branch

The Vatsagulma branch was founded by Sarvasena, the second son of Pravarasena I after his death. King Sarvasena made Vatsagulma, the present day Washim in Washim district of Maharashtra his capital. The territory ruled by this branch was between the Sahydri Range and the Godavari River. They patronized some of the Buddhist caves at Ajanta.

Sarvasena

Sarvasena (c.330-355) took the title of *Dharmamaharaja*. He is also known as the author of *Harivijaya* in Prakrit which is based on the story of bringing the *parijat* tree from heaven by Krishna. He is also known as the author of many Prakrit *Gathas*. One of his minister's name was Ravi. He was succeeded by his son Vindhyasena.

Vindhyasena

Vindhysena (c.355-400) was also known as Vindhyashakti II. He is known from the well-known Washim plates which recorded the grant of a village situated in the northern marga (sub-division) of Nandikata (presently Nanded) in his 37th regnal year. The genealogical portion of the grant is written in Sanskrit and the formal portion in Prakrit. This is the first known land grant by any Vakataka ruler. he also took the title of *Dharmamaharaja*. Vindhyasena defeated the ruler of Kuntala, his southern neighbur. One of his minister's name was Pravara. He was succeeded by his son Pravarasena II.

Pravarsena II

Pravarasena II (c.400-415) was the next ruler of whom very little is known except from the Cave XVI inscription of Ajanta, which says that he became exalted by his excellent, powerful and liberal rule. He died after a very short rule and succeeded by his minor son, who was only 8 years old when his father died. Name of this ruler is lost from the Cave XVI inscription.

The Dashakumaracharita version of the end

According to the eighth *ucchavasa%* of the *Dauakumaracarita* of Dandin, which was written probably around 125 years after the fall of the Vakataka dynasty, Harishena's son, though intelligent and accomplished in all arts, neglected the study of the *Dandaniti* (Political Science) and gave himself up to the enjoyment of pleasures and indulged in all sorts of vices. His subjects also followed him and led a vicious and dissolute life. Finding this a suitable opportunity, the ruler of the neighbouring *Ashmaka* sent his minister's son to the court of the Vakatakas.

The latter ingratiated himself with the king and egged him on in his dissolute life. He also decimated his forces by various means. Ultimately, when the country was thoroughly disorganised, the ruler of Ashmaka instigated the ruler of Vanavasi (in the North Kanara district) to invade the Vakataka territory. The king called all his feudatories and decided to fight his enemy on the bank of the Varada (Wardha). While fighting with the forces of the enemy, he was treacherously attacked in the rear by some of his own feudatories and killed. The Vakataka dynasty ended with his death.

Rulers of the Vakataka Dynasty

- Vindhyasakti (250-270)
- Pravarasena I (270-330).

The Pravarapura-Nandivardhana Branch

- Rudrasena I (330-355)
- Prithvisena I (355-380)
- Rudrasena II (380-385)
- Divakarasena (385-400)
- Prabhavatigupta (fem.), Regent (385-405)
- Damodarasena (Pravarasena II) (400-440)
- Narendrasena (440-460)
- Prithvishena II (460-480).

The Vatsagulma Branch

- Sarvasena (330-355)
- Vindhyasena (Vindhyashakti II) (355-400)
- Pravarasena II (400-415)
- Unknown (415-450)
- Devasena (450-475)
- Harishena (475-500)

4

Pallava

The Pallava dynasty ruled the Northern Tamil Nadu region and whole of Andhra Pradesh with their capital at Kanchipuram. The Pallava dynasty is a dravidian tamil dynasty. The word Pallava in Sanskrit means *branch* (kilai, tondai as in Tamil). The Tondaiman rulers were the Pallava Kings. They hail from the Royal community of Pallars. They expanded into the Guntur region of Andhra Pradesh. This area is still referred to as Palnadu or Pallava Nadu. Some historians like to speculate about the lineage of Pallava Kings by giving it an Northern Aryan and add a foreign angle tc the Pallavas origin. Though most of the historians and stone inscriptions and edicts asserts and confirm that Pallava Kings belongs to the Dravidian race and were later offshoot of Cholas. Pallavas gained prominence after the eclipse of Satavahanas of Andhra and decline of Cholas in Tamilnadu. The Pallavas patronized Tamil, Telugu and Sanskrit. Some of the most illustrious Sanskrit poets like Bharavi and Dandin and the seashore rock-cut temples of Mahabalipuram belongs to the Pallavan era.

Pallavas rose in power during the reign of Mahendravarman I (571 – 630 CE) and Narasimhavarman I (630 – 668 CE) and dominated the Telugu and northern parts of the Tamil region for about six hundred years until the end of the 9th century.

Throughout their reign they were in constant conflict with both Chalukyas of Badami in the north and the Tamil kingdoms of Chola and Pandyas in the south and were finally defeated by the Chola kings in the 8th century CE.

Pallavas are most noted for their patronage of Dravidian architecture, still seen today in Mahabalipuram. The Pallavas, who left behind magnificent sculptures and temples, established the foundations of classical Dravidian architecture. Chinese traveller Hiuen Tsang visited Kanchipuram during Pallava rule and extolled their benign rule.

Many sources describe Bodhidharma, the founder of the Zen school of Buddhism in China, as a prince of the Pallava dynasty, a contemporary of Skandavarman IV and Nandivarman I, and the son of Simhavarman II, but this is debatable.

Etymology

The word Pallava means *branch* in Sanskrit, in contrast with Chola meaning *new country*, Pandiya meaning *old country* and Chera meaning *hill country* in Sangam Tamil lexicon. The Pallavas are considered to be later offshoot of Cholas, who made Kanchipuram their capital and ruled Northern Tamil Nadu and Andhra Pradesh (till Northern Circars). They have also conquered Southern Karnataka.

Origins

But for some historians the origins of the Pallava still remains a subject of speculation and hence a mystery and so that leading to many legends. Some of those were Brahmanical legends and Puranas spun by Brahmins to give a foreign origin twist, so as to cover their foreign origins, to Pallavas, Gangas (Kongas) and many ruling dynasties in South India and Central India who were in reality native people and indigenous ruling clans and dynasties. Others were stated to be researched work by western scholars who gave it a racial and ethnic colour to divide the indigenous people of South Asia.

The Pallava were a South Indian Tamil dynasty who ruled the Northern Tamilnadu and Andhra Pradesh with their capital at Kanchipuram from the early the 4th century CE until the end of the 9th century for a period of about six hundred years. The Pallava dynasty belongs to the Thondaiman rulers. And the Pallava Kings hailed from the Royal community of Pallars.

Original Tamil Ancestry

The word *Pallava* means branch or twig in Sanskrit. The word is rendered as *Tondaiyar* in Tamil language. The Pallava kings at several places are called *Thondamans* or *Thondaiyarkon*. The territory of the Pallavas was known as *Tundaka Visaya* or *Tundaka Rashtra*. The word *Thondan* should not to be confused with a similar Tamil word which means slave, servant, follower or helper. The Chola king Karikala Chola annexed the region now referred to as Tondaimandalam after overthrowing the Kurmubar sovereignty and gave it to his valiant son Athondai Chakravarti. The region henceforth came to be known after the king *Athondai*.

Thus the Pallavas were an offshoot of the Cholas. Thus the dynasty is named *Pallava* derived from the Sanskrit word Pallavam means bud, branch refers to the separate branch of dynasty founded by the Karikala Chola's son *Athondai Chakravarti*.

On collapse of the Satvahana power, the Pallavas asserted themselves and annexed a large part of Chola territory but the epithet Tondon remained and their territory also came to be called *Thondaimandlam* literally meaning the *region of Athondai* in Tamil. R Sthainathaier seems to connect the Pallavas with ancient Pulindas, who according him, were identical to the Kurumbas of Tondamandlam. R. Sthainathaier also states that Tondamandlam was a province under Maurya king Asoka in third century BCE and later on, it was seized by the Satavahanas and thus Tondamandlam became a feudatory to the Satavahanas. He furthei believes that Tondaiyar is Tamil rendering of Pallava. After collapse of Satavahanas in about 225 AD, the Pallavas of Tondamandlam became sovereign and expanded to river Krishna river.

Sri Lankan Origin

Tamil literature relates the story of Chola king Killivalavan who moved his capital to Uraiyar after the destruction of the Chola capital of Puhar. Mudaliyar C. Rasanayagam of Colombo claims that Killi Valavan had a liaison with the daughter of Naga king Valaivanam of Manipallavanam (in Jaffna peninsula) in Ceylon. From this union was born a child who was named *Tondaiman Ilantirayan* whom his father, Killi Valavan, made the ruler of a territory which was named Tondamandlam with capital at Kanchi. It is pointed out that name Pallava derives from the last syllable of *Manipallavanam*....the land of prince's mother.

Tamil Origin

The word Pallava means bud or branch in Sanskrit. The word is rendered as Tondaiyar in Tamil language. The Pallava kings at several places are called Thondamans or Thondaiyarkon. The territory of the Pallavas is still known as Thondaimandalam literally meaning The region of Thondai in Tamil. The Chola king Karikala Chola annexed the region now referred to as Tondaimandalam after overthrowing the Kurmubar sovereignity and gave it to his valiant son Athondai Chakravarti The region henceforth came to be known after the king Athondai. Thus the Pallavas were an offshoot of the Cholas and the dynasty is named Pallava derived from the Sanskrit word Pallavam meaning bud or branch and refers to the separate branch of dynasty founded by the Karikala Chola's son Athondai Chakravarti

Aryan Origin

But for some historians the origins of the Pallava still remains a subject of speculation and hence a mystery and so that leading to many legends. Some of those were Brahmanical legends and Puranas spun by Brahmins to give a foreign origin twist, so as to cover their foreign origins, to Pallavas, Gangas (Kongas) and many ruling dynasties in South India and Central India who were in reality native people and indigenous ruling clans and dynasties. Others were stated to be researched work by western scholars who gave it a racial and ethnic colour to divide the indigenous people of South Asia. So some like Dr V. D. Mahajan has added to that view by postulating that the Pallavas belonged to the caste of *Braham-Kshatriyas* i.e. they were Brahmanas in origin and Kshatriyas by *Dharama* or profession.

Pallava Chronology

The rule of the Pallavas apparently starts as early as 275 CE, but their greatest epoch corresponds to the 7th and 8th century.

Early Pallavas

The history of the early Pallavas has not yet been satisfactorily settled. The earliest documentation on the Pallavas is the three copper-plate grants, belonging to Skandavarman I and written in Prakrit. Skandavarman appears to have been the first great ruler of the early Pallavas, though there are references to other early Pallavas who were probably predecessors of Skandavarman.

Skandavarman extended his dominions from the Krishna in the north to the Pennar in the south and to the Bellary district in the West. He performed the *Aswametha* and other Vedic sacrifices and bore the title of 'Supreme King of Kings devoted to *dharma*'.

An absence of documentation about the Pallavas following Skandavarman is broken by the Allahabad pillar inscription of Samudragupta, which indicates that he defeated the Pallava Vishnugopa (350–355 CE). With Samudragupta's expedition the Pallava eclipse set in, whereas many claim that the prince Vishnu Gopa who suffered a set back was only a governor of Pallava provinces in the Deccan and did not actually come to throne. The invasion of Kalabhras is also a myth as the literature of the period shows contrary. These assertions are further strengthened when we know from Pallava documents about an expedition to Deccan where many territories were destroyed after defeating a "treacherous ruler avery representative of age of Kali who was called Kadamban". It is very much possible that this previously mentioned Kadamban indulged in subversion against Pallavas to the advantage of Samudra Gupta. The literature of the period paints everything perfect for Pallavas.

Inasmuch as the absence of discontinuity or waning of their power, and also that of any counter expedition of the Pallavas who like other crowned kings their equals, never ever failed to send in counter expeditions with well defined objectives in case of any "attack" on them clearly showed that the face off with the Guptas was inconsequential with the initiator himself having no objectives to be met with in his move. In the reign of Simhavarman IV, who ascended the throne in 436 CE, the fallen prestige of the Pallavas was restored. He recovered the territories lost to the Vishnukundins in the north up to the mouth of the Krishna. The early Pallava history from this period onwards is furnished by a dozen or so copper-plate grants in Sanskrit. They are all dated in the regnal years of the kings.

With the accession of Nandivarman I (480-500 CE), the decline of the early Pallava family was seen. The Kadambas had their aggressions and attacked even the headquarters of the Pallavas with the Pallavas taking retaliatory measures by expelling and invading Kadamba territories in Karnataka. In coastal Andhra the Vishnukundins established their ascendency. The Pallava authority was confined to Tondaimandalam. With the accession of Simhavishnu, father of Mahendravarman I, c. 575 CE, the Pallava revival began in the south.

- Simhavarman I 275-300 CE
- Skandavarman
- Visnugopa 350-355 CE
- Kumaravishnu I 350-370 CE
- Skandavarman II 370-385 CE
- Viravarman 385-400 CE
- Skandavarman III 400-436 CE
- Simhavarman II 436-460 CE
- Skandavarman IV 460-480 CE
- Nandivarman I 480-510 CE
- Kumaravishnu II 510-530 CE
- Buddhavarman 530-540 CE
- Kumaravisnu III 540-550 CE
- Simhavarman III 550-560 CE.

Later Pallavas

The incursion of the Kalabhras and the confusion in the Tamil country was broken by the Pandya Kadungon and the Pallava Simhavishnu.

The Pallava kingdom began to gain both in territory and influence over the South Indian peninsula and were a regional power by the end of the 6th century. The Pallavas exercised control over their southern neighbours of Cholas and Pandyas. But their history is marked by the continuous conflict with the Badami Chalukyas.

Narasimhavarman I and Paramesvaravarman I were the kings who stand out with glorious achievements in both military and architectural spheres. Nandivarman II built the Shore Temple.

Simhavishnu 555-590 CE

Simhavishnu, son of Simhavarman III and one of the Pallava kings of India, was responsible for the revival of the Pallavan dynasty. He was the first Pallava monarch whose domain extended beyond Kanchipuram (Kanchi) in the South. He was portrayed as a great conqueror in *Mattavilasa Prahasana* (drunken revelry), a drama written by his son Mahendravarman I.

Reign

Hero stones of the reigns of Simhavishnu and his father Simhavarman show his highest regnal year to be the thirty-third, and on this basis he ruled for over 33 years. However, there is no exact consensus as to Simhavishnu's period on the throne. Recent epigraphical evidence supports the period of 537-570 CE, whereas older generation historians like T.V. Mahalingam claimed it to be 575-615 CE. KAN Sastri tentatively places Simhavishnu's reign between 555-590 CE.

Expansion of Kingdom

When Simhavishnu ascended the throne, the Pallava dynasty was beginning to reassert its supremacy. His father Simhavarman was an accomplished militarist who according to a grant by Rajasimha Pallava (Narasimhavarman II) in 8th century A.D, had destroyed the town and army of Ranarasika, a Chalukyan king of the Deccan.

The southern peninsula of India was then ruled by five dynasties. The Pallavas, the Cholas and the Pandyas shared the power in Tamil Nadu, Andhra Pradesh, parts of southern and eastern Karnataka border and Ceylon; the Cheras controlled Kerala and the Chalukyas controlled Karnataka. Simhavishnu, who was known for his gallant martial courage and judicial wisdom from a young age, overthrew the Kalabhras and conquered the region up to Kaveri, where he came into conflict with the Pandyas and Ceylon. He dispatched a naval expedition and occupied Malaya and Sri Lanka. ** and established Kanchipuram as his capital. The presence of the Pallavas, much before further naval expeditions to Indo-China by their illustrious succeeding and contemporary empires such as the Pandiyans and the Cholas, is attested by the existence of specimen of art bearing striking resemblance in countries like Thailand, Laos, Cambodia, as well as scores of inscriptions in those lands in the Grantha script (a script in which both Tamil and Sanskrit can be written) in which the Pallavas were the first to specialize.**

Simhavishnu led the revival of the Pallavas, and the period starting with him came to be known as the Greater Pallavas or Later Pallavas dynasty. The great struggle between the Pallavas and the Chalukyas, which would last for more than two centuries, began during the reign of Simhavishnu.

Contribution to Literature

Simhavishnu is known to have been the patron of the Sanskrit poet Bharavi, who wrote of the duel between Siva and Arjuna known as Kirata Arjuneeya, after which Lord Shiva blessed Arjuna with the divine 'Pasupata' missile. The structure of Bharavi's play suggests that it was written for *koodiyattam* plays for worship in temples during festivals. Kirata Arjuneeya is used as a subject for *koodiyattam* performances even today.

Religious Affiliation

As with most Indian monarchs, Simhavishnu also accepted his servility to the Almighty. Great endowments were given to temples across the Tamil region. His father Simhavarma also may have entered the Tamil pantheon of Saivite saints who had gained *mukti* at the feet of the lord.

Periyapuranam mentions a Pallava ruler, Aiyatikal Kaadavarkon, who at Chidambaram composed hymns in praise of the Lord in *venpaa* metre of Tamil and attained *mukti*. There is evidence that this could have been Simhavarman, as it is said that he had first gilded the temple with gold after bathing in the temple tank cured him of illness.

In the Udayendiram copper plates of Nandivarman II, Simhavishnu was a devotee of Vishnu. This is a noteworthy point as his son Mahendravarman I was a Jaina who opposed all the Saivaite practices before being converted to Saivism. Simhavishnu's portrait can be seen in the stone engraving at the Adivaraha Mandap, an elegant shrine at Mahabalipuram. The monuments and temples in Mahabalipuram are achievements of the Pallava dynasty, and they still exist in Tamil Nadu. Simhavishnu was succeeded by his son Mahendravarman I.

Mahendravarman I 590-630 CE

Mahendravarman I was a Pallava king who ruled the Northern regions of what forms present-day Tamil Nadu in India in the early 7th century. He was the son of Simhavishnu, who defeated the Kalabhras and re-established the Pallava kingdom.

During his reign, the Chalukya king Pulakesi II attacked the Pallava kingdom. The Pallavas fought a series of wars in the northern Vengi region, before Mahendravarman decimated his chief enemies at Pullalur (according to Pallava grants at Kuram, kasakudi and tadantottam). Although Mahendravarman saved his capital, he may have temporarily retreated the northern provinces to Pulakesi.This however remains a moot point. This is because latter is known to pallavas as a kingdom representative of wickedness of age of kali, to whom they accorded neither legitimacy nor recognition.The pallava crown prince and successor of Narasimhavarman I had been a very efficient strategist so defeating a pallava force under him would have been difficult without deceit.

The literature of the period both in Sanskrit and Tamil refer to an exceptionally severe falseful propaganda unleashed by duplicitous buddist and jain monks with the help of this deccan kingdom. The works of saints like sambandar and appar refer to these nefarious acts of monks of age of kali. Thus it may be possible tha what may have been a minor and partially successful skirmish for the evil kingdom may have been promoted as a defeat to pallavas through falseful propaganda. Otherwise we see from literature including periyapuranam as to how this king mahendra was contributing to development and administration through innovation.

Sri sankara in his writings says that these evil saints meticulously conspired to establish the lie as the truth through various means.

A Sanskrit work of period of king harsha says that the king's army was attacked from rear by a deccan kingdom probably same as the above as the tired soldiers were returning home. This should once again testify the wicked means of the rulers of "age of kali".

The pallava and chola literature are very clear on status of this kingdom. Rogue, truthless,degenerate and illegitimate.

Both these saints were contemporaneous to the pallava The previous as well as succeeding pallava kings were especially severe on this enemy. Thus the above mentioned face off may have only been a temporary set back for pallavas which many a brilliant regime with the exception of possibly the cholas and the pandavas sometimes suffered.

Many scholars have opined that Mahendra's patronage and liking for Jainism which had a cloak of non-voilence, in his initial years may have caused him to give up the aggressive warlike attitude that generally went alongside all of Pallava and Chola monarchs of yore and most notedly with his great warrior father Simhavishnu who had subdued all the kingdoms of the south and also Srilanka. This might in turn have encouraged his enemies the Chalukyas who exploited it well to their advantage.

Mahendravarman was succeeded to the throne by his more famous son Narasimhavarman I in 630 CE.

Patronage of Arts and Architecture

The rock-cut temples at Mamallapuram. Construction of these started in the reign of Mahendravarman I

Mahendravarman was a great patron of letters and architecture. He was the pioneer of Rock-cut Architecture amongst the Pallavas. In the inscription at the Mandagapattu rock-cut temple, it is claimed that the temple was built without wood, brick, mortar or metal. The five-celled cave temple at Pallavaram was also built during his reign.

Fine examples of his rock-cut temples can been witnessed at Mahabalipuram, Thirumayam (Satyagirinathar and Satyagirishwarar twin temples), Siyamangalam (the Siva temple Avanibhajana Pallaveswaram) in North Arcot district and the upper rock-cut temple at Trichy. Apart from the Siva temples, Mahendravarman also excavated a few Vishnu cave temples, the Mahendravishungrha at Mahendravadi, and the Ranganatha temple both at Srigavaram both in present-day North Arcot district.

The architecture of the rock-cut Narasimha and Anjaneya Temple of Namakkal in Tamil Nadu is so similar to that of Thirumayam, especially the reclusive Ranganatha shrine of Namakkal being similar to that of the Ranganatha at Thirumayam, both being of gigantic proportions with varied sculptural masterpieces chiselled on mountain rocks, they bear the unmistakable stamp of Mahendravarman I.

Mahendravarman after his re-adaption of vedism also contributed greatly to the Sanskrit dramatized dance worship in temples namely *kutiyattam*. Many Sanskrit dramas focussing on Ramayana, Mahabharatha and puranas are known to have been written by him., for example the comedy Mattavilasaprahasana. During Mahendravarman's time a dedicated task force for the study of tamil language and grammar was set up that after completing study passed several resolutions incorporating changes in grammar, structure and prosody and also one to change the script of the language. The script developed during his time is the prototype of current tamil script. The kudiyamalai (near salem) cave inscription describes his aptitude in fine arts.

Religion

Mahendravarman was initially a patron of the Jain faith, but he converted back into the Saiva faith under the influence of the Saiva saint Appar. The latter alongside a bhagavata alwar by name Tirumazhisai alwar or Bhargaavar was persecuted by the king initially as he took to jainism. At which instance sree Narayanan (lord Vishnu) who had his abode in the great city of Kanchi enshrined as sree yatotkara perumaal, is supposed to have accompanied the saint and abandoned the city. It may be noted here that this conversion took place by volition and the Saiva saint's philosophical activities were mostly targeted against Jain monks who were on a conversion spree within the kingdom. As though to further testify this some sanskrit traditions refer to a pallava invasion of pataliputra during the period of mahendra and the subsequent destruction of monasteries by of jains by their army.

The pallava edicts inform as to how the king chose to express his gratitude to lord sivan for having "given him true knowledge" by erecting on top of a mountain in trichy a temple for lord sivan. The grant metaphorically says as to how "lord Sivan expressed his wish to be enshrined on top of a mountain because he could not see in full the great power and justice of cholas from a temple situated in the land

Narasimhavarman I (Mamalla) 630-668 CE

Narasimhavarman I was one of the most famous Tamil kings of the Pallava dynasty who ruled South India from 630-668 CE. He shared his father Mahendravarman I's love of art and completed the work started by Mahendravarman in Mahabalipuram.

He avenged his father's defeat at the hands of the Chalukya king, Pulakesi II in the year 642 CE. Narasimhavarman was also known as *Mamallan* (great wrestler) and Mamallapuram (Mahabalipuram) was named after him. It was during his reign that the Chinese traveller Hsuan Tsang visited Kanchipuram.

Narasimhavarman I was a devotee of Siva. The great Nayanmar saints like Appar and Tirugnanasambandar lived during his reign.

Narasimhavarman I was succeeded by his son Mahendravarman II in the year 668 CE.

Military Conquests

Narasimhavarman I is claimed to be one of the six Indian kings who never lost on the battlefield to their enemies, the others being Karikala Chola of the Sangam age, Samudragupta, Asoka the great, Rajaraja Chola I, his great warrior son Rajendra Chola.

War with the Chalukyas

Pulakesi II, the most famous of the early Chalukya kings, had previously raided various northern Pallava provinces and forts. However, he was unable to capture the Pallava capital of Kanchipuram. This led to a long conflict between the Chalukyas and the Pallavas.

Pulakesi II again attempted to seize the Pallava capital and undertook another expedition several years later. However, the Pallava reign had moved on to Narasimhavarman II by then. Narasimhavarman defeated the Chalukyas in several battles, including one at Manimangalam 20 miles to the east of Kanchipuram. The king states that he could see the back of his dreaded enemy as he tore apart his army. Encouraged by this victory, Narasimhavarman led his army along with his general Paranjothi and invaded Vatapi, successfully defeating the Chalukya king Pulakesi II in 642 CE.

He returned victorious to Kanchipuram, and was given the title *Vatapikondan* (one who destroyed Vatapi).

His general Paranjothi a (Vikrama Kesari, also known as paradurgamarddana) was known very well for his devotion to Lord Siva and as one of the 63 Nayanmar saints, is said to have indeed personally destroyed the city of Vatapi. He is also known as 'Siruthonttar', a dutiful warrior and a practicing medic who had "mastered several treatises in medicine". This vikramakesari had at the insistence of lord sivan sacrificed his child without any qualms. There was a confusion as to whether the ganesha at a temple in chengattankudy could have been a result of this invasion but this seems not to be true because the temple and association of lord ganesha with the same are well described in sthalapuranam or the literature discussing the importance of the place.

The ganesha seems to be installed several thousands of years ago in a previous epoch.The pallava grants are very clear on how they viewed the kingdom of this enemy and the status accorded to the same. All literature of the period and hence describe them as evil, degenerate, opportunistic and untruthful kingdoms of age of kali. They are described as evil empire who are to be confronted continually and regularly and not to be treated as either subordinates or tributaries. The capital vatapi was completely destroyed and the kingdom for years never really recovered from this brutal assault by pallavas who succeeded in maintaining their hegemony all over the subcontinent and south Asia continually. Many grants refer to this event as:" kilisayoneriva vimattita vathapi" or the one who destroyed vatapi, the same way sage agastya had killed a demon by that name long ago.

It has to be noted here that even though Narasimhavarman I was punitive he was not the first of pallava kings both to confront or decimate this enemy many pallava kings through ages had been undertaking expeditions into this deccan territory. Grants of Sree Rajasimha mention the punitive, destructive expeditions undertaken by many pallavas through centuries into this territory.

Influence on Ceylon politics

The Sinhalese prince Manavamma lived at the court of Narasimhavarman and had helped him crush his enemy Pulakesi II. In return, Narasimhavarman supplied Manavamma twice with an army to invade Ceylon. The second attack was successful. Manavamma occupied Ceylon, over which he is supposed to have ruled from A. D. 691 to 726. The Kasakudi copper plates refer to Narasimhavarman's conquest of Ceylon. The *Mahavamsa* also confirms these facts.

- Mahendravarman II 668-672 CE
- Paramesvaravarman I 672-700 CE.

Parameswaravarman I was a Pallava emperor who ruled in South India in the latter half of the seventh century.

He ascended to the throne after the death of his father Mahendravarman II in 670 CE. His grandfather Narasimhavarman I had already made the Pallava empire the most powerful force in the subcontinent and destroyed the Chalukya capital at Vatapi. Parameswaravarman was an efficient and capable ruler, known for his military exploits, his love for poetry and his devotion to Siva, to whom he erected many temples.

Parameswaravarman's reign was marked by revived conflicts with the Chalukya, led by Vikramaditya I who had fought against his grandfather and was now allied with a pandyan royal prince of madurai, and many rulers of karnataka, Andhra and orissa.

In 674 CE the two armies met at Peruvalanallur near Trichinopoly and Parameswaravarman was victorious despite facing a huge coalition. Pallava sources record that the chalukyan king Vikramaditya fled the battle field alone with "only a rag" to cover and that his army was completely annihilated. The kuram grant describes this in a long and complex prose and credits the king for " In a terribly cruel war in which Rakshasas, pisachas, kushmandas made fearful noises, he unaided destroyed the army of vikramaditya who fled the battlefield unclothed to escape death.". The greatly enraged pallava emperor followed this up by re-occupying chalukyan territories (A.D.677-A.D.680), thus emulating his great ancestor Narasimha varman and withdrew the occupation forces only after chalukyan rulers agreed to pay a yearly tribute and accepted pallava overlordship, but not before the occupation army had annihilated several chalukyan princes, nobles and citizens.

The expeditionary forces returned to capital kanchi with big war booty that included "a huge quantity of fine chinese yellow silk, imported by the jain monks to clothe the idols of their saints ". The pallava forces were especially brutal and punitive as noted from the pallavas' own inscriptions that go on to say that the army as well as the territories of the "wicked rulers of age of kali" was completely destroyed. The victory enabled Pallavas to assert their hegemony over the subcontinent throughout the remaining years of Parameswaravarman's reign. He is credited with having performed aswamedha yagam to further consolidate power. Rayakota grant refers to him as "parameswara-aswamedha-yajin". To commemorate the victory he consecrated a temple and a village called Kuram (at a distance of 13km to the north east of Kanchipuram) and invited virtuous men and vedic scholars to settle and offer their services to the temple with a section dedicated to chanting the verses of ramayana and mahabharatha in temples.

Inscriptions record Parameswaravaran's generosity to temples at Vennainallur, Vriddhachalam and Chidambaram. Some grants celebrate him to be adept in chanting vedas "like true devotees of lord of thillai". Parameswaravarman was the contemporary of great saiva saint Appar. Parameswaravarman was succeeded by his illustrious son Rajasimha. Some writers have opined that the pallava king aiyatikal kaadavarkon of the saivite nayanmar galaxy may have been parameswaravarman. They have pointed to the construction of temple at kuram and the heroics in battlefield mentioned in oneline of periyapuranam as an indicator to his identity. But this conclusion is inconsistent when one looks at other factors. For example most pallava kings were foremost among warriors and so the description of valour need not be exclusive to parameswaravarman. The expertise in various fine arts like poetry etc was well exhibited by many pallavas most predominantly by mahendra who ruled 30 years before parameswaravarman. Mahendra's multifaceted genius even produced treatises in music and dance dramas for temple worship. His encounter with saint appar and his subsequent upholding of truth of vedism is well known. Also there is difference in style and language of the composition of aiyatikal kaadavarkon and great saints like sambandar and appar. If the above mentioned king indeed was parameswaravarman who was a contemporary of above mentioned saints then the language of his composition should have been the same as the above mentioned saints. This not being the case we may safely conclude that aiyatikal kaadavarkon was not parameswaravarman. In his composition aiyatikal mentions of his visit to chidambaram and the bath in the holy temple pond. An early pallava emperor by name simhavarman is known to have taken bath in the temple pond and cured of a certain afflicted disease. It is possible that that ruler may have been conferred the title aiyatikal kaadavarkon for his becoming a saint at the feet of "lord at thillai".

Narasimhavarman II (Raja Simha) 700-728 CE

Narasimhavarman II was a Pallava king who ruled in South India during the 6th century. Succeeding his father Paramesvaravarman I in the year 700 CE, he ruled for nearly 3 decades, until he was succeeded by his son Paramesvaravarman II in 728 CE.

Ascension to the Throne

By the time Rajasimha ascended the throne, the Pallavas were by the large most powerful military force in the subcontinent. His father Parameswaravarman I was among the greatest of warrior kings of ancient India, the Amaravati Pallava inscription praises him of being:'" As vigorous and strong as lord sambhu (siva).". Parameswaravarman I had subdued all his formidable enemies to extend the Pallava empire far and away. Rajasimha followed up very well. The Vayalur inscription of Pallavas issued on the eve of the coronation of Rajasimha (695.C.E-728.C.E), gives a lineage of 54 rulers through the epochs of Kritam, Dwaparam and Kali up to emperor Rajasimha, this includes 47 kings after Aswattaman, the great warrior ancestor of the Pallavas.

The Reign

Rajasimha, like of most of Pallava kings before him, was a great militarist. That the Pallavas were recognized as a major power during his period is testified by the fact that he exchanged ambassadors with China. Some inscriptions credit him of "offering to certain rulers assistance in their war against Arabs". In general his period was relatively free from major wars and Pallava domination of south east Asia continued.

Contribution to Literature

Rajasimha was a skilled dramatist and poet. He wrote many works in Sanskrit and Tamil. Most of these are missing. His Sanskrit plays had themes from Ramayana, Mahabharatha and *puranas*. *Kutiyattam,* which is presently considered as the most ancient available form of Sanskrit dance drama and still in vogue in Kerala, uses some of his plays (like *kailasodharanam*) for subject matter. another play called "kamsavadham" dealing with lord krishna's killing of kamsa also was written by the king.

The Sanskrit litterateur Dandin spent several years in his court and was patronized by the king, but we do not know about his standing as the inscriptions denote considerable level of erudition. Rajasimha himself was a great devotee who was credited for having mastered the great agamic worship rituals" like preceptor drona".

For all his accomplishments, Rajasimha is mainly remembered as a foremost devotee of lord sivan and a relentless, truthful, diehard warrior king who made sure that pallava armies remained dominant in the subcontinent. Lord sivan is famously known to have appeared in the king's dream and ordered him to adjourn his coronation because he wanted to first bless an impoverished saint poosalar. This event is very well described in most pallava grants of Rajasimha as well as the ones after him.

Religious Endowments

Rajasimha was a great devotee of Siva and constructed the Kailasanathar Temple at Kanchipuram. Rajasimha is one among the pantheon of 63 Saivite Nayanmar saints as Kazharsimha (meaning "one who is lion to crowd of evil kings") Nayanar and also contemporary to many nayanmar saints like sundarar, dandi, poosalar and his great queen Rangapataka who was known to be a pious queen. Rajasimha is greatly admired for valor. He took many titles like "ranajaya", "sivachudamani" etc.

He is further credited with the construction of the Buddhist Vihara at Nagapattinam.

Patronage of Architecture

Rajasimha's reign was marked by peace and prosperity, and he constructed several beautiful temples. Apart from the Kailasanatha Temple at Kanchipuram, Rajasimha also built several other temples, including the Vaikuntha Perumal Temple at Kanchi, Shore Temple at Mahabalipuram. He is also credited with building the Airavatesvara temple at Kanchipuram and the Talagirisvara temple at Panamalai.

Successor

Rajasimha's had two sons-Mahendravarman III and Paramesvaravarman II. However, Mahendravarman III predeceased his father, and Paramesvaravarman II succeeded to the throne in 728 CE.

Nandivarman II (Pallavamalla) 732-796 CE

In A.D 731, the Pallava king Parameswaravarman died without any heir and hence the Pallava empire was kingless. Parameswaravarman, was the last ruler of Simhavishnu line of Pallavas. That the enemies may not utilize the opportunity to invade the country, the military leaders (dandanayakas), scholars and representatives of mercantile and peasantry formed an entourage and undertook "a long journey" to reach the kingdom of kambujadesa (modern day Cambodia and Vietnam) ruled by a certain *kadavesa hari varma* who stemmed from the pallava lineage and was 6th descendant of Bhimavarman, the brother of the great *simha vishnu*. The king had four sons. The first three declined the offer (Kshatriyamalla, Sangramamalla and Rajamalla). The last one by name *pallava malla parameswara* also known as *Nandi varman*, who was then 12 years old accepted the request. Nandivarman's becoming a king at such a tender age is referred to in many inscriptions and contemporary literature (referring to him as "The one of strong arms who got the kingdom at a tender age" or the one who became king at a tender age).

Rule and Conquests

Nandivarman was an intellectual with aptitude in many arts like writing, poetry, music and philosophy. He is known for his good looks and liking for training in gymnastics.

Nandi varman inherited a kingdom that was made strong by the efforts of his illustrious predecessors like parameswaravarman and Rajasimha. The deccan enemies of pallavas who had for long been at the receiving end from successive pallava kings, used the opportunity resulting out of the anarchy and marched into pallava kingdom. Nandivarman then only 13 years old was not equipped physically and mentally to command an army and thereby the naturally imperialist pallavas for the first time in their illustrious history beat a tactical retreat.

This however, did not have a serious consequence and the pallava territories were never in any danger. As noted from many of his inscriptions, the period witnessed general peace and trade flourished. Nandi varman was successful in defeating many of his foes who mainly ruled states in deccan (a copperplate reports that he took the kingdom of certain vishnu Raja in deccan) with the help of his brave commander called udayachandran, who was a part of the entourage that accompanied him from kambujadesa and "who had long been serving in the king's special forces" in 731 A.D.

The previously mentioned king had alongside a king called prithvivyaghra nishadaraja (king of forest tribes) had arrogantly seized the horse let loose by the pallavas in course of their aswamedha sacrifice. He was also a very pious man noted for his munificence to temples at karkudi (the temple still bears his name as uyyakondan tirumalai and is mentioned in tevaram hymns), vennainallur and parameswara vinnagaram in kanchipuram.

The pandyan kings the natural enemies to both cholas and pallavas also met with defeat at his hands. A temple for goddess bhagavati (durga) was built in nagercoil by Nandivarman and this shows that the pallavas reigned supreme in south during his period. He died in 796 A.D.

- Thandivarman 775-825 CE
- Nandivarman III 825-869 CE
- Aparajitha Varman 882-901 CE.

Kadava Kingdom

Kadava was the name of a South Indian ruling dynasty who ruled parts of the Tamil country during the thirteenth and the fourteenth century CE. Kadavas were related to the Pallava dynasty and ruled from Kudalur near Cuddalore in Tamil Nadu. The Kadava kingdom was at the height of their power briefly during the reigns of Kopperunchinga I and Kopperunchinga II. These two rulers were powerful enough to challenge the waning Chola dynasty during the reign of Rajaraja Chola III and Rajendra Chola III. The two Kopperunchingas have left a large number of inscriptions mostly in the North and South Arcot districts and in the Chingleput district.

Origins of Kadava

The title Kadava is found among the several titles assumed by Mahendravarman I, Narasimhavarman I and Narasimhavarman II. The *Kadava* name with *Tondaiyar* and *Kaduvetti,* is found in Tamil literature to refer to the Pallavas. The relationship of the Kadavas to the main Pallava dynasty is documented in an inscription in Kanchipuram.

The kings of the collateral line of the Pallavas who were descended from Bhimavarman, the brother of Simhavishnu, are called the *Kadavas*. The Pallava king Nandivarman (Pallavamalla) is praised as 'one who was born to raise the prestige of the Kadava family'. The title *Kaduvetti* is also used in some inscriptions to denote the Pallavas.

Rise of Kadava Power

The Kadavas, who must have been minor chieftains under the Cholas, began to raise in power during the reign of Kulothunga Chola III (1178-1218 CE). We have very little reliable information on the various chieftains of the Kadava dynasty. In 1186 CE a Kadava chieftain named Virasekhara occupied Kudalur. Another chieftain Manavalapperumal, possibly the heir of Virasekara, was identified as a feudatory of Kulothunga Chola III. Koppernchinga I was probably Manavalaperumal's son and heir.

Kopperunchinga I (reigned c.1216-1242 CE), who was related to the Cholas through marriage, was an officer in the court of Kulothunga Chola III. When the Pandya army invaded the Chola country in 1216 CE, Kopperunchinga I strengthened his position by garrisoning the town of Sendamangalam. From this opportunity, the Kadavas gradually increased their power until Kopperunchinga I could defeat and imprison the Chola king Rajaraja Chola III with some help from the Lanka king Parakrama Bahu II. Under the reign of Kopperunchinga I's son and successor Kopperunchinga II (c.1243-1279 CE), the Kadava power further expanded. Hoysalas, who were the allies of the Cholas were absent from the Tamil country, removing one of the major influences in the region. The last Chola king Rajendra Chola III (1246-1279 CE) came to power with Kopperunchinga II's help. Their relationship was one of alternating friendship and hostility.

Religious work

The Kadava kings have donated generously to various temples. They constructed and expanded many temples and shelters, opened up new roads, founded villages and made other benefactions which are remembered in names of temples, gardens, etc. Some of these are *Alappirandisvaram-Udaiyar, Alagiya-Pallavantoppu, Alagiya-Pallavan-sandi,* and *Kopperunjigan-teru*. The fort ruins at Sendamangalam, with rampart walls, moat, palace buildings and bathing pools is an example of the past glories of this small but important Kadava principality which flourished in the 13th century CE.

Religion

Pallavas were followers of Hinduism and made gifts of land to gods and brahmins. In line with the prevalent customs, some of the rulers performed the *Aswamedha* and other Vedic sacrifices. They were, however, tolerant of other faiths. The Chinese monk Xuanzang who visited Kanchipuram during the reign of Narasimhavarman I reported that there were 100 Buddhist monasteries, and 80 temples in Kanchipuram.

Mahendravarman I was initially a patron of the Jain faith. He later re-converted to Hinduism under the influence of the Saiva saint Appar with the revival of Hinduism during the Bhakti movement in South India.

Pallava Architecture

The Pallavas were instrumental in the transition from rock-cut architecture to stone temples. The earliest examples of Pallava constructions are rock-cut temples dating from 610–690 CE and structural temples between 690–900 CE. A number of rock-cut cave temples bear the inscription of the Pallava king, Mahendravarman I and his successors.

The greatest accomplishments of the Pallava architecture are the rock-cut temples at Mahabalipuram. There are excavated pillared halls and monolithic shrines known as *rathas* in Mahabalipuram. Early temples were mostly dedicated to Shiva. The Kailasanatha temple in Kanchipuram and the Shore Temple built by Narasimhavarman II are fine examples of the Pallava style temples.

Mahabalipuram

Mahabalipuram also known as Mamallapuram is a town in Kancheepuram district in the Indian state of Tamil Nadu. It has an average elevation of 12 metres (39 feet).

Mahabalipuram was a 7th century port city of the South Indian dynasty of the Pallavas around 60 km south from the city of Chennai in Tamil Nadu. It is believed to have been named after the Pallava king Mamalla. It has various historic monuments built largely between the 7th and the 9th century, and has been classified as a UNESCO World Heritage Site.

History

The temples of Mamallapuram, built largely during the reigns of Narasimhavarman and his successor Rajasimhavarman, showcase the movement from rock-cut architecture to structural building. The mandapa or pavilions and the rathas or shrines shaped as temple chariots are hewn from the granite rock face, while the famed Shore Temple, erected half a century later, is built from dressed what makes Mamallapuram so culturally resonant are the influences it absorbs and disseminates. The Shore Temple includes many bas reliefs including one 100 ft. long and 45 ft. high carved out of granite.

All but one of the rathas from the first phase of Pallava architecture are modelled on the Budhist viharas or monasteries and chaitya halls with several cells arranged around a courtyard. Art historian Percy Brown, in fact, traces the possible roots of the Pallava Mandapa to the similar rock-cut caves of Ajanta Caves and Ellora Caves. Referring to Narasimhavarman's victory in AD 642 over the Chalukyan king Pulakesin II, Brown says the Pallava king may have brought the sculptors and artisans back to Kanchi and Mamallapuram as 'spoils of war'.

Landmarks

The monuments are mostly rock-cut and monolithic, and constitute the early stages of Dravidian architecture wherein Buddhist elements of design are prominently visible. They are constituted by cave temples, monolithic *rathas* (chariots), sculpted reliefs and structural temples. The pillars are of the Dravidian order. The sculptures are excellent examples of Pallava art.

It is believed by some that this area served as a school for young sculptors. The different sculptures, some half finished, may have been examples of different styles of architecture, probably demonstrated by instructors and practiced on by young students. This can be seen in the *Pancha Rathas* where each *Ratha* is sculpted in a different style. These five Rathas were all carved out of a single piece of granite in situ. While excavating Khajuraho Alex Evans a stone mason and sculptor recreated a stone sculpture made out of sandsstone, which is softer than granite, under 4 feet that took about 60 days to carve. the carving at Mahabalipuram must have required hundreds of highly skilled sculptors.

Some important structures include:

Thirukadalmallai-the temple dedicated to Lord Vishnu. It was also built by Pallava King in order to safeguard the sculptures from the ocean. It is told that after building this temple, the remaining architecture was preserved and was not corroded by sea.

Sthalasayana Perumal Temple-The Sthalasayana Perumal Temple is at Mahabalipuram. The Temple resides as the first and foremost of Mahabalipuram sculptures. It is one of the 108 Divya desam.

The temple

The temple stands on the shore and it was built along with the other sculptures. It is a small temple with two major Shrines for Lord Sthalasayana Perumal and Nilamangai Thayaar. This is the avatrasthalam (Birthplace) of Bhoothathazhwar, the 2nd Azhwar. There is also a separate shrine for Lord Narasimha. The architecture depicts the pallava style. This shrine was built by Pallava kings. Bhoothathazhwar was found in a tank that is opposite to the temple.

The place is also famous for its Adivaraha shrine near the seashore, where the Lord is known as "Valavendai Gnanapiran" or the Lord having His Consort on His right side unlike other places with His Consort on the left side like the nearby Thiruvidaventhai divyadesam.

Legend

Sage Pundareeka was worshipping Lord Vishnu with Lotus flowers. Once the Sage Pundareeka started piling water from the ocean in order to get the divine vision of Lord Vishnu. Seeing his devotion, Lord Vishnu came in guise as an old man and asked for food. The Sage went to get food for the old man. When he returned he found Lord Vishnu in an Ananthasayana posture and wearing the lotus flowers which was offered by the sage. He then realised that it is Lord himself had come in disguise to bless the devotee.

Descent of the Ganges

Descent of the Ganges at Mahabalipuram, in the Tamil Nadu state India, is one of a group of monuments that were designated as a World Heritage Site since 1984. Measuring 96 feet (29 m) long by 43 feet (13 m) high, it is a giant open-air relief carved of the a monolithic rock. The monuments and sanctuaries were built by the Pallava kings in the 7th and 8th centuries. The legend depicted in the relief is the story of the descent of the sacred river Ganga to earth from the heavens led by Bhagirata. The waters of Ganges are believed to possess supernatural powers. The descent of the Ganges and Arjuna's Penance are portrayed in stone at the Pallava heritage site

Two Interpretations

In one interpretation, a figure in the bas-relief who is standing on one leg is said to be Arjuna performing an austerity Tapas to receive a boon from Shiva as an aid in fighting the Mahabharata war. (The boon which Arjuna is said to have received was called Pasupata, Shiva's most powerful weapon).

The bas relief is situated on a rock with a cleft. Above the cleft was a collecting pool, and at one time, water may have flowed along the cleft. Figures within the cleft are said to represent Ganga or the River Ganges and Shiva. This provides the basis for an alternative interpretation of the mural. Rather than Arjuna, the figure performing austerities is said to be Bhagiratha. Bhagiratha is said to have performed austerities so that Ganga might descend to earth and wash over the ashes of his relatives, releasing them from their sins. To break Ganga's fall from heaven to earth, she falls onto Shiva's hair, and is divided into many streams by his tresses

Arjuna's Penance –

Arjuna's Penance or Bhagiratha's Penace is the name of a massive open air bas-relief monolith dating from the 7th century CE located in the town of Mahabalipuram in Southern India. Measuring 96 feet long by 43 feet high, the bas-relief is also known as The Descent of Ganga. The bas-relief has two names, because there is not full agreement regarding which stories the mural depicts.

Interpretations

In one interpretation, a figure in the bas-relief who is standing on one leg is said to be Arjuna performing an austerity Tapas to receive a boon from Shiva as an aid in fighting the Mahabharata war. (The boon which Arjuna is said to have received was called Pasupata, Shiva's most powerful weapon).

The bas relief is situated on a rock with a cleft. Above the cleft was a collecting pool, and at one time, water may have flowed along the cleft. Figures within the cleft are said to represent Ganga or the River Ganges and Shiva. This provides the basis for an alternative interpretation of the mural. Rather than Arjuna, the figure performing austerities is said to be Bhagiratha. Bhagiratha is said to have performed austerities so that Ganga might descend to earth and wash over the ashes of his relatives, releasing them from their sins. To break Ganga's fall from heaven to earth, she falls onto Shiva's hair, and is divided into many streams by his tresses.

Figures

One of the notable, and perhaps ironic figures in the bas-relief is the figure of a cat standing on one leg (apparently as an austerity). This may be related to the Panchatantra story of the cat who poses as an ascetic in order to lure a hare and a bird to come near. (When near, he devours them.)

Varaha Cave Temple

Varaha Cave Temple, an example of Indian rock-cut architecture dating from the late 7th century, is a rock-cut cave temple located at Mamallapuram, a tiny village south of Chennai in the state of Tamil Nadu, India. Part of the Group of Monuments at Mahabalipuram, the temple is a UNESCO World Heritage Site.

Temple

The temple is a small monolithic rock-cut temple with a mandapam dating from the 7th century. Inside the side walls have large sculptured panels depicting Vishnu as Varaha, the boar, holding up Bhudevi, the earth goddess, good examples of naturalistic Pallava art. The Pallava doorkeepers are four pillars that have lion carved into the bases. Inside, on rear wall, is the shrine with guardian figures on either

The Shore Temple

The Shore Temple (700-728 CE) is so named because it over looks the Bay of Bengal. It is a structural temple, built with blocks of granite, dating from the 8th century AD. It was built on a promontory sticking out into the Bay of Bengal at Mamallapuram, a tiny village south of Chennai in the state of Tamil Nadu, India. The village was a busy port during the 7th and 8th century reign of the Pallava dynasty during the reign of Narasimhavarman II. As one of the Group of Monuments at Mahabalipuram, it has been classified as a UNESCO World Heritage Site. It is one of the oldest structural (versus rock-cut) stone temples of South India.

Architecture

The Shore Temple is a five-storeyed structural Hindu temple rather than rock-cut as are the other monuments at the site. It is the earliest important structural temple in Southern India. Its pyramidal structure is 60 ft high and sits on a 50 ft square platform.

There is a small temple in front which was the original porch. It is made out of finely cut local granite. the shore temple is also one of the most popular temples. Recent excavations have revealed new structures here under the sand.

Shrines

The temple is a combination of three shrines. The main shrine is dedicated to Shiva as is the smaller second shrine. A small third shrine, between the two, is dedicated to a reclining Vishnu and may have had water channeled into the temple, entering the Vishnu shrine.

The two Shiva shrines are orthogonal in configuration. The entrance is through a transverse barrel vault gopuram. The two shikharas have a pyramidal outline, each individual tier is distinct with overhanging eaves that cast dark shadows. The outer wall of the shrine to Vishnu and the inner side of the boundary wall are extensively sculptured and topped by large sculptures of Nandi. The temple's outer walls are divided by plasters into bays, the lower part being carved into a series of rearing lions.

Deities

The temple has a garbhagriha in which the deity, Sivalinga, is enshrined, and a small mandapa surrounded by a heavy outer wall with little space between for circumambulation. At the rear are two shrines facing opposite directions.

The inner shrine dedicated to *Ksatriyasimnesvara* is reached through a passage while the other, dedicated to Vishnu, faces the outside. The Durga is seated on her lion *vahana*. A small shrine may have been in the cavity in the lion's chest.

Significance

The Shore Temples configuration of the two Shiva shrines with the small Vishnu shrine in between illustrates an attempt to balance the different, competing religious requirements.

Pancha Rathas (Five Chariots)

Pancha Rathas an example of monolith Indian rock-cut architecture dating from the late 7th century located at Mamallapuram, a tiny village south of Madras in the state of Tamil Nadu, India. As one of the Group of Monuments at Mahabalipuram, it has been classified as a UNESCO World Heritage Site.

The Pancha Rathas shrines were carved during the reign of King Mahendravarman I and his son Narasimhavarman I. Each temple is a monolith, carved whole from a rock outcropping of pink granite. The five monolithic pyramidal structured shrines are named after the Pandavas (Arjuna, Bhima, Yudhishtra, Nakula and Sahadeva) and Draupadi. As noted, each shrine is not assembled from cut rock but carved from one single large piece of stone. It is likely their original design traces back to wood constructions.

Underwater City

According to descriptions by early travel writers from Britain, the area near Mahabalipuram had seven pagodas by the sea. Accounts of Mahabalipuram were first written down by British traveller John Goldingham who was told of the "Seven Pagodas" when he visited in 1798.

An ancient port city and parts of a temple built in the 7th century may have been uncovered by the tsunami that resulted from the 2004 Indian Ocean earthquake. As the waves gradually receded, the force of the water removed sand deposits that had covered various rocky structures and revealed carvings of animals, which included an elaborately carved head of an elephant and a horse in flight.

A small square-shaped niche with a carved statue of a deity could be seen above the head of the elephant. In another structure, there was a sculpture of a reclining lion. The use of these animal sculptures as decorations is consistent with other decorated walls and temples from the Pallava period in the 7th and 8th centuries.

Seven Pagodas of Mahabalipuram

The Myth

The name "Seven Pagodas" has served as a nickname for the south Indian city of Mahabalipuram, also called Mamallapuram, since the first European explorers reached the city. The phrase "Seven Pagodas" refers to a myth that has circulated in India, Europe, and other parts of the world for over eleven centuries. Mahabalipuram's Shore Temple, built in the 8th century CE under the reign of Narasimhavarman II, stands at the shore of the Bay of Bengal. Legend has it that six other temples once stood with it.

An ancient Brahman legend explains the pagodas' origins in mythical terms. Prince Hiranyakasipu refused to worship the god Vishnu. The prince's son, Prahlada, loved Vishnu greatly, and criticized his father's lack of faith. Hiranyakasipu banished Prahlada, but then relented and allowed him to come home. Father and son quickly began to argue about Vishu's nature. When Prahlada stated that Vishnu was present everywhere, including in the walls of their home, his father kicked a pillar. Vishnu emerged from the pillar in the form of a man with a lion's head, and killed Hiranyakasipu. Prahlada eventually became king, and had a son named Bali. Bali founded Mahabalipuram on this site. (Adapted from Coombes, 23-4.)

Unclear Ancient Evidence

The temples' origins have been obscured by time, lack of complete written records, and storytelling. Englishman D. R. Fyson, a long-time resident of Madras (now Chennai), wrote a concise book on the city of Mahabalipuram titled *Mahabalipuram or Seven Pagodas,* which he intended as a souvenir volume for Western visitors to the city. In it, he states that the Pallava King Narasimharavarman I either began or greatly enlarged upon Mahabalipuram, circa 630 CE (Fyson 1). Archaeological evidence has not yet clearly proven whether Narasimharavarman I's city was the earliest to inhabit this location.

About 30 years prior to the founding of Narasimharavarman I's city, Pallava King Mahendravarman I had begun a series of "cave temples," which were carved into rocky hillsides (Fyson 2). Contrary to what the name suggests, they often did not begin as natural caves. Mahendravarman I and Narasimharavarman I also ordered construction of free-standing temples, called rathas in the region's language, Tamil. Nine rathas currently stand at the site (Ramaswami, 209). Construction of both types of temples in Mahabalipuram appears to have ended around 640 CE (Fyson 3). Fyson states that archaeological evidence supports the claim that a monastery, or vihara in Tamil, existed in ancient Mahabalipuram. The idea of the monastery would have been adopted from practices of the region's past Buddhist inhabitants. Fyson suggests that the monks' quarters may have been divided between a number of the city's rathas, based on their division into small rooms. Buddhist influence is also apparent in the traditional pagoda shape of the Shore Temple and other remaining architecture.

Fyson devoted only the next to the last page of his slim book to the actual myth of the Seven Pagodas. He recounts a local myth regarding the pagodas, that the god Indra became jealous of this earthly city, and sank it during a great storm, leaving only the Shore Temple above water He also recounts the assertion of local Tamil people that at least some of the other temples can be seen "glittering beneath the waves" from fishing boats. Whether the six missing pagodas exist does not seem to matter much to Fyson; the Seven Pagodas gave his beloved city its nickname and fame, and that seems to be the important part for him. However tne six missing temples have continued to fascinate locals, archaeologists, and lovers of myth alike, and have recently returned to the archaeological spotlight.

European Explorers

Indian historian N. S. Ramaswami names Marco Polo as one of the earliest European visitors to Mahabalipuram. Polo left few details of his visit, but did mark it on his Catalan Map of 1275 (Ramaswami, 210).

Many Europeans later spoke of the Seven Pagodas following travelers to their colonies in India. The first to write of them was John Goldingham, an English astronomer living in Madras in the late 18th and early 19th centuries. He wrote an account of his visit and the legend in 1798, which was later collected by Mark William Carr in his 1869 book *Descriptive and Historical Papers Relating to the Seven Pagodas on the Coromandel Coast*. Goldingham mainly described art, statues, and inscriptions found throughout the archaeological site at Mahabalipuram. He copied many of the inscriptions by hand, and included them in his essay. Goldingham interprets most of the signs as picture-symbols, and discusses what meaning their shapes may have. Interestingly, Benjamin Guy Babington, author of another essay in the same volume, identified several of the figures in Goldingham's copied inscriptions as Telugu letters. Babington's note on the text is included as a footnote to Goldingham's work.

In 1914, British writer J.W. Coombes related the common European belief on the origin of the pagoda legend. According to him, the pagodas once stood on the edge of the shore, and their copper domes reflected sunlight and served as a nautical landmark. He claims that modern people do not know for sure how many pagodas once existed. He believes that the number was close to seven.

N. S. Ramaswami places much of the responsibility for the myth's European propagation on the poet Robert Southey, who mentioned it in his poem "The Curse of Kehama," published in 1810 (Ramaswami, 205). He refers to the city by another of its popular names, Bali. In his poem, Southey clearly states that more than one of the Seven Pagodas is visible (See stanza 4). Southey told romantic tales of many cultures around the world, including India, Rome, Portugal, Paraguay, and Native American tribes, all of which were based on accounts of others' travels, and his own imagination. "The Curse of Kehama" certainly played a role in rising Orientalism.

Ramaswami's words for European explorers are not entirely negative. He notes that, before Europeans began to visit South India toward the beginning of the Raj, many of the smaller monuments at Mahabalipuram were partially or entirely covered with sand. The colonizers and their families played an important role in uncovering the archaeological site in their free time. Once early English archaeologists realized the extent and beauty of the site, toward the end of the eighteenth century, they appointed experienced antiquarians such as Colin Mackenzie to preside over the dig (Ramaswami, 210).

Is the Myth True?

Twenty-first century probes of the coast off Mahabalipuram have not yet conclusively proven the truth of the Seven Pagodas myth. They do bring archaeologists and historians closer to believing in the myth. As exploration continues, we will come closer to knowing the reality behind the pagodas.

Pallava Society

The Pallavas political history covering four centuries is tortous and complex but their contribution to society is singnificant in two ways-comletion of Aryanisation of southern India, and consmation of traditional or indigenous art.

The Aryanisation of south India as completed during the period of the Pallavas. Their grants show that the Aryan structure of society has gained frim hold on the south by the sixth century. Grants to brahmins are specifically mentioned which show that the north Indian Dharma Sastras had acquired authority in the Pallava kingdom. Sanskrit had established its sway. The university of Kanchi played to doubt a great part in India, and we know from Hiuen-Tsang that it was the greatest center of education in the south. Vatsyayana, the logician, the author of Nyaya Bhashya who lived in the fourth century. A.D, seems tohave been Pandit of Kanchi. Denage the famous Buddhist dialectian is also said to have had his training in the souther capital. In the fifth century we have epigraphic record of Nayurrasarman of the Kadamba family going for higher studies to Kanchi. In fact it can ligtimately be calimed that Kanchi of the Paalvas was the great center from which the Sanksritisation of the south as well as the Indian colonies in the far-east proceeded.

Pallavas were orthdox Hindus and they patronized the great reformation of the medival ages. Most of the kings ere brahminical Hindus devoted to the worship of Shiva. Mahendravarman was the first, who about the middle of his reign, adopted the worship of Siva and he was influenced by the famous saints of the age. He showed reverence to other Hindu gods also. But, he was intolerant of Jainism and destroyed some Jain monastries. Some Vaishnava and Saiva saints lived during his time. In general, the Pallavas were tolerant to other sects. Buddhism and Jainism lost their appeal. Indeed Hiuen-Tsang saw at Kanchi one hundred Buddhist monastries and 10,000 priests belonging to the Mahayana school but this has to be taken with a pinch of salt.

In general, the vedic tradition was super imposed on the local traditions, As brahmins were custodians of Vedic tradition, they automaticalldy enjoyed privillages. The Vedic tradition, a little later, received stimulus because of Sankarcharya. The Temples were the focal points. The out-castes were not permitted to enter the precincts of the temple.

Even then, Tamil saints of the 6th and 7th centuries, who were the progenitors of the bhakti movement, mostly belonged to the lower castes. The hymns and sermonsof the nayanaras (Shaivism) and the slvars (vaishnavism) continued the tradition. Amongst the Shaiva saints the important were Appar (supposed to have converted Mahendravarman) Sambandar, Manikkawasagar, and Sundarar. The most .... about them was the presence of women, Saints, such as Andal. This Bhakti cult was derived from the ideas in the Upanishads and also from the heterodox doctrines. Dr. Thapar opines that the concepts of comapassonate God was a resultant of the impact of Buddhist ideas particularly the bodhisttava concept, although the chirstians in malabar might have provided a new perception of religion. What the bhakti movement contributed was great. The religious hymns and music as popularized by Tamil saints were sung during temple rituals. Dancing was also included. From the Pallavi period onwards dancers were maintained by all the prosperous temples.

Regarding education, in the early days, education was imparted by Jains and Buddhists. The Jaina institutions were located at Madurai and Kanchi. Soon brahminical institutions superseded them. Ghatkias or Hindu colleges were attached to the temples. They were primarily Brahmin institutions are mostly confined themselves to advanced studies. And in the 8th century the maths also became popular, which was an ominous institutions because of its being a rest-house, a feeding center and an education center. In all these colleges Sanskrit was the medium of instruction which was also the official language. Kanchi, the capital, was a great cencentre of Sanskrit learning. The scientific works of Varahmihira and the poetry of Kalidasa and Bhairvi were-known in the Pallava country. And Parameshvaravarman I granted the Kurran copper-plate that was made for the recitation of the Mahabharata in a mandapa at the village of Kurram, near Conjeevaram.

By the beginning of the 7th century the Pallavas of Kanchi, the Chalukyas of Badami and the Pandyas of Madurai emerged as the three major states. By the time the political rule of these dynasties came to an end, an event known as the revolt of the Kalabharas took place. The Pallavas, the Kadambas (North Canara in Karnataka) and the Chalukyas of Badami along with along with a large number of their contemporaries were the protage of vedic sacrifices. Logically, the brahmins emerged as an important segment of society but at the expense of the peasantry. Possibly, this predominance was oppressive leading to the revoltof the kalabhars in the 6th century. A.D. It is also said that they overthrew in numberable kings and established their old inTamilnadu. They ended the Brahmadeva rights earlier granted to brahmins in numerous villages. It is also said that the Kalabhras patronized Buddhism. In the end, the revolt of the kalabhras could be ended only by the Joint efforts of the Pandays, the Pallavas and the Chalukays.

Pallava Administration

Kingship was attributed to define origin. The kings claimed their descent from the God Brahma. It has hereditary. Yet, on one occasion a king was elected. Most of the kings were accomplished scholars. Mahendravarman I wrote the famous burlesque, Masttavilasa Prahsana. Many of the vaishnava alvars and saiva nayanars flourished during their rule.

The kings adopted high-sounding titles like maharajadhiraja, dharma-maharjadhiraja (great king of kings rulling in accordance with the dharma), asvamedha-yaji (he who has performed the agnithtoma-vajapeya and asvamedha sacrifices) They were assisted by ministers. History shows that the ministerial council played a great part in the state policy in the later period.

A hierarchy of officials in provincial administration, the governor ofa province was assisted by district officers, who in turn worked in collaboration with automous local bodies. In local administration the meeting of assembles were frequent, and the administration the meeting of assemblies were frequent, and the assemblies were of many varieities and of many levels. Often special meetings were held. As the village levelthe assembly was the sabha which looked after almost all the matters of the village, along with endowments, irrigation, crime, maintaining census and other necessary records, Courts at villages level dealt with minor criminal cases. The judicial courts of the town and districts were presided over by government officials, climaxing with the king as the supreme arbiter of justice. The sabha worked in close association with the urar, and informal gathering of the entire village. Above this unit was a district administration. Finally, the head man of the villages was the link between the village assembly and the official administration.

Theoretically the king owned the land. The status of a village depended on the prevalent land tenure. The fist variety was the village with inter-caste population where in the people paid taxes to the king. The second was the brahmadeya village in which the entire land was donated to a single Brahmin or a group of brahmins. A variation of this village was the agrahars grant which, was an entire village settlement of brahmins. Both these forms were exempt from royal taxes. In the devadana village the revenue was donated to a temple, and the temple authorities in turn provided employment for the villagers in the temple whenever possible. In the Pallava period the first two categories of villages were in vogue.

Apart from these major points relating to land there was a special category of land, the sripatti or tank land. The revenue from such a land was sent apart for the maintenance of the village tank. The tank itself was built by the efforts of the entire village. All shared the water stored in the tank. Very many inscriptions of the Pallavas refer to the up-keep of tanks.

There are two Points about taxes. The land revenue varied from one-sixth to one tenth of the produce of the land. This was paid to the State. The local taxes that were collected in a village were spent for the needs of the village. As land revenue was necessarily small, the State revenue was supplemented by additional taxes on draught cattle, marriage-parties, potters, makers of clarified butter, textile manufacturers, washermen and weavers. The major source of revenue was from land, since the revenue from mercantile activity was not fully exploited.

Regarding expenditure, most to the revenue want for the maintenance of army. The king preferred a standing army instead of feudal levie. The army primarily consisting of food soldiers and cavalry along with a sprinkling of elephants. Indeed the Pallavas developed a navy although the mercantile activity was not great. Two dockyards were built at Mahablipuram and Nagabatnam. This pioneeringh effort of the Pallavas reached its climax during the days of cholas. The navy served a double purpose. It was meant for defence and also assisted the maritime trade with souteast Asia, particularly with the three kingdoms of Kambuja (Cambodia) Champa (Annam) and Shrivijaya (Malayan peninsula and Sumatra).

Pallava Literature

DaG in DaGin is a 6th-7th century Sanskrit author of prose romances and expounder on poetics. Although he produced literature on his own, most notably the Dauakumaracarita, first translated in 1927 as *Hindoo Tales, or The Adventures of the Ten Princes,* he is best known for composing the *Kavyadarua* ('Mirror of Poetry'), the handbook of classical Sanskrit poetics, or Kâvya. His writings were all in Sanskrit. He lived in Kanchipuram in modern-day Tamil Nadu.

Kavyadarua

The *Kavyadarua* is the earliest surviving systematic treatment of poetics in Sanskrit. It has been shown that *Kavyadarua* was strongly influenced by the Bhammikavya of Bhammi. In *Kavyadarua,* DaG

in argued that a poem's beauty derived from its use of rhetorical devices – of which he distinguished thirty-six types. He was the main proponent of *gunaprasthana,* the view that poetry needed qualities or virtues such as *shlesa* (punning), *prasada* (favour), *samata* (sameness), *madhurya* (beauty), *arthavyakti* (interpretation), and *ojah* (vigour). Poetry consisted in the presence of one of these qualities or a combination of them.

He is also known for his complex sentences and creation of very long compound words (some of his sentences ran for half a page, and some of his words for half a line).

Dauakumaracarita

The Dauakumaracarita (The Tale of the Ten Princes), translated into English as "The Adventures of the Ten Princes", is a Sanskrit *Katha* (story), written in the 6th or 7th century by a renowned Sanskrit writer DaG in. Most of the extant manuscripts of this text comprise two parts: the Purvapimhikâ and the Uttarapimhika, the proper Dauakumaracarita (though a few manuscripts do not consist the Purvapimhika). A number of manuscripts also have th.ee parts: the Purvapimhika, the Dauakumaracarita (proper) and a small separate Uttarapimhika.

Contents

The story describes the adventures of ten princes, who have been disinherited: Somadatta, Puspodbhava, Rajavahana, Apaharavarman, Upaharavarman, Arthapala, Pramati, Mitragupta, Mantragupta and Visruta and their pursuits of love and power.

The Purvapimhika, an introductory text, probably added later, comprises five *ucchavasas*. The first *ucchavasa* describes the birth of the ten princes. The second deals with the *digvijaya* (campaign) of Rajavahana. The third deals with the adventures of Somadattta and his marriage with Princes Vamalocana. The fourth *ucchavasa* narrates the adventures of Puspodbhava and his marriage with Balacandrika. The fifth *ucchavasa%* narrates the marriage of Rajavahana with Avantisundari.

The Uttarapimhika or the Dauakumaracarita (proper) consists eight *ucchavasas* which deal with the adventures of eight princes: Rajavahana, Apaharavarma, Upaharavarma, Arthapala, Pramati, Mitragupta, Mantragupta and Visruta.

The separate Uttarapimhika, found in some manuscripts, is basically a short supplement, winds up the story, which ends with the slaying of Manasara and the annexation of Malava to Puspapura and division of the empire into several principalities.

It is perhaps one of the earliest examples of a novel. In the Clay Sanskrit Series, it is translated as *What Ten Young Men Did.*

Bharavi

Bharavi was a Sanskrit poet known for his *Mahakavya* (epic), the *Kiratarjuniya* (Arjuna and the Mountain Man) in 18 cantos based on an episode from the Mahabharata.

Time and Place

As with most Sanskrit poets, very few concrete details are available about Bharavi's life, and inferences must be made from references to him. A Chalukya inscription from 634 CE mentions him and Kalidasa as famous poets of the past. In another inscription, the king Durvinita of the Western Ganga Dynasty mentions having written a commentary on the fifteenth canto of Bharavi's Kiratarjuniya. The Western Ganga Dynasty ruled from about the middle of the fourth century, and Durvinita is usually believed to have lived in the later half of the sixth century.

The poet DaGin, who was born in the middle of the seventh century, reports that his great-grandfather was a friend of Bharavi and was introduced by him to a king VicGuvardhana, before receiving patronage from Durvinita and King Simhavishnu of the Pallava dynasty. This is unlikely to be Vishnuvardhana II (673–682 CE) and is more likely to be Yasodharman Vishnuvardhana, placing Bharavi's floruit in c. 530–550 CE.

Bharavi probably belonged to Southern India. "Bharavi" means "lustre of the sun". It is reported that his original name was Dâmodara, although this may have been an error.

Work

Kiratarjuniya is a Sanskrit *kavya* by Bharavi, written in the 6th century or earlier. It is an epic poem in eighteen cantos describing the combat between Arjuna and lord Shiva in the guise of a *kirata* or mountain-dwelling hunter. Along with the *Naicadhacarita* and the *Uiupalavadha*, it is considered to be one of the three best among the six Sanskrit *mahakavyas*, or great epics.

Synopsis and Appraisal

The *Kiratarjuniya* predominantly features the *Vîra rasa*, or the mood of valour., and expands upon a minor episode in the *Vana Parva* ("Forest book") in the *Mahabharata*. While the Pandavas are exiled in the forest, Draupadi and Bhima incite Yudhisthira to declare war with the Kauravas, while he does not relent. Finally, Arjuna, at the instruction of Indra, propitiates Lord Shiva with penance (*tapasya*) in the forest. Pleased by his austerities, Lord Shiva decides to reward him. When a demon named Muka, in the form of a wild boar, charges toward Arjuna, Shiva appears in the form of a Kirata, a wild mountaineer. Arjuna and the Kirata simultaneously shoot an arrow at the boar, and kill it. They argue over who shot first, and a battle ensues. They fight for a long time, and Arjuna is shocked that he cannot conquer this Kirata. Finally, he recognises the god, and surrenders to him. Shiva, pleased with his bravery, gives him the powerful weapon, the Pashupatastra, which later in the *Mahabharata* aids him against Karna and the Kauravas during the Kurukshetra war.

Over a tenth of the verses from this work are quoted in various anthologies and works on poetics. The most popular verse is the 37th from the eighth canto, which describes nymphs bathing in a river, and is noted for its beauty. Another verse from the fifth canto (*utphulla sthalanalini...*) is noted for its imagery, and has given Bharavi the sobriquet of "Chhatra Bharavi", as he describes the pollen of the lotus flowers being blown by the wind into a golden umbrella (*Chhatra*) in the sky. Thus, for having verses that are pleasing to lay people as well as clever verses appreciated by scholars, the work is considered to have 'harmony' or 'appropriateness' at all levels, and has been said to possess *samastalokarañjakatva*, the quality of delighting all the people.

The *Kiratarjuniya* is the only known work of Bharavi. It "is regarded to be the most powerful poem in the Sanskrit language". A. K. Warder considers it the "most perfect epic available to us", over Aœvaghoca's *Buddhacarita*, noting its greater force of expression, with more concentration and polish in every detail. Despite using extremely difficult language and rejoicing in the finer points of Sanskrit grammar, Bharavi achieves conciseness and directness. His alliteration, "crisp texture of sound", and choice of metre closely correspond to the narrative.

Offshoots and Commentaries

Bharavi's "power of description and dignity of style" were an inspiration for Magha's *Shishupala Vadha*, which is modelled after the *Kiratarjuniya* and seeks to surpass it. While Bharavi uses 19 different types of metres, Magha uses 23; while Bharavi praises Shiva, Magha extols Vishnu; and he has his own instances of one-consonant and *sarvatobhadra* palindromic verses.

A *vyayoga* (a kind of play), also named *Kiratarjuniya* and based on Bharavi's work, was produced by the Sanskrit dramatist Vatsaraja in the 12th or 13th century.

The authoritative commentary on the *Kiratarjuniya*, as on the other five *mahakayvas*, is by Mallinatha. His commentary on the *Kiratarjuniya* is known as the *GhaGmâpatha* (*the Bell-Road*) and explains the multiple layers of compounds and figures of speech present in the verses.

The first Western translation of the poem was by Carl Cappeller into German, published by the Harvard Oriental Series in 1912. There have since been six or more partial translations into English.

5

Notable Temples

Mahadeva Temple

The Mahadeva Temple at Itagi dedicated to Shiva is among the larger temples built by the Western Chalukyas and perhaps the most famous. The Mahadeva Temple was built based on The general plan of the Amruteshwara Temple at Annigeri (used as the prototype). The Mahadeva Temple has the same architectural components and there is a differences in their articulation.

The Mahadeva Temple at Itagi was built in c. 1112 CE by Mahadeva, a commander (*dandanayaka*) in the army of the Western Chalukya King Vikramaditya VI. Itagi is located about 22 miles (35 km) east of Gadag and 40 miles (64 km) west of Hampi. The temple is dedicated to Hindu God Shiva. The well-executed sculptures, finely crafted carvings on walls, pillars and the tower make it a good example of complete Western Chalukyan art which speaks volumes about the taste of the Chalukyan artisans. An inscription dated 1112 CE in the temple calls it "Emperor among Temples" (*Devalaya Chakravarti*). Art critic Henry Cousens has called this monument the "finest in Kannada country after Halebidu". These Western Chalukya monuments, regional variants of pre-existing dravida (South Indian) temples, defined the *Karnata dravida* tradition. The Mahadeva temple is officially protected as a national monument by the Archaeological Survey of India.

Details

Temple plan: The temple plan consists of a shrine (cella) which is connected to a closed *mantapa* (hall) by a vestibule (antechamber). The closed *mantapa* leads to an open pillared *mantapa,* with the temple as a whole facing the east. Some parts of the temple, such as the cornice and parapet over the outer edge of the roof of the open *mantapa* are missing. The main temple, the sanctum of which has a *linga* (symbol of Shiva), is surrounded by thirteen minor shrines, each with its own *linga*. The temple has two other shrines, dedicated to Murthinarayana and Chandraleshwari, parents of Mahadeva, the Chalukya commander who consecrated the temple.

Mantapa (Hall)

The closed *mantapa* has a doorway on each side, with the eastern doorway leading to the open *mantapa,* and the western doorway to the sanctum. The door panels are well wrought and the ceiling of the porches have a ribbed design in them. The decoration of the outer walls follows the same pattern as that of the shrine. The great open *mantapa* has 64 pillars, 24 of which are full pillars which start from the floor and support the main ceiling. The remaining are half pillars (or "dwarf pillars") which start from the bench (parapet wall) that surrounds the *mantapa* and support the sloping eaves. The pillars in this hall bear similarities to the porch pillars at the Dodda Basappa Temple at Dambal and the lathe-turned pillars (whose rounded sections are lathe turned) at the Kasivisvesvara Temple at Lakkundi.

The square ceiling of the open *mantapa* which are supported by the four central pillars exhibits interesting fretted stonework. The ceiling here has been worked into a decorative arabesque foliage and *makaras* (mythical beasts) which flow from the mouth of a *Kirtimukha* (gargoyle or demon face). This type of stonework is considered as high a quality as any. In stark contrast, the interior of the closed *mantapa* and the sanctum are plain and simple. It is believed that bracket figures that once adorned the outside pillars are now missing. These forward leaning bracket figures (Salabhanjika), which normally represent female forms in various poses (such as dancing or adorning themselves), would have rested on small blocks on the shaft of the pillars (capital), finding support from the underside of the overhanging cornice via a slot in their upper end.

Inscription in Medieval Kannada

Inscription in medieval Kannada on a huge stone adjacent to the temple describes the style of rule of Chalukyan kings and details on the construction of the temple. Inscription describes Mahadeva temple as Emperor of Temples of the Chalukya period built in 1112 A.D. by Mahadeva, an army general of King Vikramaditya VI.

Puskarni and Open well

The Mahadeva temple has a puskarani (teertha) on its front side (it is under renovation), which is still in use. An open well with steps (renovated) behind the temple.

Siddhesvara Temple

The Siddhesvara Temple (or Siddheshvara Temple) is located in the town of Haveri in Haveri district, Karnataka state, India. It is considered an ornate example of 12th century Western Chalukyan art and is well-known for the many loose sculptures of Hindu deities that exist in it, and is the finest testimonial for Vishwakarma Brahmin sthapathis in sculting this temple. However, inscriptional evidence would suggest that the initial consecration of the temple was in late 11th century. An interesting aspect about the temple is that it faces west, instead of facing the rising sun in the east–a standard in Chalukyan constructions. Though it is currently used as a Shaiva temple dedicated to God Shiva, historians are unsure by which faith or sect the temple was originally consecrated and to which deity. This uncertainty perhaps stems from the many loose sculptures of deities that exist and the degradation of primary wall images.

Temple Plan

The Siddhesvara temple, which is built of soapstone, is located at the east end of the town. From inscriptions, Haveri was originally called Nalapuri and was one of the oldest *agraharas* (place of learning) in modern Karnataka. An inscription dated 1067 CE in the town mentions the grant of the village to 400 Brahmins. The temple bears close resemblance to a few other Chalukyan temples in the vicinity of Haveri; the Muktesvara temple at Chavudayyadanapura, the Somesvara temple at Haralhalli and the Siddharamesvara temple at Niralgi. The entire basement of this temple has sunk by a few feet, making it necessary to descend into the open *mantapa* (hall). The temple may have been consecrated initially as a Vaishnava temple (to the God Vishnu), later taken over by Jains who may have removed some images from the temple and eventually become a Shaiva temple after coming under the procession of the worshippers of God Shiva. This conclusion is drawn because the image of the Sun God Surya exists below the little *Kirthimukhas* (gargoyle faces) on the eastern wall (back wall) of the temple, though, an image of Shiva, sculpted out of an independent slab of stone and mounted in front of the *Sikhara* (superstructure) above the *mantapa* roof, would suggest otherwise. Overall, the temple plan bears all the hallmarks of a standard 11th century Chalukyan construction with *dravida* architectural articulation to which some innovative 12th century elements such as aedicules, miniature decorative towers on pilasters, were added.

Sculptures

The *mantapa* (hall) in the temple contains sculptures of *Uma Mahesvara* (Shiva with his consort Uma), Vishnu and his consort Lakshmi, the Sun God Surya, Naga-Nagini (the male and female snake goddess), Ganapati and Kartikeya, the sons of Shiva. Shiva is depicted with four arms, holding his attributes: the *damaru* (drum), the *aksamala* (chain of beads) and the *trishul* (trident) in three arms. His lower left arm rests on Uma, who is seated on Shiva's lap, embracing him with her right arm while gazing into his face. The sculpture of Uma is well decorated with garlands, large earrings and curly hair. The Naga and Nagini, with their tails intertwined, appear on the side of the door to the vestibule (antechamber) along with an image of Parvati. A niche depicts a curious male figure with six hands, the two lower hands each hold a *linga* (the symbol of Shiva) and the middle left hand holds a *chakra* (wheel).

The architrave above the vestibule entrance bears images of Brahma, Shiva and Vishnu, with Shiva in the centre. Ganapati and Kartikeya flank Brahma and Vishnu. On either side of the doorway is a perforated stone worked window, and the main shrine (*garbhagriha* or cella) has a plain *linga* (the symbol of Shiva). Some ceiling panels contain images of the *saptamatrika* ("seven mothers") while a square column contains images of the *ashtadikpalas* ("eight guardians") along with the Hindu *trimurthy* ("three forms") and Surya. The *saptamatrikas* are also carved into the wall of a step well outside. The *saptamatrika* sculptures on friezes has the female deities, generally each with a child on the lap to denote motherhood and are identified by the *vahana* (vehicle) of their male counterpart, found under them. At one end of the frieze is Shiva and at the other is Ganapati.

Next to Shiva are the Matrika ("mother") goddessses: Brahmi (or Brahmani), Brahma's consort, with a goose; Maheshvari, the consort of Shiva has a Nandi (bull); Vaishnavi, the consort of Vishnu has a Garuda (eagle); Kaumari, the consort of Kartikeya has a peacock; Varahi, the consort of Varaha, has a buffalo (instead of a boar); Indrani, the consort of Indra, has an elephant; and the last "mother" could be a skeletal image of Chamunda with a dog or could be a dead body. Other loose sculptures in niches worthy of mention are those of Surya canopied by a seven hooded snake, and the Mahishasuramardini (a form of Durga). Within the temple premises are several old-Kannada inscriptions recording grants, the earliest of which is inscribed on a beam inside the temple and is dated to 1087 CE while another stone inscription (*shilashasana*) dated to 1108 CE stands outside.

Kasivisvesvara Temple, Lakkundi

The Kasivisvesvara temple (also spelt Kashivishveshvara) and sometimes called *Kashivishvanatha* temple is located in Lakkundi (Gadag district), Karnataka state, India. It is 11 km from Gadag city, 24 km from Dambal and about 50 km from Kuknur.

The centre of cultural and temple-building activity of the Western Chalukya Empire lay in the Tungabhadra river region, where large medieval workshops built numerous monuments, and the entire architectural wonders at this location are ultimate testimonial for Vishwakarma Brahmin sthapathis for planning and sculpting this architectural wonder. These monuments, regional variants of pre-existing dravida (South Indian) temples, defined the *Karnata dravida* tradition. Lakkundi in particular was the location of the mature phase of the Western Chalukya architecture, and the Kasivisvesvara temple marks a high point of these achievements. According the Henry Cousens, it is one of the most ornate temples in the Kannada spoken region of India.

The existence of a 1087 CE inscription on a beam in the temple mantapa (hall) and the plainness of that part of the temple suggests that the original construction may have been simpler and that the profusion of decoration may have been added to the other parts of the temple at a later period, with the end of Chola invasions of Chalukyan territory. Most of the inscriptions in Lakkundi date from 1170 CE onwards. It is known that Hoysala king Veera Ballala II annexed Lakkundi (also known as Lokkigundi) from the Seunas of Devagiri and made it his capital around 1193 CE. It is possible that the temple may have received embellishment during his rule.

Temple Plan

This is a double shrined temple (*dvikuta*). The shrine facing east is dedicated to Kasivisvesvara (Hindu god Shiva) whose universal symbol, a *linga,* stands three feet tall in the sanctum. The other shrine, which faces the main shrine is dedicated to the sun god Surya and is called *Suryanarayana.* The Surya shrine faces west, an unusual occurrence among Surya temples, which normally face east. The Kasivisvesvara temple epitomises the shift in Chalukyan artistic achievements, towards sharper and crisper stone work not seen in earlier constructions, taking full advantage of the effect of light and shade. Special attention was paid to mouldings, arches and other details on the tower, and decorations on door jambs and lintels.

The architects in the Karnataka region seem to have been inspired by architectural developments in northern India. This is evidenced by the fact that they incorporated decorative miniature towers (multi-aedicular towers depicting superstructures) of the *Sekhari* and *Bhumija* types, supported on pilasters, almost simultaneously with these developments in the temples in northern India. The miniature towers represented shrines, which in turn represented deities. Sculptural depictions of deities were generally discreet although not uncommon. Other northern ideas they incorporated were the pillar bodies that appeared as wall projections. Well-known constructions incorporating these features are found at the Kasivisvesvara Temple and the nearby Nannesvara Temple.

Decorative Features

The doorpost mouldings on the southern and eastern doorway are worthy of mention. On both sides of the southern doorway are four inner bands of scrolls which run up the sides and around the lower part of the entablature above. Next to these bands, on either side, in the centre, are tall columns or pilasters supporting the lower cornice above. Beyond these columns, on either side, are four more bands of decorative mouldings. On the lintel of the doorway is a dedicatory block containing an image of Gaja-Lakshmi with an elephant on either side. In fact, in the Kannada spoken regions, it is common to find the image of Lakshmi in the dedicatory block on the lintel irrespective of the temple's original dedication; whether the principle deity was Shiva, Vishnu or Jaina.

Above the lower cornice, the entablature consists of small figures, now numbering only three (must have been eleven originally) standing under cusped arches. The decoration on the eastern doorway, though not a fine as on the southern doorway, is worthy of praise for its filigree work. The doorway to the shrine (sanctum) rivals the exterior ones in finish. The dedicatory block on the lintel has an image of Gaja-Lakshmi and her elephants. Above the cornice is a procession of men and animals. These images, which are barely six inches tall, include horsemen and musicians. Above these images are the trinity of Hindu gods; Brahma, Vishnu and Shiva.

The ornamentation on the outer wall of the shrine consists of prominent central niches above which is a miniature tower (sikhara or aedicule) which is purely *nagara* (north Indian) in style and cuts through the principle cornice.

The decorative arch above the miniature tower is a conspicuous ornamental feature of the superstructure. The miniature tower–arch combination is repeated up the superstructure of the shrine. The finial (*kalasha*) and the capping structure of the tower is missing. In the temple hall, the pillars. The artisans fully availed the workable properties of finely grained stone (soapstone) to produce polished pillars whose shafts have a rounded appearance obtained by using a lathe.

Doddabasappa Temple

The Doddabasappa Temple is a 12th century Western Chalukyan architectural innovation in Dambal, Karnataka state, India. The temple is located about 20 km (13 miles) south–east of Gadag city and 24 km (16 miles) south–west of Ittagi in Koppal district. The sanctum contains a Shiva *linga*, the symbol of the presiding deity, God Shiva. The temple interior is a standard construction and consists of a sanctum (cella), a vestibule (*antarala*) and a main *mantapa* (also called *navaranga* or hall). The vestibule connects the sanctum to the *mantapa.* The Western Chalukya monuments, regional variants of pre-existing dravida (South Indian) temples, defined the *Karnata dravida* architectural tradition.

Temple plan

Stellate plan: The temple is based on a very original 24-pointed uninterrupted stellate plan (star shaped) and uses soapstone as its basic building material. Contemporary stellate plans of the Bhumija shrines in central India from where the inspiration for this temple came from, were all 32-pointed interrupted types. No temples of the 6-, 12-, or 24-pointed stellate plans are known to exist anywhere in Karnataka or Maharashtra, with the exception of the Doddabasappa temple, which can be described as a 24-pointed uninterrupted plan. In an 'interrupted' stellate plan, the stellate outline is interrupted by orthogonal (right-angle) projections in the cardinal directions, resulting in star points that have been skipped.

The Doddabasappa temple marks the mature development of the Chalukyan art which originated from basic *dravida* architecture of South India. Its departure from conventional *dravida* plan used in the Virupaksha temple in Pattadakal is so extreme that it would be very difficult to find similarities without detailed examination. A star shape is obtained by rotating a square about its centre. The star points form equidistant projections. The angles and re-entrant angles thus formed make the perimeter of the outerwall of the shrine.

The star projections are carried right up the superstructure (tower over the shrine–*Sikhara*), giving it an exotic look, though it loses strength in comparison to the square superstructures found in conventional *dravida* plans. The storied arrangement of the superstructure found in *dravida* plans is not easily distinguishable here. The upper tiers of the seven-tiered (*tala*) superstructure look like cogged wheels with 48 dents.

Other details

The pillars in this temple are finely chiselled and "complicated" but lack the elegance of those at the Kasivisvesvara Temple in Lakkundi. The entrance to the shrine has above it a decorative architrave with space for images (now missing) of the Hindu Gods Brahma, Vishnu and Shiva. Depending on the dedication of the temple, either Vishnu or Shiva would take the central position in this arrangement. The entrance to the sanctum is elaborately decorated on either side with designs that are floral containing tiny images of dancers, musicians and even a mithuna couple (Gemini). In the main mantapa (hall) there are three images, one of the "five headed" Brahma and his vehicle (*vahana*), the goose, and two images are of Surya, the Sun God. The temple has two doorways each with a porch, one facing south and the other facing east. The east facing door has on either side the remains of what must have been elegant lintel decoration, and an open hall type of pillared extension containing a large recumbent image of Nandi (bull) which faces the shrine.

Some temples, in a departure from the norm, were dedicated to deities other than Shiva or Vishnu. These include the Surya (portrayed as 'Suryanarayana') shrine at the Kasi Vishveshwara temple complex and a Jain temple dedicated to Mahavira, both at Lakkundi; the Taradevi temple (built in a Buddhist architectural style) at Dambal in the Gadag district; the Mahamaya temple dedicated to a tantric goddess at Kuknur in the Koppal district, and the Durga temple at Hirekerur in the Haveri district.

Chalukyas of Vengi

Eastern Chalukyas were a South Indian dynasty whose kingdom was located in the present day Andhra Pradesh. Their capital was Vengi and their dynasty lasted for around 500 years from the 7th century until c. 1130 C.E. when the Vengi kingdom merged with the Chola empire. The Vengi kingdom was continued to be ruled by Eastern Chalukyan kings under the protection of the Chola empire until 1189 C.E., when the kingdom succumbed to the Hoysalas and the Yadavas. They had their capital originally at Vengi now (Pedavegi, Chinavegi and Denduluru) near Eluru of the West Godavari district end later changed to Rajamahendravaram (Rajamundry).

Eastern Chalukyas were closely related to the Chalukyas of Vatapi (Badami). Throughout their history they were the cause of many wars between the more powerful Cholas and Western Chalukyas over the control of the strategic Vengi country. The five centuries of the Eastern Chalukya rule of Vengi saw not only the consolidation of this region into a unified whole, but also saw the efflorescence of Telugu culture, literature, poetry and art during the later half of their rule. It can be said to be the golden period of Andhra history.

Origin of Eastern Chalukyas

Pulakesin II (608–644 C.E), the greatest Badami Chalukya king, conquered the eastern Deccan, corresponding to the coastal districts of Andhra Pradesh 616 C.E., defeating the remnants of the Vishnukundina Empire. He appointed his brother Kubja Vishnu Vardhana as Viceroy. On the death of Pulakesin II, the Vengi Viceroyalty developed into an independent kingdom. Eastern Chalukyas of Vengi outlived the main Vatapi dynasty by many generations.

Between 641 C.E. and 705 C.E. some kings, except Jayasimha I and Mangi Yuvaraja, ruled for very short durations. Then followed a period of unrest characterised by family feuds and weak rulers. Meanwhile, the Rashtrakutas of Malkhed ousted Western Chalukyas of Badami.

The weak rulers of Vengi had to meet the challenge of the Rashtrakutas, who overran their kingdom more than once. There was no Eastern Chalukya ruler who could check them until Gunaga Vijayaditya III came to power in 848 C.E. The then Rashtrakuta ruler Amoghavarsha treated him as his ally and after Amoghavarsha's death, Vijayaditya proclaimed independence.

List of Eastern Chalukya Kings:

- Kubja Vishnuvardhana (624 – 641 C.E.)
- Jayasimha I (641 – 673 C.E.)
- Indra Bhattaraka (673 C.E.)
- Vishnuvardhana II (673 – 682 C.E.)
- Mangi Yuvaraja (682 – 706 C.E.)
- Jayasimha II (706 – 718 C.E.)
- Vishnuvardhana III (719 – 755 C.E.)
- Vijayaditya I (755 – 772 C.E.)
- Vishnuvardhana IV (772 – 808 C.E.)
- Vijayaditya II (808 – 847 C.E.)
- Vishnuvardhana V (847– 849 C.E.)
- Vijayaditya III (848 – 892 C.E.)

- Chalukya Bhima I (892 – 921 C.E.)
- Vijayaditya IV (921 C.E.)
- Amma I (921 – 927 C.E.)
- Vikramaditya II (927 – 928 C.E.)
- Yuddamalla II (928 – 935 C.E.)
- Chalukya Bhima II (935 – 947 C.E.)
- Amma II (947 – 970 C.E.)
- Danamava (970 – 973 C.E.)
- Jata Choda Bhima (973-1000 C.E.)
- Saktivarman I (1000-1011 C.E.)
- Vimaladitya (1011 – 1018 C.E.)
- Rajaraja Narendra (1018 – 1061 C.E.)
- Saktivarman II (1062 C.E.)
- Vijayaditya VII (1063 – 1068 C.E., 1072 – 1075 C.E.).

Administration

In its early life, the Eastern Chalukya court was essentially a republic of Badami, and as generations passed, local factors gained in strength and the Vengi monarchy developed features of its own. External influences still continued to be present as the Eastern Chalukyas had long and intimate contact, either friendly or hostile, with the Pallavas, the Rashtrakutas, the Cholas and the Chalukyas of Kalyani.

Type of Government

The Eastern Chalukyan government was a monarchy based on the Hindu philosophy. The inscriptions refer to the traditional seven components of the state (Saptanga), and the eighteen Tirthas (Offices), such as:

- Mantri (Minister)
- Purohita (Chaplain)
- Senapati (Commander)
- Yuvaraja (Heir-apparent)
- Dauvarika (Door keeper)
- Pradhana (Chief)
- Adhyaksha (Head of department) and so on.

No information is available as to how the work of administration was carried out. The *Vishaya* and *Kottam* were the administrative subdivisions known from records. The *Karmarashtra* and the *Boya-Kottams* are examples of these. The royal edicts (recording gifts of lands or villages) are addressed to all *Naiyogi Kavallabhas*, a general term containing no indication of their duties, as well as to the *Grameyakas*, the residents of the village granted. The *Manneyas* are also occasionally referred in inscriptions. They held assignments of land or revenue in different villages.

Fratricidal wars and foreign invasions frequently disturbed the land.

The territory was parcelled out into many small principalities (estates) held by the nobility consisting of collateral branches of the ruling house such as those of Elamanchili, Pithapuram and Mudigonda, and a few other families such as the Kona Haihayas (Heheya, Kalachuris), Kolanu Saronathas, Chagis, Parichedas, Kota Vamsas, Velanadus and Kondapadamatis, closely connected by marriage ties with the Eastern Chalukyas and families who were raised to high position for their loyal services. When the Vengi ruler was strong, the nobility paid allegiance and tribute to him, but when the weakness was apparent, they were ready to join hands with the enemies against the royal house.

Society

The population in the Vengi country was heterogeneous in character. Yuan Chwang, who travelled in the Andhra country after the establishment of the Eastern Chalukya kingdom, noted that the people were of a violent character, were of a dark complexion and were fond of arts. The society was based on hereditary caste system. Even the Buddhists and Jains who originally disregarded caste, adopted it. Besides the four traditional castes, minor communities like Boyas and Savaras (Tribal groups) also existed.

The Brahmins were held in high esteem in the society. They were proficient in Vedas and Shastras and were given gifts of land and money. They held lucrative posts such as councillors, ministers and members of civil service. They even entered the army and some of them rose to positions of high command. The Kshatriyas were the ruling class. Their love of intrigue and fighting was responsible for civil war for two centuries. The Komatis (Vaisyas) was flourishing trading community. Their organisation into a powerful guild (Nakaram) which had its headquarters in Penugonda (West Godavari) and branches in seventeen other centres had its beginnings in this period. It seems there used to be a minister for communal affairs (Samaya Mantri) in the government. The Sudras constituted the bulk of the population and there were several sub-castes among them. The army furnished a career for most of them and some of them acquired the status of Samanta Raju and Mandalika.

Religion

Buddhism, which was dominant during the Satavahanas was in decline. Its monasteries were practically deserted. Due to their love of sacred relics in stupas, a few might have lingered on, Yuan Chwang noticed some twenty or more Buddhist monasteries in which more than three thousand monks lived. Jainism, unlike Buddhism, continued to enjoy some support from the people. This is evident from the several deserted images in ruined villages all over Andhra.

The inscriptions also record the construction of Jain temples and grants of land for their support from the monarchs and the people. The rulers like Kubja Vishnuvardhana, Vishnuvardhana III and Amma II patronised Jainism. Vimaladitya even became a declared follower of the doctrine of Mahavira. Vijayawada, Jenupadu, Penugonda (West Godavari) and Munugodu were the famous Jain centres of the period. Hinduism was the official religion throughout the Chalukya period. Of the Hindu sects, Saivism was more popular than Vaishnavism.

Some of the rulers, declared themselves as *Parama Maheswaras* (Emperors). The Buddhist religious centres eventually attained great celebrity as Siva pilgrim centres. Eastern Chalukya rulers like Vijayaditya II, Yuddhamalla I, Vijayaditya III and Bhima I took active interest in the construction of many temples. The temple establishments like dancers and musicians show that during this period, temples were not only a centre of religious worship but a fostering ground for fine arts.

Literature

Telugu literature owes its origin to the Eastern Chalukyas. Poetry makes its first appearance in the Addanki and Kandukur inscriptions of Panduranga in the time of Vijayaditya II in the later half of the ninth century. However no literary work of any value appeared until 11th century C.E. Nannaya Bhatta's *Mahabharata* is the earliest extant work of Telugu literature. Nannaya was the poet-laureate of Rajaraja Narendra in the middle of the eleventh century C.E. An erudite scholar, he was well-versed in the Vedas, Sastras and the ancient epics, he undertook to translation of the Mahabharata in to Telugu. The fact that Narayana Bhatta who was proficient in eight languages assisted him in his endeavour. Though incomplete, his work is universally acclaimed as a masterpiece of Telugu literature. It remains unrivaled for its graceful end dignified diction and sweet and elegant verses.

6

Pala Empire

The Pala Empire was a Buddhist dynasty as well as one of the major middle kingdoms of India that ruled from the north-eastern region of the Indian subcontinent. The Palas were often described by opponents as the *Lords of Gauda*. The name *Pala* means *protector* and was used as an ending to the names of all Pala monarchs. The Palas were followers of the Mahayana and Tantric schools of Buddhism. Gopala was the first ruler from the dynasty. He came to power in 750 in Gour by a democratic election. This event is recognized as one of the first democratic elections in South Asia since the time of the Mahâ Janapadas. He reigned from 750-770 and consolidated his position by extending his control over all of Bengal. The Buddhist dynasty lasted for four centuries (750-1120 AD) and ushered in a period of stability and prosperity in Bengal. They created many temples and works of art as well as supported the Universities of Nalanda and Vikramashila. Somapura Mahavihara built by Dharmapala is the greatest Buddhist Vihara in the Indian Subcontinent.

The empire reached its peak under Dharmapala and Devapala. Dharmapala extended the empire into the northern parts of the Indian Subcontinent. This triggered once again the power struggle for the control of the subcontinent. Devapala, successor of Dharmapala, expanded the empire to cover much of South Asia and beyond. His empire stretched from Assam and Utkala in the east, Kamboja (modern day Afghanistan) in the north-west and Deccan in the south. According to Pala copperplate inscription Devapala exterminated the Utkalas, conquered the Pragjyotisha (Assam), shattered the pride of the Huna, and humbled the lords of Pratiharas, Gurjara and the Dravidas.

The death of Devapala ended the period of ascendancy of the Pala Empire and several independent dynasties and kingdoms emerged during this time. However, Mahipala I rejuvenated the reign of the Palas. He recovered control over all of Bengal and expanded the empire. He survived the invasions of Rajendra Chola and the Chalukyas. After Mahipala I the Pala dynasty again saw its decline until Ramapala, the last great ruler of the dynasty, managed to retrieve the position of the dynasty to some extent. He crushed the Varendra rebellion and extended his empire farther to Kamarupa, Orissa and Northern India.

The Pala Empire can be considered as the golden era of Bengal. Never had the Bengali people reached such height of power and glory to that extent. Palas were responsible for the introduction of Mahayana Buddhism in Tibet, Bhutan and Myanmar. The Palas had extensive trade as well as influence in south-east Asia. This can be seen in the sculptures and architectural style of the Sailendra Empire (present-day Malaya, Java, Sumatra). The Pala Empire eventually disintegrated in the 12th century under the attack of the Sena dynasty.

Origin of the Palas

The Ramacharitam of Sandhyakar Nandi attests that Varendra (or North Bengal) was the fatherland (*Janakabhu*) of the Palas. In the Bangarh Copperplate of Mahipala I, it has been stated that Mahipala recovered his ancestral homeland (*Rajyam Pitram*) from the usurpers (which was until that time occupied by the Kamboja-Pala Kingdom).

Caste

The caste origin of the Palas is not clearly stated in any of the numerous Pala records. The Khalimpur Plate of Dharmapala, the second Pala emperor, states that Gopala I was a son of a warrior (*Khanditarat*) named Vapyata, grandson of a highly educated man (*Saryavidyavadat*) named Dayitavishnu, and he himself was elected to the throne of Bengal, therefore he was not initially of a distinguished royal blood from the Hindu point of view.

The Kamauli Copper Plate inscription of king Vaidyadeva of Kamarupa (Assam) connects the Palas to the Kshatriyas of "*Mihirasya vamsa*" (Surya lineage). Balla-Carita says that the "The Palas were low-born Kshatriya", a claim reiterated by the historian

Taranatha in his "History of Buddhism in India" as well as Ghanarama in "Dharma Mangala" (both written in the 16th century CE). The Ramacharitam also attests the fifteenth Pala emperor, Ramapala, as a Kshatriya. As Gopala I was a Buddhist, he was also branded as a Œudra king in some sources. According to Manjuuree Mulakalpa, Gopala I was a Uudra.

Arabic accounts tell us that Palas were not kings of noble origin. According to Abu'l-Fazl ibn Mubarak (in Ain-i-Akbari), the Palas were Kayasthas. There are even accounts that claim Gopala may have been from a Brahmin lineage.

Matsyanyaya and the Ascendancy of the Palas

After Shashanka's reign, Bengal was shrouded in obscurity and was shattered by repeated invasions. During the reign of Manava, Bengal was invaded and divided between Harshavardhana and Bhaskaravarman. In 730 CE Jayavardhana of the Shaila Dynasty from Central India invaded Bengal and killed the king of Pundra Kingdom. Yasovarman (725-752) of Kannauj killed the king of Magadha and Gauda. Later Lalitaditya Muktapida (724-760) of Kashmir who defeated Yasovarmana invaded Bengal. Sri Harsha of Kamarupa conquered Anga, Vanga, Kalinga and Odra. The social and political structure of Bengal was devastated. According to Taranatha:

Every single Brahman, every Kshatriya, every Elite became all powerful in their areas and surrounding regions. This condition has been described by him as Matsyanyam (Eating of small fish by the big fish) or the Dark Age of Bengal. Disgusted at the situation the desperate people of Bengal made a bold move which marked a glorious period in the history of the sub-continent. They elected Gopala, a popular military leader, as their king by a democratic election which was probably the only democratic election in medieval India.

Buddhism

After the Buddhist king Harsha Vardhana, Buddhism faced the possibility of extinction. The Palas emerged as the champion of Buddhism, and they patronized Mahayana Buddhism. The Palas supported the Universities of Vikramashila and Nalanda which became the premier seats of learning in Asia. The Nalanda University which is considered one of the first great universities in recorded history, reached its height under the patronage of the Palas..

The Palas were responsible for the spread of Mahayana Buddhism to Tibet, Nepal, Bhutan, Myanmar and the Malay archipelago. Bengal became famous in the Buddhist world for the cultivation of Buddhist religion, culture and other knowledge in the various centres that grew under the patronage of the Pala rulers. Buddhist scholars from the Pala empire travelled from Bengal to the Far-East and propagated Buddhism. A few outstanding individuals among them are Shantarakshit, Padmanava, Dansree, Bimalamitra, Jinamitra, Muktiinitra, Sugatasree, Dansheel, Sambhogabajra, Virachan, Manjughosh and many others. But the most prominent was Atish Dipankar Srigyan who reformed Buddhism in Tibet after it had been destroyed by king Langdharma. Although the Palas were Vaishnavas, they had also given support to Saiva ascetics, typically the ones associated with the Golagi-Math. Many of the Pala Dynasty's coins also bear the image of Shiva and his bull. Besides sculptures of Vaishnava deities, they had also constructed statues of Siva and Saraswati.

Main Pala Rulers

Gopala I (756-781)

Gopala (ruled 750 – 770 CE) was the founder of the Pala Dynasty of Bengal. The last morpheme of his name *Pala* means "protector" and was used as an ending for the names of all the Pala monarchs. Pala does not suggest or indicate any ethnic or caste considerations of the Pala dynasty.

Democratic Election of Gopala

Gopala was the first independent Buddhist king of Bengal and came to power in 750 CE in Gaur by democratic election as per evidence furnished by Taranatha. After the death of famous Gauda ruler *Sasanka,* there ensued a century of anarchy and confusion in Bengal. Tired of ceaseless political chaos and anarchy (known as *matsyanyaya*), the various independent chieftains of Bengal, in 750 CE, selected a person named Gopala to put an end to this sorry state of affairs. Gopala was already a leading military general and had made a mark as a great ruler. In the Khalimpur copper plate inscription (dated 32nd regnal year of Dharmapala) Gopala's father Vapyata is described as a noted military chief of his time and his grandfather Dayita Vishnu is described as a learned man of no military distinctions. Scholars state that Vapyata came into east from north-west Panjab, which if true, definitely means Gandhara/ Kamboja region.

Life Sketch of Gopala

Not much is known about the life or military career of king Gopla but at the time of his death, Gopala had bequeathed a legacy which facilitated the creation of a great dynasty of the future by his son Dharmapala of Bengal. He is believed to have consolidated his hold on the whole of Bengal. His reign-period is not precisely known but is believed to have spanned 750 CE through 770 CE. It was his son and successor Dharmapala (770-810 CE) who really made the Palas a pre-dominant power of Northern India.

Religious Leanings

Taranatha, a Tibetan historian, attests that Gopala was a staunch Buddhist and had built famous Buddhist monastery at Otantapura.

Ethnicity of Gopala

The ethnicity of Gopala or his progeny is not clearly stated in any of the numerous Pala records. According to *Manjuuree Mulakalpa,* Gopala I was a Œudra. But Gopala is also stated to have belonged to Kshatriya lineage. *Khalimpur Plate* of Dharmapala, son of Gopala I (the founder of the dynasty), states that Gopala was a son of a warrior (*Khanditarat*) Vapyata and grandson of a highly educated (*Saryavidyavadat*) Dayitavishnu. According to Taranath, Gopala was born of a Kshatriya family (of low origin) near *Pundravardhan* (north Bengal) and was later selected a ruler of Bhangala (Vangala).

Ramacharita of *Sandhyakar Nandi,* a court poet of later Palas, states that the Pala dynasty belonged to *Samudrakula* or Ocean lineage. It is not clear what this really means. Probably, this holds a clue that the ancestors of the Palas belonged to a shipping community of *Kshatriya cum-trading group* who conducted trade via sea with other nations. This may allude to their probable links with the northwest Kambojas who are also attested to have been both a Kshatriyas as well as traders class (*varatta-shastropajivins*).

The *Kamauli Grant* of king *Vaidyadeva* of Kamarupa (modern Assam) connects the Palas to 'Surya lineage' (*Mihirasya vamsa*).

This may again imply their probable connections with the ancient Kambojas who were indisputably of *Mihirasya vamsa* i.e. Sun/Fire worshipping Iranians.. As stated above, Gopala's father Vapyata, is said to have come into east (probably as mercenary military adventurer), from north-west Panjab which, if true, also links the Palas with the Gandhara/Kamboja lineage.

Ramachrita further states that Varendri or North Bengal was the fatherland (*Janakabhu*) of the Palas. Mention may be made here of the fact that there was a flourishing city named Gour in Iran (Firuzabad). Another fact that complicates history is that there was also a Kanauj (Kohnouj) here. As in the case of his son, Gopala's dominion may also have included the Yavana lands.

The Pala relations with Kambojas also appear probable from the fact that Pala king Devapala had brought *Viradeva,* a renowned scholar from Nagarahara, Jalalabad near Kabul (Kamboja) and appointed him to a very important and prestigious post of Abbot of Nalanda in south Bihar. Probably, Devapala had brought Viradeva during his military expedition to Kamboja in north-west.

Dharmapala (781-821)

Dharamapala (rule: 770 AD-810 AD) was the second ruler of the Pala Empire of Bengal. He was the son and succeessor of Gopala (rule: 750 AD-770 AD), the founder of the Pala Dynasty. He greatly expanded the boundaries of the Pala Empire founded by his father and made the Palas the most dominant power in the northern and eastern Indian subcontinent. He was succeeded by his son Devapala who further expanded the empire.

Military Career

When Dharmapala ascended the throne of Bengal, the political horizon was very gloomy. At the very outset, Dharmapala was locked in severe power struggle with the Pratiharas of Malwa and Rajputana as well as the Rashtrakutas of the Deccan who were both desirous of establishing their own hegemony over northern India. So, shortly he was involved in cut-throat power struggle with them. Dharmapal defeated the Pratihara king Indraraja or Indrayudha of Kanauj and deposed him, and placed Chakrayudha on the throne of Kanauj. It is pointed out that Dharmapala had held a court in Kanauj after this victory which was attended by rulers from Bhoja (*Berar*), Matsya (*Jaipur*), Madra (*Central Punjab*),

Kuru (*Thaneswar*), Yadu (*Mathura & Dwaraka*), Avanti (*Malava*), Yavana, Gandhara (*Kabol valley = Kamboja*) and Kira (*Kangra*). These chiefs not only approved of his military action but also paid respectful obeisance to him. It seems that Dharmapala had made himself the supreme leader in of Northern India since he calls himself as *Uttarapathasvamin* or *Lord of Northern India*.

Later, however, Dharmapala was defeated by Vatsaraja of the Pratihara dynasty who deprived him of the Gaur. But Vatsaraja himself was soon defeated by King Dhruva of the Rashtrakutas who later also clashed with Dharmapala and defeated him but Dhruva soon left for Deccan and thus Dharmapal did not lose much in this quick chain of events, but these events had left the Pratiharas badly mauled which indirectly helped Dharmapala. He fully availed this golden opportunity and truly made himself the Lord of Northern India (Uttarapathasvamin).

Later, Nagabhatta II of Pratihara had deposed Chakrayudha of Kanauj, a protégé of Dharmapala, which event brought Dhrampala into military conflict with Nagabhata at Monghyr. Dharmapala suffered a defeat but curiously enough, history repeated itself and Pratihara invader Nagabhata was himself soon knocked out by Govinda III of the Rashtrakuta dynasty.

The invasion by Nagabhata was of transitory nature and did not leave any permanent mark so Dharamapala practically retained the supreme power in North till the end of his life.

Sphere of Influence

Dharamapala had full control of Bengal and Bihar. Kingdom of Kanauj was his feudatory. The kingdoms of Madra, Kamboja/ Gandhara, Rajputana, Malava and Berar were vassal states which paid him tributes and acknowdged his mastery over them. Even Nepal is said to have been his vassal state. The strong influence of Indian art(Buddhist) in eastern Iran has been noted by R.N. Frye Sandhyakar Nandi, a court poet of later Palas, states that the Pala dynasty belonged to Samudrakula or Ocean lineage. The Kamauli Grant of king Vaidyadeva of Assam also connects the Palas to *Mihirasya vamsa* or 'Surya lineage' (Sun/Fire worshipers).

Religious Leanings

Dharmapala was a great patron of Buddhism and had founded the Vikramshila university which later evolved into a great learning center of Buddhism. He built the great Vihara at Somapuri in Verendri, Vihara in Paharpur and a splendid monastery at Odantapuri in Bihar. He is said to have founded fifty religious schools for the teachings of Buddhism.

Devapala (821-861)

Devapala (ruled 810 AD-850 AD) was a powerful emperor from the Pala Empire of Bengal. He was the third king in the line and had succeeded his father, king Dharamapala (ruled 770-810 AD). He inherited a great empire built by his father but he also made his own contributions to it to expand its frontiers.

Military Career of Devapala

Though not much is known about the details of his military campaigns, he is said to have exacted tributes from whole of northern India from Himalayas to Vindhyas and from east to west ocean. More specifically, the inscriptions reveal that his victorious military compaigns led him as far as to Kamboja of northwest and Deccan in the south and that he exterminated the Utkalas, conquered the Pragjyotisha (Assam), shattered the pride of the Hunas, and humbled the lords of Gurjara Pratiharas and the Dravidas.

Information provided by these inscriptions bears witness to Devapala's encounter with the Kambojas of Kabol valley, which nation, since remote antiquity, had been known for its quality war horses. The *Monghyr Charter* also bears witness to the fact that the Palas recruited their war horses from this Kamboja of the northwest. King Devapala definitely had some sort of relations with the north-west borderland of India (i.e. Kamboja) which fact also appears probable from his connections with *Viradeva,* a scholar from Nagarahara, Jalalabad near Kabul whom he had appointed to a very important and prestigious post of Abbot of Nalanda in south Bihar. Probably, Devapala had brought Viradeva during his military expedition to Kamboja in north-west.

Imperialistic and Expanionistic Policies

According to "Age of Imperial Kanauj" (*History and Culture of Indian People*), the above inscriptional statements attest that Devapala had followed imperialistic and expansionistic policy and in his military compaigns under his real cousin General

Jayapala, the Pala army invaded Pragjyotisha (Assam) where the king submitted without giving a fight and the Utkalas whose king fled from his capital city. On the opposite frontiers of the empire, were the Hunas located in south-east Punjab in Uttarapatha who became the next target of Devapala's fury. From there, the Pala forces had proceeded further to Kamboja of North-West Frontiers (Trans-Indus territory). Unfortunately, no details of his campaign or extent of success against the Kambojas is available from these inscriptions (Dr R. C. Majumdar). It is not known if Pala army had actually engaged in fight with the Kambojas and subjugated them or not. Thereafter, Devapala reduced king Ramabhadra of the Pratiharas and later he defeated Mihir Bhoja. It also pointed out that Devapala had vanquished the Rashtrakuta ruler Amoghavarsha. It is further claimed that he humbled the rulers of Dravida too.

Religious Leanings

Devapala was a staunch Buddhist and is stated to have granted five villages to Buddhist monasteries for the promotion of Buddhism and the welfare & comforts of the Bhikshus. He is said to have got constructed many temples and monasteries in Magadha.

Successor of Devapala

Devapala had ruled for about 40 years and was succeeded by his son Mahendrapala, who was succeded by Vigrahapala, his nephew according to one view and his son according the other.

Estimate of Devapala

It is stated that the reigns of Dharmapala and Devapala constituted the most brilliant period of Bengal. Under the Palas, Bengal played a very important role in the history of India.

Mahendrapala, Shurapala I, Vigrahapala I (861-866)

Mahendrapala was the fourth emperor of the Pala dynasty. He succeeded his father Devapala. We came to know about him and his *mahasenapati* (general) Vajradeva from the Jagjivanpur copper plate grant dated in his 7th regnal year and issued from the Kuddalakhataka *jayaskandhavara* (the camp of victory). He was succeeded by his second cousin Vigrahapala. Vigrahapala was the fifth emperor of the Pala dynasty and the successor of Mahendrapala, the son and successor of Devapala. He reigned for

1 year. Vigrahapala was grandson of Dharmapala's younger brother Vakapala and son of Jayapala. He was succeeded by his son, Narayanapala. The information about him and his ancestors are found in the Bhagalpur copper-plate inscription of his son, Narayanapala

Narayanapala (866-920)

Narayanapala (855-908) was the sixth emperor of the Pala dynasty of eastern India, mainly the Bengal and Bihar regions. The Gaya temple inscription dated in his 7th regnal year, the Indian Museum (found in the erstwhile Patna district) stone inscription dated in his 9th regnal year, the Bhagalpur copper-plate grant dated in his 17th regnal year, Bihar votive image inscription dated in his 54th regnal year and the Badal pillar inscription of his minister Bhatta Guravamishra provide information about his reign.

Rajyapala (920-952)

Rajyapala was the seventh emperor of the Pala dynasty. He succeeded his father Narayanapala. He reigned for 32 years. Bargaon inscription is dated in his 24th regnal year. He was succeeded by his son Gopala II.

Gopala II (952-969)

Gopala II was the successor to the Pala king Rajyapala, and eighth ruler of the Pala line reigning for 20 years. He was succeeded by Vigrahapala II.

Vigrahapala II (969-995)

Vigrahapala II was the successor to the Pala king Gopala II, and ninth ruler of the Pala line reigning for 22 years. He was succeeded by the famed Mahipala.

Mahipala I (995-1043)

Mahipala I (c. 995-1043 C.E.) is considered the second founder of the Pala dynasty. Gopala I established the dynastic rule of the Palas in the middle of the 8th century C.E. The Pala Dynasty ruled Bengal and Bihar for about four centuries from the middle of the 8th century AD. Mahipala succeeded in recovering the lost fortune of the dynasty and in checking the forces of disintegration for the time being, but could not totally remove them. But his success gave the dynastic rule of the Palas a second lease on life. During the reigns of Gopala II and Vigrahapala II, the two immediate predecessors of Mahipala, Bengal had to face repeated invasions of the Chandellas and the Kalachuris, the new powers that arose out of the ruins of the Pratihara empire in northern India.

Conquests

Mahipala seems to have a long reign as his two Imadpur inscriptions are dated in his 48th year. Mahipala, on his accession, found the Pala empire confined to southern Bihar and in his early years he fought successfully to recover northern and western Bengal from the Kambojas. Towards the close of his reign he succeeded in spreading Pala authority in northern Bihar. He must be given the credit for re-establishing Pala authority over their original kingdom, except a portion of southern west Bengal, where Ranasura and Dharmapala ruled.

The Belwa and Bangarh copperplates claim that Mahipala, by slaying all his enemies, obtained his paternal kingdom which had been snatched away through pride of prowess by people who had no claim to it. It is possible that the Mahipala lost his rightful Pala throne sometime during the early part of his reign. Mahipala's success in recovering the paternal kingdom was his most important achievement, since it gave a new lease of life to the Pala Empire.

Mahipala held authority over southern Bihar (Magadha) and towards the close of his reign over northern Bihar. Scholars also ascribe to him conquests beyond Bihar on the basis of his Sarnath inscription.

The inscription, dated c. 1083 or 1026 C.E., is of a purely religious nature and records the construction and rebuilding of religious edifices at the famous Buddhist site near Benares. Mahipala cannot be taken to have possessed Benares solely on the basis of this inscription.

Battle with Rajendra Chola

The Chola inscription (Tirumulai inscription), which records Rajendra Chola's invasion of Bengal some time in between 1021 and 1024 C.E., throws further light on the condition of Bengal. The inscription records that after conquering Orissa the Chola general seized Dandabhukti after having destroyed Dharmapala (possibly belonging to the Kamboja line) and reached southern Radha where he met Ranashura. Then the army reached *Vangaladesha,* where the 'rainwater never stopped'.

Civic Works

Mahipala was better known for his peaceful pursuits. A number of towns and large tanks still bear his name. *Mahiganj* in Rangpur district, *Mahipur* in Bogra district, *Mahisantosa* in Dinajpur district and *Mahipala* in Murshidabad district; *Mahipaladighi* (tank) in Dinajpur and Mahipala's *Sagardighi* in Murshidabad-all these still bear testimony to his deeds and the high esteem in which the people held him. It is further reflected in the numerous ballads believed to exist in Bengal commemorating his name. Brindaban Das wrote in his Chaitanya Bhagavat (c. 1572 C.E.) that the people of Bengal in the early part of the 16th century were very fond of these songs of Mahipala. The popularity of these songs and the name of Mahipala are reflected in the common saying, *Dhan bhante Mahipaler git* (songs of Mahipala while husking rice), which is still prevalent in rural Bengal.

Possibly after early years of war Mahipala devoted himself to peaceful pursuits and religious activities. His public works endeared him to the hearts of the people of Bengal. The excavations at Paharpur have revealed the revival of Pala power under Mahipala as manifest in the wholesale renovation of the main temple and in the monastic cells and in the numerous votive stupas at the shrine of Tara in the Satyapir Bhita.

Nayapala (1043-1058)

Naya Pala (1038-1055) is the name of eleventh ruler of the Pala dynasty of eastern Indian Subcontinent, mainly the Bengal and Bihar regions.

Vigrahapala III (1058-1075)

Vigrahapala III was the successor to the Pala king Nayapala, and twelfth ruler of the Pala line reigning for 15 years. He was succeeded by Mahipala II

Mahipala II (1075-1080)

Mahipala II was the successor to the Pala king Vigrahapala III, and thirteenth ruler of the Pala line reigning for 5 years. He was succeeded by Shurapala II.

Shurapala II (1080-1082)

Shurapala II (reigned ca. 1075-1077) was a ruler of the Pala Empire in northeast India. He was the successor to the Pala king Mahipala II and fourteenth ruler of the Pala line, reigning for two years. He was succeeded by Ramapala.

Ramapala (1082-1124)

Ramapala was the successor to the Pala king Shurapala II, and fifteenth ruler of the Pala line reigning for 53 years. He is recognised as the last great ruler of the dynasty, managing to restore much of the past glory of the Pala lineage.

He crushed the Varendra rebellion and extended his empire farther to Kamarupa, Orissa and Northern India. He was succeeded by Kumarapala. According to Bengali legend he died by walking into the sea.

Kumarapala (1124-1129)

Kumarapala was the successor to the Pala king Ramapala, and sixteenth ruler of the Pala line reigning for 10 years. During his reign he put down an uprising in Kamarupa by the governor Timgyadeva, eventually replacing him with Vaidyadeva (who would rebel four years after the death of Kumarapala). He was succeeded by Gopala III.

Gopala III (1129-1143)

Gopala III was the successor to the Pala king Kumarapala, and seventeenth ruler of the Pala line reigning for 4 years. He was succeeded by Madanapala.

Madanapala (1143-1162)

Madanapala was the successor to the Pala king Gopala III, and eighteenth and final ruler of Pala lineage reigning for 18 years. He was succeeded by Govindapala, whose lineage of that name is questionable.

Govindapala (1162-1174)

Govindapala is believed to be the successsor of Madanapala the last ruler of the Pala dynasty. However the lineage of that name is questionable.

Peace and Expansion

Gopala united all of Bengal and brought peace and prosperity in the region. The period of anarchy ended with his election. The Pala kings devoted themselves in public welfare and social reform. The Palas adopted the policy of religious toleration and co-existence of the Buddhists and the Hindus. Pala kings won the heart of the people by welfare activities like digging tanks establishing towns and took place in many folklores in the rural areas of Bengal. The *Mahipala Geet* (Songs of Mahipala) is still popular in the rural areas.

Palas adopted aggressive policy and began the period of expansion under Dharmapala and Devapala. At its height Dharmapala's empire covered most of northern and central region of the Indian Subcontinent. His successor Devapala extended the boundaries of the empire further to Assam in the east, Kamboja in the north-wast and the Deccan in the south. Devapala united much of South Asia under his rule, a feat only achieved before by Ashoka the Great. The successors of Devapala had to contend with the Gurjara-Pratihara and the Rashtrakutas for the supremacy of the Kannauj Triangle. After Narayanpala the Pala empire declined but was revived once more under the vigorous reigns of Mahipala and Ramapala.

Pala Administration

Pala rule was Monarchial. King or Monarch was the centre of all power. Pala kings would adopt Imperial titles like *Parameshwar, Paramvattaraka, Maharajadhiraja.* Pala kings appointed Prime Ministers. The Line of Garga served as the Prime Ministers of the Palas for 100 years. Garga I Darvapani I Someshwar I Kedarmisra I Vatt Guravmisra Pala Empire was divided into separate Vuktis (Provinces), Vuktis into Vishaya (Divisions) and Mandala Districts. Smaller units were *Khandala, Bhaga, Avritti, Chaturaka,* and Pattaka. Administration covered widespread area from the grass root level to the imperial court.

The Pala copperplates mention following administrative Posts:*Raja, Rajanyaka, Rajanaka, Ranaka, Samanta* and *Mahasamanta* (Vassal kings), *Mahasandhi-vigrahika* (Foreign minister), *Duta* (Head Ambassador), *Rajasthaniya* (Deputy), *Aggaraksa* (Chief guard), *Sasthadhikrta* (Tax collector), *Chauroddharanika* (Police tax), *Shaulkaka* (Trade tax), *Dashaparadhika* (Collector of penalties), and *Tarika* (Toll collector for river crossings), *Mahaksapatalika* (Accountant), *Jyesthakayastha* (Dealing documents), the *Ksetrapa* (Head of land use division) and *Pramatr* (Head of land measurements), the *Mahadandanayaka* or *Dharmadhikara* (Chief justice), the *Mahapratihara, Dandika, Dandapashika,* and *Dandashakti* (Police forces), *Khola* (Secret service). Agricultural posts like *Gavadhakshya* (Head of dairy farms), *Chhagadhyakshya* (Head of goat farms), *Meshadyakshya* (Head of sheep farms), *Mahishadyakshya* (Head of Buffalo farms) and many other like *Vogpati, Vishayapati, Shashtadhikruta, Dauhshashadhanika, Nakadhyakshya.*

Pala Literature

The proto-Bangla language was born during the reign of the Palas. The Buddhist texts of the Charyapada were the earliest form of Bangla language. This Proto-Bangla language was used as the official language in Tibet, Myanmar, Java and Sumatra. Books on every aspect of knowledge were compiled during the Pala Rule. On philosophy: *Agaman Shastra* by Gaudapada, *Nyay Kundali* by Sridhar Bhatta, *Karmanushthan Paddhati* by Bhatta Bhavadeva; On Medicine: *Chikitsa Sangraha, Ayurvedidwipika, Bhanumati, Shabdachandrika, Dravya Gunasangraha* by Chakrapani Dutt; *Shabda-Pradip, Vrikkhayurveda, Lohpaddhati* by Sureshwar; *Chikitsa Sarsangraha* by Vangasena; *Sushrata* by Gadadha Vaidya; *Daybhaga, Byabohar-Matrika, Kalvivek* by Jimutvahan etc. Atisha compiled more than 200 books. The great epic Ramacharitam written by Sandhyakar Nandi the court poet of Madanpala was another masterpiece of the Pala literature. The Pala copperplate inscriptions were of excellent literary value. This distinctive inscriptions were called *Gaudiya Style.*

Atisha

Aticea Dipankara Shrijnana (980-1054 CE) was a Buddhist teacher from the Pala Empire who, along with Konchog Gyalpo and Marpa, was one of the major figures in the establishment of the Sarma lineages in Tibet after the repression of Buddhism by King Langdarma (Glang Darma).

Early Life

Atisha is most commonly said to have been born in the year 980 in Vajrayogini village in Bikrampur, the northeastern region of Bengal (located in modern day Bangladesh). His homestead in the village is still known to the local people as the "Ponditer bhita" (the homestead of the Pundit-a learned man). The exact year of his birth and death is widely disputed. Some sources indicate that Atisha was born in 982 and died in 1054, while more recent studies contend that his life began in 980 and ended in 1052. In any case, it is unanimously recognized that Atisha lived to the age of seventy-two. It is noteworthy that, while no direct connections can be made to the birth of Atisha, the year 980 also saw a major power shift in Bengali politics as the resurgent Pala dynasty seized control of the region, disposing of the incumbent Kamboja rulers. Atisha was allegedly born into royalty, and it would be intriguing to know if his royal status stemmed from one of these two contemporaneous contending powers.

The city of Vikramapura, the most probable candidate for Atisha's birthplace, was the capital of the ancient kingdoms of Southeast Bengal. Though the city's exact location is not certain, it presently lies in the Munshiganj District of Bangladesh, and continues to be celebrated as an early center of Buddhist cultural, academic, and political life. Similar to Shakyamuni Buddha, Atisha was born into royalty; the palace in which he was raised, aptly named the Golden Banner Palace, "had a golden victory banner encircled by countless houses and there were great numbers of bathing-pools encircled by 720 magnificent gardens, forests of Tal(Borassus flabellifer) trees, seven concentric walls, 363 connecting bridges, innumerable golden victory banners, thirteen roofs to the central palace and thousands of noblemen". His father was the king of Bengal known as Kalyana Shri, and his mother was Shri Prabhavati. One of three royal brothers, Atisha went by the name of Chandragarbha during the first part of his life. In fact, it was not until he traveled to Tibet and encountered the king Jangchub O (Byang Chub Od) that he was given the name of Atisha, a Tibetan reference to peace.

The prince's birth is often described in traditional accounts as an auspicious or promising episode. For example, it is said that as Atisha was born "flowers rained down upon the city [of Vikramapura], a rainbow canopy appeared, and the gods sang hymns which brought gladness and joy to all the people". This particular description is loaded with several themes distinctly typical of Buddhist literature. The image of flowers falling from the sky appears in the episode of Shakyamuni Buddha's attainment of perfect enlightenment, and the emergence of a rainbow canopy symbolizes the reincarnation of a Bodhisattva. Most importantly, however, is that the arrival of Atisha brought certain happiness to sentient beings. This effect of Atisha's birth corresponds directly with the Buddhist concept of dedicating one's life to the uplifting and enlightenment of all conscious beings.

For the first eighteen months of his life, Atisha was sheltered and attended to by eight nurses in the royal palace of the capital city, Vikramapura. At eighteen months old, it is said that his parents then brought him into public for the first time, on a visit to a local temple in Kamalapuri. It was here that Atisha's potential as an extraordinary religious and spiritual leader initially emerged. People from all over the region gathered to witness his appearance. When Atisha learned from his parents of the crowd's status as his own subjects, he prayed that they may "be possessed of merit like that of [his] parents, rule kingdoms that reach the summit of prosperity, be reborn as sons of kings [and] be sustained by holy and virtuous deeds." Atisha then proceeded independently to worship the holy objects both inside and surrounding the temple, renouncing his ties to the world and his family and committing himself to religious pursuit.

Such an interpretation of Atisha's first public appearance, found in Buddhist texts and historical accounts, strongly reinforces a couple of critical components of Buddhist philosophy. The story clearly gives an impression of Atisha as a spiritually advanced and relatively enlightened individual at only eighteen months old. As such, the prince is seen to have acquired enough merit through virtuous actions in previous lives such that it carried over to dictate both his favorable experience as a venerated prince and enlightened personality as a compassionate individual. Moreover, Atisha's spiritual proficiency at this point is demonstrated through both kindness towards his subjects and non-attachment towards his familial, social, and overall life situation.

Mirroring the life of Shakyamuni Buddha, the young prince is depicted as having a natural capacity for swift learning in multiple fields and the practice of Dharma at a young age. He had become "well-versed in astrology, writing and Sanskrit" by the age of three, "able to distinguish between the Buddhist and non-Buddhist doctrines" by the age of ten, and would eventually become a master of the teachings of Mahayana, Hinayana, and

Vajrayana Buddhism under the guidance of over 100 different instructors. As time elapsed Atisha's wish to enter the religious life strengthened, but his parents identified him as the brightest of their sons and natural successor to power. Therefore, as he turned the customary age of eleven years old, surrounding him with the luxuries and extravagance of royalty, Atisha's parents commenced the decorative courtship and matrimonial preparations so that the prince might find a bride among the kingdom's beautiful young women of nobility.

Atisha's response to his parents' proposal as documented in Buddhist biographical texts evidences the level of commitment the young prince had for religious pursuit and enlightenment. On the eve of his wedding, Atisha experienced a momentous encounter with the Vajrayana goddess Tara, who would continue with him as a guiding spirit until the end of his life. Tara explained to the prince that in his past lives he had been a devout monk. Accordingly, he should not be overwhelmed by the lure of ephemeral pleasures in the world. If he should acquiesce, Tara continued, then "as an elephant sinks deeply into the swamp, [he], a hero, [would] sink in the mire of lust." Essentially, Tara's manifestation is symbolic for the prince's meaningful realization of his own karmic potential. The deity's metaphor is illuminating: as an elephant's enormous weight prevents it from escaping the mud, so the prince's wealth and extravagance would prevent him from spiritual awakening. With this revelation at the forefront of his consciousness, Atisha renounced his kingdom, family, and social status in order to find a spiritual teacher—or as he told his parents—to go on a hunting trip.

Buddhist sources assert that, while feigning a hunting trip, an adolescent Atisha made the acquaintance of the brahmin Jetari, a Buddhist recluse and renowned teacher. Jetari taught the young man three things: 1) taking refuge in the Three Jewels of Buddha, 2) Dharma and Sangha and 3) bodhichitta, described as the mind-oriented aspiration towards enlightenment with the intent of benefiting all sentient beings. Upon educating the young Atisha in the basic principles of Mahayana Buddhism, Jetari advised that he go to Nalanda, a Buddhist center for learning in northeastern India. In Nalanda, Atashi received once again brief instruction regarding the Bodhisattva vows under the spiritual guide Bodhibhadra, who in turn advised him to seek out a teacher renowned for his perfect meditation of perceiving emptiness, Vidyakokila.

Atisha's acquisition of the wisdom to perceive emptiness is particularly significant. It is during this stage of study that Atisha became aware of pure human nature and the fundamental freedom inherent to every sentient being's existence; a freedom exclusive of physical attachments and mental bondage. Buddhist narratives recount one story in which Atisha comes across a women alternately crying and laughing. Confused with her behavior, he inquires about her condition, and she responds: "[O]ne's own mind has been a Buddha from beginningless time. By not knowing this, great complications follow from such a small base of error for hundreds of thousands of sentient beings.... Not being able to bear the suffering for so many beings, I cry. And then, I laugh because when this small basis of error is known—when one knows one's own mind—one is freed." Coming from a background of nobility and material wealth, Atisha's realization of value as a freely determined product of perception represents a relative challenge and an alteration of life principles with substantial ontological ramifications.

Upon completing his training for meditations on nothingness and emptiness, Atisha was advised to go study with Avadhutipa, a Vajrayana master. Though Avadhutipa consented to instruct the still young Atisha, he required that the prince first consult the Black Mountain Yogi. The Black Mountain Yogi tested Atisha in numerous ways. First, he cast a lightening bolt in Atisha's direction as he first approached. He then granted the prince thirteen days of instruction, teaching him the Hevajra lineage and bestowing him with the code name Indestructible Wisdom. Finally, the Black Mountain Yogi insisted that before Atisha continue in his studies that he gain permission from his parents to be formally acquitted of royal responsibility, summoning eight naked yogis and yoginis to escort the prince back to Vikramapura.

Returning to the royal palace, Atisha's parents and subjects believed he had gone mad during his jungle refuge. He explained to his parents, however, that his pursuit of Dharma was for the greater benefit of all sentient beings and that "if [he] had become a king [he] would be with [them] only for this life. In future lives [they] would never meet, and this life, for all its luxury and wealth would have been for nothing". Essentially, Atisha's motivation in renouncing the wealth and luxury in his life was to repay his parents and fellow beings. In understanding his reasons and remembering the religious signs that accompanied the prince's birth, Atisha's mother willingly gave her consent and approved her son's decision to pursue the Dharma. Atisha's father, on the other hand, was much harder to convince and, like the Shakyamuni Buddha's own father, only conceded after multiple requests.

Driven forth by his parent's approval, Atisha went back to Avadhutipa to continue his studies, learning the Madhyamaka middle way and various tantra practices. At one point, he assumed a slight amount of pride in his accomplishments. Such an assumption was immediately met with a reminder that he knew relatively little through the visit from a dakini in a vision. Consequently, Atisha's unnecessary pride was reduced to humbleness overnight and he continued towards the path of enlightenment.

One day, as Atisha considered practicing his tantra with all the energy he could summon until he achieved his full potential he was confronted by a contending voice. The Black Mountain Yogi appeared to him in a dream, and advised him to take his time through steady practice in order to achieve the enlightenment he was seeking. Rather than extend all his powers at once, the Black Mountain Yogi warned, he should endeavor to become a "spiritual seeker who has renounced family life", a monk. Therefore, in his twenty-ninth year, Atisha was formally declared a monk under an ordination of the great Shilarakshita, and given the new name of Dipamkara Srijnana, meaning "He Whose Deep Awareness Acts as a Lamp."

Even as a monk, Dipamkara Srijnana yearned for the fastest and most direct means of attaining perfect enlightenment. He made a pilgrimage to Bodhgaya and, as he was circumambulating the great stupa there, had a vision consisting of two materializations of Tara. One asked the other what the most important practice for attaining enlightenment was, and the other duly replied that "the practice of bodhichitta, supported by loving kindness and great compassion is most important." Atisha thenceforth dedicated himself to refining his understanding and practice of bodhichitta.

Thus, at the age of thirty-one, the monk arranged for a perilous journey, traveling for thirteen months to Sumatra in order to study under the reputable Suvarnadvipi Dharmakirti, sometimes called Dharmarakshita and known in Tibetan as *Serlingpa* (Wylie:*Gser-gling-pa*), a supposed master of bodhichitta. Under the guidance of Dharmarakshita, Atisha remained on the island of Sumatra for twelve years studying bodhichitta and exclusive mind training techniques of oral origination. Finally, after over a decade of intensive training, Dharmarakshita advised Atisha to "go to the north. In the north is the Land of Snows." Dharmarakshita was referring to Tibet, a region with a Buddhist tradition forever changed after the arrival of Atisha Dipamkara Srijnana. From his Master, Dharmarakshita, Atisha learnt one meditation that became one of Tibetans fundamental meditation techniques, ie. Tongleng Meditation. A meditation that aims to recycle supposedly negative energy into loving and healing energy.

Studies

According to Tibetan sources, Atisha was ordained into the Mahasamghika lineage at the age of twenty-eight by the Abbot Shilarakshita and studied almost all Buddhist and non-Buddhist schools of his time, including teachings from Vishnu, Shiva, Tantric Hinduism and other beliefs. He also studied the sixty-four kinds of art, the art of music and the art of logic and accomplished these studies until the age of twenty-two. Among the many Buddhist lineages he studied, practiced and transmitted the three main lineages were the *Lineage of the Profound Action* transmitted by Maitreya/Asanga, Vasubandhu, the *Lineage of Profound View* transmitted by Manjushri/Nagarjuna, Chandrakirti, and the *Lineage of Profound Experience* transmitted by Vajradhara/Tilopa, Naropa. It is said that Atisha had more than 150 teachers, but one prominent teacher above all else was Dharmakirti from Sumatra, Indonesia.

Preaching in Sumatra and Tibet

Before journeying to Tibet, however, Atisha first returned to India. Once back, the increasingly knowledgeable monk received much attention for his teachings and skills in debate and philosophy. On three separate occasions, the monk Atisha was acclaimed for defeating non-Buddhist extremists in debate. When he came into contact with what he perceived to be a misled or deteriorating form of Buddhism he would quickly and effectively implement reforms. Soon enough he was appointed to the position of steward, or abbot, at the venerable Buddhist college Vikramasila, established by the King Dharmapala of Bengal. Atisha's return from Sumatra and rise to prominence in India coincided with a flourishing of Buddhist culture and the practice of Dharma in the region, and in many ways Atisha's influence contributed to these developments. As Dharmarakshita had predicted, however, Buddhism in Tibet was in desperate need of resuscitation. Some Tibetans, for example, believed that "ethical self-discipline and tantra were mutually exclusive and that enlightenment could be achieved through intoxication and various forms of sexual misconduct." The politically unstable rule of King Langdarma had suppressed Tibetan Buddhism's teachings and persecuted its followers for over seventy years. According to the Blue Annals, new king of the Western Tibetan kingdom of Guge by the name of Lha Lama Yeshe Yod, however, was a strict believer in Dharma and so sent his academic followers to learn and translate some of the Sanskrit Buddhist texts. Among these academics was Nagtso, who was eventually sent to Vikramasila college to study Sanskrit and plead with Atisha to come teach the Dharma in his homeland.

At first, Atisha declined the offer to come reintroduce the Buddha's teachings in Tibet. He believed that he was getting too old for travel and had much unfinished work at the monastic college. On the evening following his declination, however, he received a vision in which his tutelary guide Tara informed him that his trip to Tibet would be very successful: not only would he greatly honour and assist the Tibetans, but he would also find a dedicated disciple and further contribute to the spread of Dharma. In exchange for these benefits, however, he would only live to seventy-two years.

In truth, Atisha's undertaking in Tibet was never in doubt. Prophecies of the impending departure begin with Dharmarakshita in Sumatra and follow Atisha's story up until his vision of Tara. During his travels across the perilous Himalayas, the Tibetan scholar Nagtso "vaguely realized that [...] miraculous manifestations assisted me in an uninterrupted flow." Nagtso was referring, whether he knew it or not, to the numerous assistances provided by Avalokitesvara throughout his trip to Vikramasila. As such, it seems as though Atisha's two-year journey to Tibet is interpreted within the Buddhist tradition as a fulfillment of destiny.

Once he arrived, Atisha grasped very quickly the Tibetan peoples' enthusiasm for the Dharma, but relative lack of comprehension. At Ngari, he was very impressed with the king's request for "a teaching of the people [...] had [Atisha] been asked for advanced empowerments into tantric deity systems [...] he would have been far less pleased". It was during the three years Atisha spent in this town that he compiled his teachings into his most influential scholarly work, *A Lamp for the Path to Enlightenment,* and encountered the disciple forecast by Tara, Dromtonpa.

According to Jamgon Kongtrul, when Atisha discovered the store of Sanskrit texts at Pekar Kordzoling, the library of Samye, "he said that the degree to which the Vajrayana had spread in Tibet was unparalleled, even in India. After saying this, he reverently folded his hands and praised the great dharma kings, translators, and panditas of the previous centuries."

Death

As he grew old, Atisha moved on from Ngari and accepted an invitation from Dromtonpa to explore Central Tibet. In Nyetang, a town near Lhasa, Atisha spent nine years during which he discovered Tibetan libraries with impressive collections written in both Sanskrit and Tibetan. The venerable monk moved around the region for another five years before passing away in 1052 at the prophesied age of seventy-two. He was enshrined near his last permanent home in the town of Nyetang.

After staying for thirteen years in Tibet, Atisha died in 1052 CE in a village called Lethan, near Lhasa. The site of his last rites at Lethan has turned into a shrine. His ashes were brought to Dhaka, Bangladesh on 28 June 1978 and placed in Dharmarajika Bauddha Vihara.

Legacy

Atisha remains an important figure in the Tibetan Buddhist tradition for several reasons. First, he refined, systematized, and compiled an innovative and thorough approach to bodhichitta known as "mind training" (Tib. *lojong*), in such texts as *A Lamp for the Path to Enlightenment,* and established the primacy of bodhichitta to the Mahayana tradition in Tibet. In this sense, Atisha not only dictated a scholarly model for bodhichitta but acted as a living human example.

Second, after King Langdarma's intolerant reign, the monastic Buddhist tradition of Tibet had been nearly wiped out. Atisha's closest disciple, Dromtönpa, is considered the founder of the Kadam school, which later evolved into the Gelug, one of the four main school of Tibetan Buddhism. Although monasticism and the lojong teachings were of greatest centrality to the Kadam/Gelug, they were incorporated into the other three schools—the Nyingma, Kagyu, Sakya—as well.

Finally, Atisha mobilized his influence in India towards the goal of reforming the impurities and redirecting the development of Buddhism there, in the native country of the Shakayumi Buddha. For these reasons and more, Atisha remains a central figure in the history and religious study of Buddhism.

Writings

Atisha wrote, translated and edited more than two hundred books, which helped spread Buddhism in Tibet. He discovered several Sanskrit manuscripts in Tibet and copied them himself. He translated many books from Sanskrit to Tibetan. He also wrote several books on Buddhist scriptures, medical science and technical science in Tibetan. Dipamkara wrote several books in Sanskrit, but only their Tibetan translations are extant now. Seventy-nine of his compositions have been preserved in Tibetan translation in the Tengyur (bstan-sgyur).

Following are his most notable books:

- Bodhi-patha-pradipa or *Bodhipathapradîpa* (Tib. Byang-chub lam-gyi sgron-ma)
- Charya-sanggraha-pradipa
- Satya-dvayavatara
- Bodhi-sattva-manyavali
- Madhyamaka-ratna-pradipa
- Mahayana-patha-sadhana-sanggraha
- Shiksa-samuchchaya Abhisamya
- Prajna-paramita-pindartha-pradipa
- Ekavira-sadhana
- Vimala-ratna-lekha.

Vimalaratnalekha is a Sanskrit letter to Nayapala, king of Magadha. *Charyasamgrahapradipa* contains some kirtan verses composed by Atisha.

Charyapada

The Charyapada is a collection of 8th-12th century Vajrayana Buddhist caryagiti, or mystical poems from the tantric tradition in eastern India. Being caryagiti, or 'songs of realization' the Charyapada were intended to be sung. These songs of realization were spontaneously composed verses that expressed a practitioner's experience of the enlightened state. Miranda Shaw describes how caryagiti were an element of the ritual gathering of practitioners in a tantric feast: The feast culminates in the performance of tantric dances and music that must never be disclosed to outsiders. The revelers may also improvise "songs of realization" (*caryagiti*) to express their heightened clarity and blissful raptures in spontaneous verse. A manuscript was discovered in the early 20th century. It provides the early examples of the Assamese, Oriya and Bengali languages. The writers of the Charyapada, the Mahasiddhas or *Siddhacharyas*, belonged to the various regions of Assam, Bengal, Orissa and Bihar. A Tibetan translation of the Charyapada was also preserved in the Tibetan Buddhist canon.

Manuscripts of the Charyapada

The original palm-leaf manuscript of the Charyapada, or *Charyacharyavinishchayah*, consisting of an anthology of 47 Padas (verses) along with a Sanskrit commentary, was discovered by Haraprasad Shastri at the Nepal Royal Court Library in 1907. This manuscript was edited by Shastri and published by the Bangiya Sahitya Parishad as a part of his *Hajar Bacharer Purano Bangala Bhasay Bauddhagan O Doha* (The Buddhist Songs and Couplets in a thousand years old Bengali Language) in 1916 under the name of *Charyacharyavinishchayah*.

This manuscript is presently located at the National Archives of Nepal. Later Prabodhchandra Bagchi published a manuscript of a Tibetan translation containing 50 verses.

The Tibetan translation of the Charyapada provided additional information. It names the Sanskrit commentary as the *Charyageetikoshavritti*, the writer as *Munidatta* and the translator as Chandrakirti, the 7th century abbot of the Buddhist monastery at Nalanda.

Poets of the Charyapada

The manuscript of the Charyapada discovered by Haraprasad

Shastri from Nepal consists of 47 Pada or verses. The title-page, the colophon-page,the pages 36, 37, 38, 39 and 66 containing the Padas (verses) 24, 25 and 48 and their commentaries were missing in this manuscript. The 47 verses of this manuscript were written by 22 Mahasiddha, or Siddhacharyas, whose names are mentioned at the beginning of each Pada (except the first Pada). In the Tibetan Buddhist canon version of the text and its commentary there are another 3 Padas, the complete form of Pada 23 and the Siddhacharya poet Tantripada is also mentioned. The names of the Siddhacharyas are given in Sanskrit (or its Tibetan language equivalent) prior to each Pada as follows:

Poet	Pada
Luipâda	1, 29
Kukkuripâda	2, 20, 48
Virubâpâda	3
Gundaripâda	4
Chatillapâda	5
Bhusukupâda	6, 21, 23, 27, 30, 41, 43, 49
Kânhapâda	7, 9, 10, 11, 12, 13, 18, 19, 24, 36, 40, 42, 45
Kambalâmbarapâda	8
Dombipada	14
Shantipada	15, 26
Mahidharapada	16
Vinapada	17
Sarahapada	22, 32, 38, 39
Shabarapada	28, 50
Aryadevapada	31
Dhendhanapada	33
Darikapada	34
Bhadepada	35
Tadakápada	37
Kankanapada	44
Jayanandipada	46
Dhamapada	47
Tantripada	25

The name of another Siddhacharya poet, Ladidombipada, is mentioned by Munidatta in his commentary on Pada 10, but no Pada written by him has been discovered so far.

Probably, the Sanskrit names of the Siddhacharya poets were assigned to each Pada by the commentator Munidatta. Modern scholars doubt whether these assignments are proper on the basis of the internal evidences and other literary sources. Controversies also exist amongst the scholars as to the original names of these Siddhacharya.

Language of the Charyapada

Haraprasad Shastri in his introduction to the *Charyacharyavinishchaya* referred to the enigmatic language of its verses as 'Twilight Language' (Sanskrit: *Sandhya-bhasha*), or *Alo-andhari* (half expressed and half concealed) based on the Sanskrit commentary of Munidatta. But later Vidhushekhara Shastri on the basis of evidences from a number of Buddhist texts referred to this language as 'Intentional Language' (Sanskrit: *Sandha-bhasha*)..

The Charyapadas were written by poets from different regions, and it is natural that they would display linguistic affinities from these regions. Different scholars claimed the affinities of the language of *Charyapada* with Assamese, Bengali, Maithili and Oriya.

Affinities with Assamese

Luipa, also known as Matsyendranath, was from Kamarupa and wrote two *charyas*. Sarahapa, another poet, is said to have been from Rani, a place close to present-day Guwahati. Some of the affinities with Assamese are:

Negatives — the negative particle in Assamese comes ahead of the verb: *na jāi* (No. 2, 15, 20, 29); *na jivami* (No. 4); *na chadaa, na jani, na disaa* (No. 6). *Charya* 15 has 9 such forms.

Present participles — the suffix-*ante* is used as in Assamese of the Vaishnava period: *jvante* (while living, No. 22); *sunante* (while listening, No. 30) etc.

Incomplete verb forms — suffixes-*i* and-*iya* used in modern and old Assamese respectively: *kari* (3, 38); *cumbi* (4); *maria* (11); *laia* (28) etc.

Present indefinite verb forms —-*ai*: *bhanai* (1); *tarai* (5); *pivai* (6).

Future — the-*iva* suffix: *haiba* (5); *kariba* (7).

Nominative case ending — case ending in *e*: *kumbhire khaa, core nila* (2).

Instrumental case ending — case ending-*e* and-*era*: *uju bate gela* (15); *kuthare chijaa* (45).

The vocabulary of the Charyapadas includes non-*tatsama* words which are typically Assamese, such as *dala* (1), *thira kari* (3, 38), *tai* (4), *uju* (15), *caka* (14) etc.

Affinities with Oriya

The beginnings of Oriya poetry coincide with the development of Charya Sahitya, the literature thus started by Mahayana Buddhist poets..This literature was written in a specific metaphor named "Sandhya Bhasha" and the poets like Luipa, Kanhupa are from the territory of Orissa. The language of Charya was considered as Prakrita.

In one of his poem, an author, Kanhupa wrote:

"Your hut stands outside the city

Oh, untouchable maid

The bald Brahmin passes sneaking close by

Oh, my maid, I would make you my companion

Kanha is a kapali, a yogi

He is naked and has no disgust

There is a lotus with sixty-four petals

Upon that the maid will climb with this poor self and dance."

The language of Kanhupa's poetry bears a very strong resemblance to modern Oriya. For example :

"Ekaso padumo chowshathi pakhudi

Tahin chadhi nachao dombi bapudi"

Padumo (Padma:Lotus), *Chowshathi* (64), *Pakhudi* (petals) *Tahin* (there), *Chadhi* (rise), *nachao* (to dance), *Dombi* (a female of Orissa from untouchable caste), *Bapudi* (a very colloqual Oriya language to apply as 'poor fellow') or

"Hali Dombi,Tote puchhami sadbhabe.

Isisi jasi dombi kahari nabe."

These passages do not require any translation into modern Oriya.

Affinities with Bengali

A number of Siddhacharyas who wrote the verses of Charyapada were from Bengal. Shabarpa, Kukkuripa and Bhusukupa were born in different parts of Bengal. Some of the affinities with Bengali can be found from the genitive in-*era,-ara;* the dative in *–re;* the locative in *–ta;* post-positional words like *maajha, antara, saanga;* past and future bases in *–il-,-ib-;* present participle in *–anta;* conjunctive indeclinable in *–iaa;* conjunctive conditional in *–ite;* passive in *–ia*-and substantive roots *aach* and *thaak.*

Melodies of the Charyapada

From the mention of the name of the Raga (melody) for the each Pada at the beginning of it in the manuscript, it seems that these Padas were actually sung. All 50 Padas were set to the tunes of different Rages.

The most common Raga for Charyapada songs was *Patamanjari.*

Raga	*Pada*
Patamanjari	1, 6, 7, 9, 11, 17, 20, 29, 31, 33, 36
Gabada or Gauda	2, 3, 18
Aru	4
Gurjari, Gunjari or Kanha-Gunjari	5, 22, 41, 47
Devakri	8
Deshakha	10, 32
Kamod	13, 27, 37, 42
Dhanasi or Dhanashri	14
Râmakri	15, 50
Balâddi or Baradi	21, 23, 28, 34
Shabari	26, 46
Mallari	30, 35, 44, 45, 49
Malasi	39
Malasi-Gabura	40
Bengal	43
Bhairavi	12, 16, 19, 38

While, some of these Rages are extinct, the names of some of these Rages may be actually the variants of the names of the popular Rages as we know them today.

Glimpses of Social Life

Many poems provide a realistic picture of early medieval society in eastern India by describing different occupations of people such as hunters, boatmen, and potters. It also describes the some popular musical instruments such as kada-nakada, drums, and tom-toms. The custom of dowry was prevalent. Cows were common domestic animals and elephants were common as well. Girls used to wear peacock feathers, flower garlands, and earrings.

The Ramacharitam is a great epic poem written in Sanskrit in *Arya metre* by Sandhyakar Nandi during Pala Empire between the second half of the 11th and the first half of the 12th century CE. This work simultaneously narrates the story of the Ramayana and details the historical events in Bengal from the assassination of the Pala emperor Mahipala II by Divya, a rebel Kaivarta officer up to the reign of Madanapala in 215 verses, by using a figure of speech, the *Shlesha* (double-meaning words) in each verse.

The poet, Sandhyakar Nandi, was born in a kayastha family of Vrihadvatu village near Pundravardhanapura in Varendra (North Bengal). He was grandson of Pinaka Nandi and son of Prajapati Nandi, the *Sandhi-Vigrahika* (minister of peace and war) of the Pala emperor Ramapala.

A palm-leaf manuscript of the *Ramacharitam* discovered by Haraprasad Shastri is preserved in the museum of the Asiatic Society, Kolkata.

Pala art and Architecture

The most brilliant side of the Pala Empire was the excellence of its art and sculptures. Palas created a distinctive form of Buddhist art known as the "Pala School of Sculptural Art." The gigantic structures of Vikramshila Vihar, Odantpuri Vihar, and Jagaddal Vihar were masterpieces of the Palas. These mammoth structures were mistaken by the forces of Bakhtiar Khilji as fortified castles and were demolished. The Somapura Mahaviharaa, a creation of Dharmapala, at Paharpur, Bangladesh, is the largest Buddhist Vihara in the Indian subcontinent, and has been described as a "pleasure to the eyes of the world." UNESCO made it World

Heritage Site in 1985. Sompur Bihara, also built by Dharmapala, is a monastery with 21 acre (85,000 m^2) complex has 177 cells, numerous stupas, temples and a number of other ancillary buildings. In 1985, the UN included the Sompur Bihara site in the world Cultural Heritage list.

The Pala architectural style was followed throughout south-eastern Asia, China, Japan and Tibet. Bengal rightfully earned the name "Mistress of the East". Dr. Stella Kramrisch says: "The art of Bihar and Bengal exercised a lasting influence on that of Nepal, Burma, Ceylon and Java". Dhiman and Vittpala were two celebrated Pala sculptors. About Sompura Mahavihara, Mr. J.C. French says with grief: "For the research of the Pyramids of Egypt we spend millions of dollars every year. But had we spent only one percent of that money for the excavation of Sompura Mahavihara, who knows what extraordinary discoveries could have been made." — "The Art of the Pala Empire of Bengal".

Somapura Mahavihara

Somapura Mahavihara in Paharpur, Naogaon, Bangladesh is among the best known Buddhist viharas in the Indian Subcontinent and is one of the most important archeological sites in the country. It was designated a UNESCO World Heritage Site in 1985.

Architecture

The quadrangular structure consists of 177 cells and a traditional Buddhist stupa in the center. The rooms were used by the monks for accommodation and meditation. In addition to the large number of stupas and shrines of various sizes and shapes, terracotta plaques, stone sculptures, inscriptions, coins, ceramics etc. have been discovered.

The site houses the architectural remains of a vast Buddhist monastery, Somapura Mahavihara, covering 27 acres. It was an important intellectual centre for Dharmic Traditions such as Buddhists (Buddha Dharma), Jains (Jaina Dharma) and Hindus (Sanatana Dharma) alike. The 21 acre (85,000 m^2) complex has 177 cells, viharas, numerous stupas, temples and a number of other ancillary buildings. The outside walls with ornamental terracotta palques still display the influence of these three religions. In terms of acreage, Somapura was the largest of the mahaviharas. It was also quite unusual architecturally. As one scholar described, the complex was dominated by a temple, which was not typical, and further, the temple had "none of the characteristic features of Indian temple architecture, but is strongly reminiscent of Buddhist temples of Burma, Java and Cambodia, reproducing the cruciform basement, terraced structure with inset chambers and gradually dwindling pyramid form.. during the age of the Palas some sort of intercourse between eastern India and south-east Asia existed.. but how this temple type, represented in India by this solitary example, became the standard of Buddhist temple architecture is not known." Another commented, "there can be no doubt that this style of architecture has most profoundly influenced that of Burma, Java and Cambodia. The nearest approximation to the plan and the superstructure of the Paharpur temple is afforded by the temples known as Chandi Loro Jongrang and Chandi Sevu of Prambanam in Central Java."

History

A number of monasteries grew up during the Pala period in ancient Bengal and Magadha. According to Tibetan sources, five great Mahaviharas stood out: Vikramashila, the premier univeristy of the era; Nalanda, past its prime but still illustrious, Somapura Mahavihara, Odantapura, and Jaggadala. The five monasteries formed a network; "all of them were under state supervision" and their existed "a system of co-ordination among them.. it seems from the evidence that the different seats of Buddhist learning that functioned in eastern India under the Pala were regarded together as forming a network, an interlinked group of institutions," and it was common for great scholars to move easily from position to position among them.

The excavation at Paharpur, and the finding of seals bearing the inscription *Shri-Somapure-Shri-Dharmapaladeva-Mahavihariyarya-bhiksu-sangghasya,* has identified the Somapura Mahavihara as built by the second Pala king Dharmapala (*circa* 781-821) of Pala Dynasty. Some clay seals from the ruins bear the inscription Shri-Somapure-Shri-Dharmapaladeva-Mahavihariyarya-bhiksu-sangghasya. Tibetan sources, including Tibetan translations of *Dharmakayavidhi* and *Madhyamaka Ratnapradipa,* Taranatha's history and *Pag-Sam-Jon-Zang,* mention that Dharmapala's successor Devapala (*circa* 810—850) built it after his conquest of Varendra. The Paharpur pillar inscription bears the mention of 5th regnal year of Devapala's successor Mahendrapala (*circa* 850—854) along with the name of Bhiksu Ajayagarbha. Taranatha's *Pag Sam Jon Zang* records that the monastery was repaired and renovated during the reign of Mahipala (*circa* 995—1043 AD).

The Nalanda inscription of Vipulashrimitra records that the monastery was destroyed by fire, which also killed Vipulashrimitra's ancestor Karunashrimitra, during a conquest by the Vanga army in the 11th century, assumed to be an army of the Varman rulers. About a century later Vipulashrimitra renovated the vihara and added a temple of Tara. The restoration work was alluded to as *jagatang netraika vishrama bhuh* (a singular feast to the eyes of the world).

Atisha Dipankar Srijnan stayed here for many years and translated the *Madhyamaka Ratnapradipa* into Tibetan. Over time Atish's spiritual preceptor, Ratnakara Shanti served as a sthavira of the vihara, Mahapanditacharya Bodhibhadra served as a resident monk, and several other scholars spent some part of their lives at this monastery including Kalamahapada, Viryendra and Karunashrimitra.. Many Tibetan monks visited the Somapura between 9th and 12th centuries

During the rule of the Sena dynasty, known as *Karnatadeshatagata Brahmaksatriya,* in the second half of the 12th century the vihara started to decline for the last time. It was finally abandoned during the 13th century, when the area came under Muslim occupation. One scholar writes, "The ruins of the temple and monasteries at Pahapur do not bear any evident marks of large-scale destruction. The downfall of the establishment, by desertion or destruction, must have been sometime in the midst of the widespread unrest and displacement of population consequent on the Muslim invasion."

Pala Foreign Relations

Palas came in contact with distant lands through their conquests and trades. The Sailendra Empire of Java, Sumatra and Malaya was a colony of the Palas. Devapala granted five villages at the request of the Sailendra king Balputradeva of Java for the upkeeping of the matha established at Nalanda for the scholars of that country. The Prime minister of the Balputradeva Kumar Ghosha was from Gauda. Dharmapala who extended his empire to the boundary of the Abbasid Empire had diplomatic relations with the caliph Harun

Al-Rashid. Coins of Harun-al-Rashid have been found in Mahasthangarh.

Palas maintained diplomatic and religious relation with Tibet. During the military expeditions of the Pala kings the Pala generals would establish kingdoms of their own in Punjab and Afghanistan. Recent discoveries in the Punjab hills showed the influence of the Pala Dynasty. There is a strong and continuous tradition that the ruling families in certain states are descended from the "Rajas of Gaur in Bengal". These states are Suket, Keonthal, Kashtwar and Mandi. In the ancient Rajput states tradition has immense force and accuracy. Of Kashtwar it is related that Kahan Pal — the founder of the state — with a small band of followers arrived in the hills in order to conquer a kingdom for himself. He is said to have come from Gaur, the ancient capital of Bengal and to have been a cadet of the ruling family of the place. The demise of the Turkshahi rule in Gandhar and the rise of the Hindushahi dynasty in that region might have connection to the invasion of the Palas in that region.

Pala Armed Forces

The Palas of Bengal in comparison with other contemporary empires such as the Rashtrakutas of Deccan and the Pratiharas of Malwa in the focal point of "Kanauj Triangle."

Palas had fourfold army consisting of: infantry, cavalry, elephants and chariots. In the copperplates of Vatsaraja Dharmapala had been mentioned as the owner of unlimited number of horses, elephants and chariots. It is amazing that when the use of chariots had been backdated in India and other parts of the world the kings of Bengal still depended on four-horsed heavy chariots. Being a riverine land and swarthy climate Bengal was not good enough for breeding quality war-horses. So the Palas had to depend upon their vassal kings for war horses. Pala copperplate inscriptions reveal that mercenary forces were recruited from the Kamboja, Khasa, Huna, Malwa, Gujarat, and Karnata.

The Kamboja cavalry were the cream of the Pala army who would later become as powerful as the Janissary army of the Ottoman Empire. The Kamboja forces maintained smaller confederates (Sanghas) among themselves and were staunch follower of their commander. Palas had the army divided into following posts: Senapati or Mahasenapati (General) controlling foot soldiers, cavalry, soldiers riding elephants and camels, and the navy, and the various army posts like Kottapala (Fort guards) and Prantapala (Border guards). Palas had a huge army and the legend of "Nava Lakkha Shainya" (Nine lac soldiers) were popular during the reigns of Dharmapala and Devapala. According to Hudud al-Alam a Persian text written in 982-983 Dharmapala possessed an army of 300,000 soldiers. According to Sulaiman the Arab traveller Devapala set out for his every military expedition with an army of 50,000 elephants and his army had 10,000-15,000 slaves for the maintenance and caretaking of his armies.

Legacy

Palas legacy gets remembered not much in Bengal but elsewhere in Asia. Tibet's modern culture and religion is heavily influenced by Palas. Palas are credited with spreading Buddhism to Tibet and around the world through missionaries. Atisa, a Palan, is a celebrated figure in the Tibetan Buddhism in tradition and in establishment. Atisa also invented bodhichitta or known as "mind training" that is practiced around the world today. Another important Palan figure in Tibetan Buddhism is Tilopa who founded the Kagyu lineage of Tibetan Buddhism and developed the Mahamudra method, a set of spiritual practices that greatly accelerated the process of attaining bodhi (enlightenment). Palas literature is widely studied by Buddhist around the world. Pala architectural style was copied throughout south-eastern Asia, China, Japan, and Tibet. Nalanda University and Vikramshila University are two of the greatest Buddhist universities ever recorded in history.

The Sen Dynasty

The original home of the Sen family must have been in Karnataka in South India. This is indicated by the Deopara inscription and is supported by other archaeological evidence. The Deopara inscription speaks of one of the founders in the South, Samanta Sen, whose successor was Hemanta Sen, the first of the family to whom royal epithets are given in the family records. The family records describe the Sens as Kshtriyas or as "Karnataka Kshytriyas". They might have been mercenaries under the imperial Palas who settled in Bengal and gradually established themselves in some portions of western Bengal. Or they might have come to Bengal in the wake of an invasion by a southern invader. His son, Bijaya Sen (C 1095-1158), followed Hemanta Sen.

Bijaysen, the first of the three great rulers of Sen dynasty, must have started consolidating and extending his hold in the Rar area, i.e., West Bengal, almost at the same time when Rampal was carrying on his campaign against Bhim, the Kaibarta rule in North Bengal. He married Vilasdevi, a princess of Sura family, and this dynastic marriage must have increased his position and power enormously. We have two important inscriptions in his name, viz., Deopara inscription, which is a eulogy (prasasti) by the poet Umapatidhar, and Barrackpore copperplate, which describes him as Maharaja dhiraja. From the combined evidence of these two inscriptions, even deducting the eulogistic elements, it seems reasonably certain that he defeated a number of chieftains like Nanya, Veera, Raghav Vardhan and, eventually, the sovereigns of Gaur, Kamrup and Kalinga. Nanya was Karnataka chieftain who conquered Mithila round AD 1097 and thereafter submitted to Bijaysen.

The lord of Gaur who, according to Deopara inscription, fled before Bijaya was probably Madanpal I, the last ruler f the Pala dynasty, by that time confined only to portions of North Bengal. Bijaysen could not complete the process for conquest of Gaur, and left it t his son and successor Ballalsen to complete this task and assume the title Gaureswara. But there is evidence that some pretenders to the Palla throne continued to linger on in South Bihar. That Bijaysen eventually established his rule in East Bengal is proved by the fact that some of his land grants were issued from Bikrampur, the capital city of Banga, and it was here that the queen of Bijaysen performed a sacrifice called *Tulapurasha Mahadana.*

The Deopara inscription also speaks of Bijaysen's military success against the king of Kamrup, although it does not unnecessarily show that he conquered Kamrup. Probably he repulsed an invasion of Bengal by the Kamrup king. The inscription also claims Bijaysen's conquest of Kalinga, although some historians have doubted this. The Deopara inscription also speaks of the advance of Bijaysen's fleet to the West along the Ganges, although this could not have been a campaign of much consequence. Bijaysen's long rule of nearly sixty years, restored peace and prosperity to Bengal and made a deep impression among its people.

The tributes paid to him in the beautiful poem of Umapatidhar in Deopara stone slab and the reference to him in poet Sriharsha's *Vijay Prasasti* (Eulogy of Vijay) no doubt reflected the people's feelings by and large in relation to him.

His son and successor, Ballalsen, the best-known Sen ruler (AD 1158-1179) consolidated the kingdom. He might have completed the conquest of North Bengal and also conquered Magadha and Mithila. According to a tradition in Bengal, Ballalsen's kingdom consisted of five provinces, viz., Banga, Barendra, Rar, Bagri (possibly a portion of lower Bengal) and Mithila. But neither the two inscriptions that survive from this region, nor the two great literary works, which were attributed to him, viz., *Dan Sagar* and *Adbhut Sagar*, allude to his military victories. On the other hand these refer to his scholastic activities and social reforms. Ballalsen is associated with the revival of orthodox Hindu practices in Bengal, in particular with the establishment of the reactionary tradition of Kulinism, but there is no historical authenticity.

He married Ramadevi, the Chalukya princess. This also indicates that the Sens maintained the kingdom inherited from his father, which included the present day Bangladesh, the whole of West Bengal and Mithila, i.e., portions of North Bihar. According to a cryptic passage in *Adbhut Sagar*, Ballalsen, along with his queen, retired in his old age to the confluence of the Ganges and the Yamuna leaving his son, Lakshman Sen, with the task of both maintaining his kingdom and completing his literary work. The book certainly remained uncompleted, but there is not historical evidence that Ballalsen abdicated in favour of his son Lakshmansen. It is reasonably certain, however, that his rule ended around AD 1170. Whether he died at that time, or abdicated and spent his last days in retirement, is not known.

There is considerable weight of historical evidence to suggest that during the rule of Sen dynasty there was a relapse into Brahmanical orthodoxy. According to Nihar Ranjan Ray, north Indian Aryan Brahmanism, which for centuries did not find an easy entry into Bengal now got an "open door" during the Sen dynasty. The Sen dynasty came from outside Bengal and in a short time was able to establish its power with the assistance from the Brahmans. Under the social system created by Ballalsen, the Brahmans became all in all in the land, and arbiters of both life and the life after death. The Sur dynasty was well established in East Bengal before the Sen dynasty. However, due to a marriage alliance with the Sen dynasty, the authority of the kings and the Brahmans got strengthened in Bengal. It was from the Sen period that greater Bengal became a narrower Bengal. Exchanges with the outside world stopped. Traveling across the seas was forbidden, and Bengal was turned into a frog-in-the-well. Intensive quarrels, fear of going out of the frontiers of Bengal and the strong desire to enjoy the comforts of a stay-at-home life forgetting the world outside were the reasons for the national degeneration. "Who could have foreseen that the gentle breeze of enjoyment at home for the sake of which we had become inert would eventually turn into a tornado making us in our own land beggars and dependent on others"

Lakshmansen (AD 1178-1207), son of Ballalsen and Ramadevi, must have been fairly old, about sixty years, when he succeeded his father. Seven copperplate inscriptions have been found in different parts of Bengal, five of them issued early in his reign from Bikrampur. This shows that Bikrampur was the center of his empire in his early days. These inscriptions show him as a great military leader as also a patron of learning. On his accession he assumed the title of *Ariraja-Madana-Sankara*. Along with the traditional title of *Gaureswara,* he also assumed the title *Paramvaishnava* in place of the earlier epithet of *Paramaeshwara* used by both Bijaysen and Ballalsen.

This indicates that Lakshmansen was a devout Vaishnav, unlike his father and grandfather, who were proclaimed Shaivas. This is also supported by the fact that all the official proclamations from then on started with an invocation to Narayana. Lakshmansen's court was adorned by Jaidev (the famous poet of Bengal), Dhoyi and Umapati Dhar among other distinguished poets. His Prime Minister, Halayudha, was himself a great poet. The king himself was a man of letters ad completed the work *Adbhut Sagar* begun by his father according to tradition.

Thus the military glory of the Sen dynasty reached its climax under Lakshmansen, in a way the last flicker before its inglorious end. According to his own copperplates, he achieved victories over the neighboring kings in all directions. In particular, his victories over the kings of Gaur, Kamrupa, Kalinga and Kashi are referred to. He is reported to have erected pillars commemorating his military activities at Puri, Benares and Allahabad. It is also quite certain that he liquidated the army of the Pala ruler in the West and carried on his campaign successfully against the Gahadavalas who had established themselves in Magadha. He was the first Bengal ruler to extend his suzerainty beyond Benares. Some inscriptions found in Gaya shortly after his reign attest to his rule in the Gaya region. But his rule also marked the beginning of the end of the Sen age.

Contemporary sources provide enough evidence to indicate that the disintegration of the Sen kingdom began in the later part of Lakshamansen's reign, both through centrifugal forces within and through the invasion by Central Asian invaders of Turkish origin and of Islamic faith. There is inscriptional evidence of an independent kingdom being established in the western Sunderbans in South Bengal by one Damanpal around AD 1196. Both Orissa and Kamrup also probably threw away the Sen suzerainty. Another challenge came from the rise of the kingdom of Pattikera in Tippera region under Ranabankarnalla Harikaladeva who ascended the throne around 1201-1203 and ruled till at lest 1217. This is known from an inscription discovered at Mainamati Hills near Comilla. It also appears that anther powerful kingdom under the Deva family rose in the territory beyond the Meghna river.

Archaeology of the Pala-Sen Age

The archaeology of the Pala-Sen period in Bengal has been of great interest to archaeologists and historians since the 1830s. The process of deciphering the inscriptions began with Wilkins who first read inscriptions from Bengal and Bihar belonging to the Pala period. The study of inscriptions went hand in hand with the study of coins and the study of the Buddhist literary sources for the dynastic history of the Buddhist period and its chronology. The archaeologists studying the early medieval period of Bengal's history have also highlighted the transition from the Buddhist motifs in the Pala period to orthodox Hindu motifs during the rule of the Sens. Simultaneously there has been a return of classical Sanskrit in contrast to Pali-Prahrit during the Pal dynasty. The most important aspects of material culture were sculptural pieces which were found in large number in the region. Sculptures were analyzed in modern times by Broadley, Beglar, Kittoe and Cunningham in the course of their surveys but the first real discussion of Pala-Sena sculptures was found in the catalogue by John Anderson and by T. Bloch.

A few works attempted to deal with these sculptures as a continuous development and relate them to the reigns of the Pala-Sena kings (French 1928; Kramarisch 1929; Banerji 1933; and in recent times Huntingdon 1984). Sculptures form the most major evidence of Pala-Sen or "early medieval" material culture today. Other aspects of material culture were also looked into as part of region-wise surveys carried out by the British officers. Buddhism's major value for the 19 century British scholars was an antithesis to the "degenerate" Brahmanical religion they came across in both India's past and present. Cunningham brought home the "greater" benefits involved in his project of searching out the Buddhist ruins of India.

The first person to deal in depth with material remains was Francis Buchanan. He described the Paharpur remains as that of a temple and "its great steepness and height induce me to suppose that it had been solid, like many temples of Buddha in Ava and Nepal". He also visited Mahasthangar and surmised that these were Buddhist remains (Bychanan-Hamilton 1833). Westmacott explored parts of southeastern Dinajpur and the neighboring parts of Bogra and found remains of Buddhism and the Buddhist Pala kings. He described Paharpur as a tall brick mound which was once a Buddhist stupa. Beveridge traveling in Bagura found nothing Buddhist in Mahasthan (Beveridge 1878). Cunningham tracing the routes of Hieun Tsang undertook tours of North Bengal in order to look for the site of the ancient capital called Paundra Vardhana. He identified it as Mahasthan on the basis of the distance and bearing from the neighbourhood of Rajmahal and partly on the basis of the immediate vicinity of Bhasu Bihar which corresponds exactly with Hieun Tsang's account of the Buddhist monastery of Po-shi-po west of the capital. He was fortunate enough to discover the site of the ancient site of Mahasthan on the Karatoya river.

Considerable work was carried out by the Varendra Research Society in order to bring to light the rich heritage of Varendra. Paharpur was excavated by the society along with the University of Calcutta. The monuments, writes A.K. Maitra, belong to two principal classes, *architectural* and *iconographic,* both of which fall under the general head, *devotional*. "In an age in which freedom of faith and observance used to be kept under cruel control ...religious toleration appears to have been a noteworthy characteristic of this land. Maitra's efforts in reconstructing to some extent the material culture of the people of Varendra was followed by Nihar Ranjan Ray's monumental work, viz., *Bangalir Itihas* (History of the Bengalee People) where there was an effort to "excite a degree of hope in their lives. It can offer some direction for the future, if it can arouse love and reverence for the land and its people."

S.K. Saraswati and H.E. Stapleton toured the area in Maldah and Dinajpur districts and discovered many 'sites' and sculptured pieces of the 'early medieval' period. Stapleton writes that the main objects of the tour were to make enquiries about Ekadala and the battle between Sikandar Shah and his son amongst other aspects. The emphasis was on remains of the Sultanate and subsequent dynasties (Stapleton 1932).

Saraswati on the other hand was more interested to show the Hindu antecedents of the Muslim monuments. He remarked how an examination of the stones used in the construction of the Adina mosque reveals the fact that most of them came from temples. "A study of every Muslim settlement of some antiquity reveals the story how they all sprang up on around earlier sites.

The ancient town of Devikot was leveled to the ground in the early days of the Muslim rule. Such was also the story of Gaur, of Mahasthan and practically of every Muhammadan establishment which were so frequently found perched on ancient mounds (Saraswati 1932a; 175). The emphasis was on the Hindu past and not on particular dynasties. Mostly sculptural fragments were used to give a tentative date to the material remains in this region. The excavation of Bangarh was carried out to understand the pre-Muhammadan remains, structures and 'major' antiquities were recorded.

Of special significance is B. Morrison's work on settlements in Mainamati near Comilla in Bangladesh (Morrison 1977). It concentrates on a holistic approach to a site in general. The excavations of Jagjivanpur and several other cities in Habibpur in Malda district in West Bengal are also of significance. The site of Jagjivanpur is a single culture site dating from AD 9th century belonging to the early medieval period where excavations have been undertaken. All this archaeological evidence points to a rich ancient archaeological heritage from the stone age to the recorded history.

Turkish Invasion

The biggest challenge to the Sen rule came from an invasion by Muhammad Bakhtiar Khilji, a Turkish adventurer in AD 1202. His invasion is described in *Tabaquat-I-Nasiri* written by Minhas-ud-Din. Before we come to this event, a little bit of digression is necessary. After the rise of Islam in Arabia in AD 7th century the South Asian subcontinent had seen a prolonged occupation of Sind by the Arabs under the Abblasid Caliphate for several centuries from 8th century onwards. But this was more an episode in this subcontinent's history than a development that had continuity in the mainstream. It was not the Abblasid Caliphate, but Turkish dynasties of trans-Oxian Central Asia, who were destined to bring the standard of Islam to the heartland of the Indian subcontinent.

One of these dynasties was the Yemeni dynasty which arose in Ghazni in the 10th century. Under its two rulers, Subuktgin and Mahmud, it carried on a relentless war against the Shahi kingdom of Udbhandpur (Und) which ruled over western Punjab and the northwestern frontier up to the Hindukush mountains. The Ghaznavid campaign against the Shahi rulers, Jaipal and Anandapal, was inspired by both a fiery zeal to spread Islam and a strong temptation to plunder the untold wealth of Hindustan. Sultan Mahmud (AD 998-1030) led a large number of expeditions, at least 17, to North India, including places as far as Kashmir, Kangra, Mathura, Kanauj and Somnath, destroyed the power of the Hindu rulers of these regions over time, and carried away immense riches to his native Ghazni.

The Ghaznavid invasion and occupation of Punjab and Afghanistan was followed a century later by another invasion, this time by another Turkish power, the Ghurids from Ghur in Afghanistan. The Ghurid General, Shihabuddin Mohammad invaded India several times. He had an unsuccessful encounter with Prithviraj, the Chauhan ruler of Delhi around AD 1190-91. He was, in fact, defeated and captured by Prithviraj, but released and allowed to return to his homeland. In 1192, Mohammad returned to India and defeated and killed Prithviraj Chauhan at the well-known battle of Tarain. This led to the establishment of the Delhi Sultanate a few years later under Mohammad Chauri's general, Qutab-ud-Din Aibak (AD 1206). It was Muhammad Bakhtiar Khilji, one of Aibak's associates and a reckless adventurer, who was responsible for bringing Islam and Turkish rule to Bengal.

Muhammed Bakhtiar Khilji, traditionally held as conqueror of Bengal but described by contemporary sources as conqueror of the Kingdom of Lakhanauti, belonged to a Turkman tribe called Khilji, which migrated from the Oxus region to Afghanistan in the 12th century. He, like many other adventurers, moved eastwards to the fabled Hindustan in quest of fortune. All of them aspired after carving out kingdoms in Hindustan, taking advantage of the political disunity and vulnerability of the numerous Hindu princes in the face of better horsemanship, better training in swords and guns, better speed and military techniques of the Central Asian tribes.

The invaders were also strongly motivated by the Islamic fervour to spread the new religion. Indeed, Bengal, along with the whole of North India, had become, in the 12th century, a playground for the Turkish-Afghan adventurers. Bakhtiar, who was physically deformed, first came to Ghazni around AD 1195, moved to Delhi shortly thereafter, seeking fortune unsuccessfully everywhere. He moved further east and landed on a soldier's job under Hassan Adib of Badayun in AD 1193 and thereafter took charge of a small *jagir* in Mirzapur district under the governor of Oudh. Soon he gathered around himself a sizeable body of Khilji and Turkish adventurers wandering around North India in search of wealth and fortune and began regular forays into the open country to the east of Karmnasa river, not defended by the army of any large kingdom.

The object was to seize as much booty as possible at a minimum of risk and bloodshed. After one o two years of plundering, he was involved in the melodramatic incident of capturing the so-called fortress for Bihar (which was in reality a Buddhist monastery, possibly the famous monastery of Odantapura). It was only after storming the massive structure of the *vihara* and killing the "shaven soldiers" that the invaders discovered that they were not soldiers but monks living n a monastery. It is to this fortuitous event that the Indian State of Bihar (Vihara) owes its name, as the Turkish conquerors started referring to this whole territory as Bihar. After occupation of Bihar and consolidation for a year through establishing *thanas* or military camps, Bakhtiar's attention inevitably turned to fabled Bengal. Meanwhile, he also visited Aibak, the sultan of Delhi, at Badaun, and paid homage. It was in the year 1201 that Bakhtiar made his famous and well-described raid into the heart of Bengal, then ruled by the aged Lakshman Sen. He led a cavalry not through the usual route of Rajmahal, but through the hills and jungles of Jharkhand and made a sudden appearance before Nadiya or Navadeep where Lakshman Sen was camping at that time. Presumably, this was already a well-known place of pilgrimage where orthodox people used to go for bathing in the sacred Ganges. According to Minhas' *Tabaqat-I-Nasiri*, many of the residents of Nadiya panicked at the news of the sudden appearance of Bakhtiar's horsemen and left the city. The vanguard of 18 horsemen entered into the town without any resistance.

Perhaps some of the local people even mistook them as horse dealers from Central Asia. They suddenly attacked the rulers and residents causing panic and all round confusion. Lakshman Sen was taking his mid-day lunch when "a loud cry rose from the gate of the palace and from the interior of the town". This shows that the main body of the Turkish troops had followed the reconnaissance party into the town almost immediately. The aged Lakshman Sen, taken by surprise, left the palace by boat together with his retinue leaving the town in possession of the daredevil invaders. He withdrew to riverine East Bengal which was beyond the reach of the Turks. Thus Bakhtiar's men had a walkover as far as Navadwip was concerned. This is the famous event described traditionally as Bakhtiar's conquest of Bengal with only 18 horsemen. The process of actual conquest of Bengal took many more years. For the present Bakhtiar had only occupied a holy place on the river Bhagirathi where religious minded people often stayed in order to have regular dips in the holy river. Navadwip was not the capital of Bengal, nor close to the capital Gaur, also called the capital of Lakshnavati; but Bakhtiar must have followed up the conquest of Nadia by occupying the central part of Bengal around Lakshmanvati.

Lakshamn Sen continued to rule in East Bengal for several years after AD 1201. Several land grants issued by him from East Bengal (e.g., Bhawal Pargana grant, AD 1205) clearly attest to this. There is also a laudatory reference to Lakshman Sen's victory against the Mlechha king and also to the victory of his sons over

Yavanas. Even the author of *Tabaqat* uses a very complimentary term in relation to him and describes him as the great Rai of Bengal comparable to Sultan Qutab-ud-Din of Delhi. Lakshman Sen must have died around AD 1206. His two sons, Biswarup Sen and Keshav Sen, ruled in succession in East Bengal with usual imperial titles. Thereafter there is no reference to them, although, in general, Eastern Bengal stayed outside Delhi's rule for nearly half a century even up to the time of Balban. According to Minhas Ghiyas-ud-din Iwaz, the Sultan of Lakhanavati, made an abortive attempt in 1226 to conquer Banga. Perhaps this invasion was followed by Biswarup Sen. Keshav Sen also claimed victory in his inscription, over invaders from the West, possibly Malik Saifuddin (AD 1231-33) of Gaur, who sent an expedition to Banga which brought some elephants, according to Minhas. Minhas also informs us that the Sens occupied the throne of Banga up to AD 1245. Both Biswarup and Keshav worshipped the Sun god. There is also evidence about a Buddhist ruler, Madhu Sen, who ruled portions of East Bengal around AD 1289.

It was the rise of the Pattikera kingdom and the Deva family beyond the Meghna river which perhaps brought about the final end of the Sen Dynasty around AD 1250. The memories of the mysterious Pattikera kingdom are generally lost except in the ruins of its capital city at Mainamati Hills near Comilla, in the Burmese chronicles from the time of King Anarotha of Burma (AD 1044-1077) which speak of the close and friendly relations between Burma and her western neighbour, Pattikera, the reference to the city of Pattikera in a Nepalese manuscript of AD 1015 and the name of a Paragana called Pattikera near the Mainamati Hills. We know the name of only one king of this dynasty from an inscription in Mainamati Hills. He must have ruled between AD 1202 and 1219.

The Deva dynasty that followed, and possibly gave the final *coup de grace* to the Sen dynasty, consisted of Purushottam, who rose from the position of a village headman (*gramani*). His son, Madhusudan, took the title of king (*nripati*). Other subsequent rulers were Vasudev and Damodar who might have destroyed the Pattikera rule, and Danuja Madhav Dasaratha Deve, who claimed to have wrested Gaur through the grace of god Naryana and who issued an inscription from Bikrampur. He entered into a treaty with Balban, the Sultan of Delhi, in AD 1293 on equal terms. The meeting between Balban and Danuj Rai at Sonargaon is vividly described in *Tarih-I-Mubarak Shahi.*

Jayadeva

Jayadeva was a Sanskrit poet, who lived in what is now Orissa, circa 1200 AD. He is most known for his composition, the epic poem *Gita Govinda,* which depicts the divine love of the Hindu deity *Krishna* and his consort, *Radha,* and is considered an important text in the Bhakti movement of Hinduism. He was born to an Utkala Brahmin family in a village called *Kenduli Sasan* in Orissa.

Biography

Jayadeva was born in *Kenduli Sasan* (formerly *Kendubilva*), in the Prachi valley, Khurda district in Orissa. *Kenduli Sasan* is a village near the famous temple city of Puri. At the time of Jayadeva's birth, Orissa was under the rule of Ganga dynasty king *Chodaganga Deva.* It was during the reign of this monarch and his son and successor, *Raghava,* that Jayadeva composed his Sanskrit epics. Chodaganga Deva, originally a *Shaiva,* was strongly influenced by the devotion to Krishna in and around Puri and became a *Vaishnava* devotee of Krishna himself. The poet's parents were named *Bhojdeva* and *Vamadevi.* From temple inscriptions it is now known that Jayadeva received his education in Sanskrit poetry from a place called *Kurmapataka,* possibly near Konark in Orissa. Later on, Jayadeva married *Padmavathi,* who according to temple inscriptions, may have been an accomplished temple dancer on her own right.

Prachi valley has a long history of worshipping *Madhava,* another name for Krishna. During Jayadeva's period, it was known as a religious place dominated by Vaishnava Brahmins. Even today, the village of Kenduli Sasan is replete with images of Madhava. Undoubtedly, the great poet must have been influenced by the devotional milieu in that area when he composed his magnum opus, the Gita Govinda.

Historical Records on Jayadeva's Life

Inscriptions at Lingaraj temple, and the more recently discovered Madhukeswar temple and Simhachal temple that were read and interpreted by Dr. Satyanarayan Rajaguru shed some light on Jayadeva's early life. These inscriptions narrate how Jayadeva had been a member of the teaching faculty of the school at Kurmapataka. He might have studied there as well. It must have been right after his childhood education in Kenduli Sasan that he left for Kurmapataka and gained experience in composing poetry, music and dancing. The earliest mention of Jayadeva outside Orissa are by Chand Bardai, the court poet of Prithviraj Chauhan. The next earliest reference outside Orissa is found in an inscription of Raja Sarangadev in the year 1201 A.D. These records establish that the Gita Govinda became popular throughout India within a brief perid of its composition, perhaps because it was regularly performed in the Jagannath temple of Puri.

Some further details about Jayadeva have been garnered from a book by an Oriya Vaishnava poet Madhava Patnaik, who was contemporaneous to Chaitanya in the fifteenth century. Madhava Patnaik's book gives a clear account of Chaitanya's visit to Puri. He mentions that Chaitanya paid a visit to Kenduli Sasan near Puri to pay homage to Jayadeva and to chant passages from the Gita Govinda. The book mentions that Kenduli Sasan was in fact the birthplace of the illustrious poet. Madhava Patnaik's book also gives an account of Jayadeva's early life from the legends around Puri. It mentions Jayadeva as excelling in the Shastras and the Puranas from early childhood. He is a great contemporary.

Literary Contributions

Jayadeva has had a profound influence on the religious practices of Hinduism. The classic *Tribhangi* (three-fold) posture of Krishna playing the flute gained popularity due to him.

Dashavatara

Jayadeva was instrumental in popularizing the *Dasavatara,* the ten incarnations of Vishnu in his composition, *Dasakritikrite.* Additionally, the Gita Govinda begins with a Dasavatara stotra. It should be noted that in Jayadeva's version of Dasavatara, Buddha as an incarnation of Vishnu, while Krishna is not incorporated. This was possibly due to the fact that from the poets perspective, Krishna was synonymous with Vishnu. In July 2009, the government of India's Department of Posts has decided to release 11 stamps in Bhubaneswar to commemorate the birth of Jayadeva. One stamp depicts the poet himself, while the other ten depict the Dasavatara. Chief Minister Naveen Patnaik unveiled the stamps at a special function in Jayadev Bhawan. The stamps are in the denomination of Rs 5. A total of 800,000 stamps were released for sale in Orissa.

Hymns in the Guru Granth Sahib

Two hymns composed by Jayadeva have been incorporated in the Guru Granth Sahib, the holy book of the Sikh religion. Although it is not clear how these medieval Orissan hymns found their way to the Sikh religion, there are records narrating how Jayadeva's work had a profound influence on Guru Nanak during his visit to Puri.

Music and Dance

Odissi dance: In the opinion of researcher scholars, Jayadeva is among the centralmost figures in Oriya culture. Jayadeva's ashtapadis that are sung in dance performances of Odissi, the classical dance of Orissa.

Classical Music of Orissa

Oriya bhajans (devotional songs) are based on rages and talas specified by Jayadeva's hymns. Jayadeva was a devotee of Krishna, and Krishna in the form of Jagannath is the central deity of Orissa.

Fine Arts

Jayadeva and his Gita Govinda had gained considerable popularity and had emerged as a painter's theme by the late 15th century itself, though no such early paintings are available now. The earliest reported Gita Govinda paintings are from Mewar between 1590-1600 A.D.

Patachitra Paintings

The Gita Govinda composed by Jayadeva is one of the popular themes in the traditional *patachitra* paintings of Orissa.

Pahari Paintings

Jayadeva had a profound influence on the Pahari school during the 17th-19th centuries, which was prevalent throughout northern India bordering the Hiimalayas (from Jammu through Himachal Pradesh). In paricular, Jayadeva's Radha and Krishna served as popular themes for Basohli Painting in Jammu and Kashmir.

7

Rashtrakuta Dynasty

The Rashtrakuta Empire was a royal Indian dynasty ruling large parts of southern, central and northern India between the sixth and the tenth centuries. During this period they ruled as several closely related, but individual clans. The earliest known Rashtrakuta inscription is a seventh century copper plate grant that mentions their rule from Manpur in the Malwa region of modern Madhya Pradesh. Other ruling Rashtrakuta clans from the same period mentioned in inscriptions were the kings of Achalapur which is modern Elichpur in Maharashtra and the rulers of Kannauj. Several controversies exist regarding the origin of these early Rashtrakutas, their native home and their language.

The clan that ruled from Elichpur was a feudatory of the Badami Chalukyas and during the rule of Dantidurga, it overthrew Chalukya Kirtivarman II and went on to build an impressive empire with the Gulbarga region in modern Karnataka as its base. This clan came to be known as the Rashtrakutas of Manyakheta, rising to power in South India in 753. At the same time the Pala dynasty of Bengal and the Prathihara dynasty of Malwa were gaining force in eastern and northwestern India respectively.

This period, between the eight and the tenth centuries, saw a tripartite struggle for the resources of the rich Gangetic plains, each of these three empires annexing the seat of power at Kannauj for short periods of time. At their peak the Rashtrakutas of Manyakheta ruled a vast empire stretching from the Ganga River and Yamuna River doab in the north to Cape Comorin in the south, a fruitful time of political expansion, architectural achievements and famous literary contributions. The early kings of this dynasty were Hindu but the later kings were strongly influenced by Jainism. During their rule, Jain mathematicians and scholars contributed important works in Kannada and Sanskrit. Amoghavarsha I was the most famous king of this dynasty and wrote *Kavirajamarga,* a landmark literary work in the Kannada language. Architecture reached a milestone in the Dravidian style, the finest example of which is seen in the Kailasanath Temple at Ellora. Other important contributions are the sculptures of Elephanta Caves in modern Maharashtra as well as the Kashivishvanatha temple and the Jain Narayana temple at Pattadakal in modern Karnataka, all of which are UNESCO World Heritage Sites.

History

The origin of the Rashtrakuta Dynasty has been a controversial topic and has been debated over the past decades by historians, but it is said that the Rashtrakuat Dynasty was started when a warioir in charge named as Dantidurga defeated the Chalukya overloard.

The differing opinions mostly revolve around issues such as the home of the earliest ancestors of the medieval Rashtrakutas, a possible southern migration during the early part of the first millennium and the relationship between the several Rashtrakuta dynasties that ruled small kingdoms in northern and central India and the Deccan in the 6th century-7th century. Further, the relationship of these medieval Rashtrakutas to the most important and famous dynasty, the Rashtrakutas of Manyakheta of the 8th century-10th century time period has also been debated. Also contested is whether the Rashtrakutas of Manyakheta were related by ancestry to the early Kannada, Maratha, Reddi, Rajput or Punjabi communities of the Deccan and northern India.

While the history of the early Rashtrakutas has caused much debate, the history of the Rashtrakutas of Manyakheta (in present day Gulbarga) of the 8th-10th centuries can be accurately constructed because numerous contemporaneous inscriptions and texts refer to them. The crux of the Manyakheta empire extended from the Kaveri river in the south to the Narmada in the north. At their peak they were the only south Indian empire that conquered regions in far northern India (Kannauj) as well as the extreme south (Tamilakam). The Lata branch of the empire (in present day Gujarat) was an important dynasty belonging to the

Manyakheta family line which later merged with the Manyakheta kingdom during the 9th century.

Research

Sources: The study of the history of the early Rashtrakutas and the Rashtrakutas of Manyakheta has been made possible by the availability of numerous inscriptions spread all over the Deccan, ancient literature in Pali, contemporaneous Kannada literature such as *Kavirajamarga* (850) and *Vikramarjuna Vijaya* (941), Sanskrit writings by Somadeva, Rajashekara, Gunabhadra, Jinasena and others and the notes of Arab travellers of those times such as Suleiman, Ibn Haukal, Al Masudi, Al Istakhri and others. Scholars have left no topic unstudied in an effort to accurately propose the history of the Rashtrakutas. Theories about their lineage (*Surya Vamsa* or *Chandra Vamsa*), native region and ancestral home have been proposed using clues from inscriptions, royal emblems, ancient clan names such as "Rashtrika", epithets such as *Ratta, Rashtrakuta, Lattalura Puravaradhiswara,* names of royalty, coins and contemporaneous literature. These theories from noted scholars have resulted in claims that the Rashtrakutas were from either Rajput, Kannadiga, Reddi, Maratha, or Punjabi origin.

Epithets

The appearance of the terms *Rathika, Ristika* (*Rashtrika*) or *Lathika* in conjunction with the terms *Kambhoja* and *Gandhara* in some Ashokan inscriptions of 2nd century BCE from Mansera and Shahbazgarhi in North Western Frontier Province (present day Pakistan), Girnar (Saurashtra) and Dhavali (Kalinga) and the use of the epithet "Ratta" in many later inscriptions has prompted a claim that the earliest Rashtrakutas were descendants of the *Arattas,* natives of the Punjab region from the time of Mahabharata who later migrated south and set up kingdoms there, while another theory points more generally to north western regions of India. Based on this theory, the Arattas may have become natives of the Deccan having arrived there during the early centuries of the first millennium.

This is counter to the argument by other scholars that the term *Rishtika* used together with *Petenika* in the Ashokan inscriptions implied they were hereditary ruling clans from modern Maharashtra region and the term "Ratta" implied *Maharatta* ruling families from modern Maharashtra region. But this has been rejected on the basis that from ancient books such as *Dipavamsha* and *Mahavamsha* in Pali language it is known the term *Maharatta* and not *Rashtrika* has been used to signify hereditary ruling clans from modern Maharashtra region and the terms *Rashtrika* and *Petenika* appear to be two different displaced ruling tribes.

It is noted by another scholar that ruling clans called *Rathis* and *Maharathis* were in power in parts of present day Karnataka as well in the early centuries of the Christian era, which is known inscriptions from the region and further proven by the discovery of lead coins from the middle of 3rd century bearing *Sadakana Kalalaya Maharathi* in the heart of modern Karnataka region near Chitradurga. In the face of these facts it is claimed it can no longer be maintained that the *Rathi* and *Maharathi* families were confined only to present day Maharashtra. It is claimed there is sufficient inscriptional evidence that several *Maharathi* families were related to Kannadiga families by marriage and they were naga worshippers, a form of worship very popular in the Mysore region (modern Karnataka). Also, no evidence to confirm that these families were either Aryan or non-Aryan is available.

The epithet *Ratta*, it is also claimed is a Kannada word from which the word *Rashtrakuta* has been derived. The use of the word *Rattagudlu* (meaning an office) has been found in inscriptions from present day Andhra Pradesh dated prior to the 8th century indicating it was a South Indian word. From the Deoli plates and Karhad records it is argued there was a prince called Ratta and his son was called Rashtrakuta. Hence it has been argued the Rashtrakutas were of Kannada origin. It is also said the term *Rashtra* means "kingdom" and *Kuta* means "lofty" or *Rashtra* means province and *Kuta* means chieftain.

Another epithet used in inscriptions of Amoghavarsha I was *Lattalura Puravaradhiswara*. It is proposed that it refers to their original home *Lattalur*, modern day Latur in Maharashtra state, bordering Karnataka. This area it is claimed was predominantly Kannada speaking based on surviving vestiges of place names, inscriptions and cultural relics. It is explained that *Latta* is a Prakrit variation of *Ratta* and hence Rattana-ur became Lattana-ur and finally Lattalur. Another theory is that Latalurapura is modern day Ratnapur in Bilaspur district of central India.

Royal Names and Signatures

In linking possible connections between the medieval Rashtrakuta families to the imperial family of Manyakheta it has been pointed out that only the family members ruling from Elichpur (Berar or modern Amravati district, modern Maharashtra) had names that were very similar to the names of Kings of the Manyakheta dynasty. From the Tivarkhed and Multhai inscriptions it is clear that the kings of this family were Durgaraja, Govindaraja, Svamikaraja and Nannaraja. These names closely resemble the names of Manyakheta kings or their extended family, the name Govindaraja appearing multiple times among the Manyakheta line. These names also appear in the Gujarat line of Rashtrakutas whose family ties with the Manyakheta family is well known.

It has been noted that princes and princesses of the Rashtrakuta family used pure Kannada names such as Kambarasa, Asagavve, Revakka and Abbalabbe as their personal names indicating that they were native Kannadigas. It has been pointed out that princesses of family lineage belonging to Gujarat signed their royal edicts in Kannada even in their Sanskrit inscriptions. Some examples of this are the Navsari and Baroda plates of Karka I and the Baroda plates of his son Dhruva II. It has been attested by a scholar that the Gujarat Rashtrakuta princes signed their inscriptions in the language of their native home and the race they belonged to. It is well known that the Gujarat line of Rashtrakutas were from the same family as the Manyakheta line.

It is argued that if the Rashtrakutas were originally a Marathi speaking family, then the Gujarat Rashtrakutas would not have signed their inscriptions in Kannada language and that too in far away Gujarat. The theory that under the rule of the Badami Chalukyas of Kannada country, Kannada speaking dynasties were established in the far corners of the Chalukyan empire in Gujarat, Andhra and Berar (present day Vidharba region in modern Maharashtra) and hence the ancestors of King Dantidurga, the founder of the Manyakheta empire were Kannadigas. It is further claimed there is proof that in the locality where Dantidurga lived Kannada was the spoken language.

Emblems

Several Rashtrakuta families ruled India during the 6th century-7th century period. Scholars have tried to understand their relationship with the Rashtrakutas of Manyakheta by a comparative study of the emblems.

The only Rashtrakuta family whose royal emblem is similar to that of the rulers of Manyakheta, the golden eagle or Garuda *lanchhana* (emblem) is that of the family that ruled from Amravathi district of modern Maharashtra. It has been theorised that this line may possibly have been ancestors of the Manyakheta kings. Their inscriptions (Tivarkhed and Multhai) were issued from Achalapura (modern Elichpur) which may have been their capital. Another Rashtrakuta family ruling from Manapur in Malwa region with its founder King Abhimanyu had the emblem of a lion. This makes it improbable that they were the ancestors of the Manyakheta family.

While the Garuda is normally indicative Vaishnavite leanings, it has to be observed here that earlier coins belonging to King Krishna I's period use the legend *Parama Maheshwara,* which in turn indicate staunch Shaivite leanings. This change in symbology has been used to theorise that the Rashtrakutas may have originally been Shaivites and embraced Vaishnavism later.

Vamsha(Genealogy)

With regards to their *vamsha* (whether they belonged to *Surya Vamsha* (solar lineage) or *Chandra Vamsha* (lunar lineage), Rashtrakuta inscriptions remained silent on the issue, until about 860. Some 75 inscriptions have been found thereafter in the Deccan and Gujarat which speak about their *vamsha.* Of these, only 8 lay claim that they belonged to the Yadava line. While one inscription of 860 claims that King Dantidurga was born to the *Yadava Satyaki,* 1800 coins of King Krishna I (772), his successor calls him *Parama Mahesvara* indicating his solar lineage origin and Shaiva faith. An inscription of King Govinda III (808) mentions "by the birth of this virtuous king, the Rashtrakuta dynasty became invincible just as the Yadava dynasty by the birth of Lord Krishna". This is considered only a comparative statement. Only a few records attest to a possible Yadava connection and even the descendants of the Rashtrakutas such as the Gahadavalas of Kanauj, Rathors of Rajasthan claim to be from *Surya Vamsha* (solar lineage), a sure sign the Rashtrakutas belonged to the *Surya Vamsha.* The opinion that the Rashtrakutas did not belong to the Yadava line is supported by another scholar as well.

Language

While the linguistic leanings of the early Rashtrakutas has caused considerable debate, the history and language of the Rashtrakutas of Manyakheta has been free of such confusion. It is clear from inscriptions, coinage and prolific contemporaneous literature that the court of these Rashtrakutas was multi-lingual, used Sanskrit and Kannada as their administrative languages and encouraged literature in Sanskrit and Kannada. However this period was the very end of the classical era of literary Sanskrit and Prakrit. As such, from the Kavirajamarga of 9th century, it is known that Kannada was popular from Kaveri river up to the Godavari river, an area covering large territory in modern Maharashtra.

The Rashtrakuta inscriptions call them the vanquishers of the *Karnatabala,* a sobriquet used to refer to the near invincibility of the Chalukyas of Badami. This however it is claimed should not be construed to mean that the Rashtrakutas themselves were not Kannadigas. Their patronage and love of the Kannada language is apparent in that most of their inscriptions within modern Karnataka are in Kannada, while their inscriptions outside of modern Karnataka tended to be in Sanskrit. An inscription in classical Kannada of King Krishna III has also been found as far away as Jabalpur in modern Madhya Pradesh which further supports the view of their affinity to the language.

Adikavi Pampa, Sri Ponna, Shivakotiacharya and King Amoghavarsha I were among the noteworthy scholars in Kannada, the Apabhramsha poet Pushpadanta wrote several works and famous Sanskrit scholars such as Jinasena and Virasena (both of who were theologians), mathematician Mahaviracharya and poets such as Trivikrama and Gunabhadra adorned their courts. The earliest extant Kannada literature belongs to this time. These Rashtrakuta kings married princess from Northern and Southern India and several Rashtrakuta branches emerged in Northern India during the their imperialistic expansion in the 9th century.

The argument that the Rashtrakutas were either Marathi speaking Marathas or Telugu speaking Reddies in origin has been rejected. Reddy's in that time period had not come into martial prominence even in the Telugu speaking regions of Andhra, being largely an agrarian society of cultivators who only much later (in the 14th century-15th century) came to control regions in the Krishna-Rajamundry districts.

The Rashtrakuta period did not produce any Marathi inscriptions or literature (with the exception of a 981 CE Shravanabelagola inscription which some historians argue was inscribed later). In addition very few literary works in Prakrit language are available from this period. Jainism which played such an important role in giving patronage to early Kannada literature did not flourish as much in the present day Maharashtra region which is why no Marathi literature emerged during this period. Hence Marathi as the language of the Rashtrakutas, it is claimed, is not an acceptable argument.

Rashtrakutas and Rajputs

The Rashtrakutas emerged before the term "Rajput" came to be used as a community. The emergence of Rajputs in Rajasthan and Gujarat coincides with the arrival of the Rashtrakutas and Chalukyas in the region.

Branches of Rashtrakuta Dynasty

Several Branches of the Rashtrakuta Dynasty were created by the kings, commanders and relatives of the Rashtrakuta family during their expansion into central and northern India in the eighth to the tenth centuries.

These kingdoms ruled during the reign of the parent empire or continued to rule for centuries after the its fall or came to power much later. Well known among these were the Rashtrakutas of Gujarat (757-888), the Rattas of Saundatti (875-1230) in modern Karnataka, the Gahadavalas of Kannauj (1068-1223), the Rashtrakutas of Rajasthan (known as Rajputana) and ruling from Hastikundi or Hathundi (893-996), Dahal (near Jabalpur), Mandore (near Jodhpur), the Rathores of Dhanop, Rashtraudha dynasty of Mayuragiri in modern Maharashtra and Rashtrakutas of Kannauj.

Rashtrakuta Branches

These branches emerged as a result of Rashtrakuta conquest of North India.

Rashtrakutas of Lata (Gujarat):

- Indra (807-818) (brother of Govinda III above)

- Karka and Govinda (818-826)
- Dhruva II (835-845)
- Akalavarsha Shubhatunga (867)
- Dhruva III (-871)
- Direct rule from Manyakhet by Krishna II.

Rashtrakutas of Hastikundi (Hathundi) (Jodhpur) :

- Harivarma
- Vidagdha (916-938)
- Mammata (939)
- Balaprasada (997)
- The Hathundi Rathores (descendants).

Rashtrakutas of Dahal (near Jabalpur) (Madhya Pradesh) :

- Golhanadeva (1023).

Rashtrakutas of Kanauj (11th. century-13th. century):

- Gopal (4th king)
- Tribhuvana
- Madanapala (1119)
- Devapala (Lost Shravasti to Gahadavalas in 1128)
- Bhimapala
- Surapala
- Amritapala
- Lakhanpala (In 1202 defeated byQutub-ud-din)
- Mahasamanta Barahadeva (under Gahadavala Adakkhamalla).

Rashtrakutas of Mandore/Jodhpur:

- The lineage of Rathors 1226-To date (Mandore/Jodhpur).

Descendants Of Rashtrakuta

Their descendants are spread out over large areas of India. The Rashtraudha dynasty of Mayuragiri, Maharashtra, described in the Rashtraudha Kavya (1596) of Rudrakavi, the Rathors Rajputs of Rajasthan and the Rattas of Saundatti in Karnataka also claim descent from them.

Rashtrakuta Kings (753-982)

Dantidurga (735-756)

Dantidurga (735-756) C.E. also known as Dantivarman or Dantidurga II was the founder of the Rashtrakuta empire of Manyakheta. His capital was based in Gulbarga region of Karnataka. He was succeeded by his uncle Krishna I who extended his kingdom to all of Karnataka.

The Ellora record of Dantidurga says he defeated the Chalukyas in 753 and took the titles *Rajadhiraja* and *Parameshvara*. The inscription calls him son of Indra II. The Samangad inscription (modern Kholapur district, Maharashtra) states his mother was a Chalukya princess from Gujarat called Bhavanaga. The same inscription states he defeated the invincible *KarnataBala* of the Badami Chalukyas. Further he defeated the kings Lata (Gujarat), Malwa, Tanka, Kalinga and Sheshas (Nagas) in central India and performed many sacrifices. Though he conquered the Chalukya kingdom it is clear from the Vakkaleri inscription of 757 that the Chalukya King Kirtivarman II retained control over his southern provinces up to 757. His daughter was married to a Pallava King Nandivarman II of Kanchi. Dantidurga helped Nandivarman recover Kanchi by warring against the Chalukyas..

Krishna I (756-774)

Krishna I (756-774)C.E. an uncle of Dantidurga took charge of the growing Rashtrakuta empire by defeating the last Badami Chalukya king Kirtivarman II in 757. This is known from the copper plate grant of King Govinda III of 807 and a copper plate grant of the Gujarat Rashtrakuta King Karka from Baroda. He is also known as Kannara or Kannesvara and took the titles *Akalavarsha, Shubatunga, Prithvivallabha* and *Shrivallabha*. He patronised the famous Jain logician Akalanka Bhatta, the author of *Rajavartika.*

Some historians are of the opinion that Krishna I usurped the throne from his nephew Dantidurga. But others disagree as the term "demise of Dantidurga" occur in the Kavi and Navasari copper plates indicating Krishna I mush have ascended the throne after the death of Dantidurga. However from the Baroda inscription it seems that Krishna I may have had to subdue another claimant to the throne, perhaps a Rashtrakuta princes or a son of Dantidurga.

He successfully fought the Western Ganga Dynasty king Sripurusha and acquired some territory in Gangavadi (Southern Karnataka) and the Shilaharas of south Konkan. He defeated the Eastern Chalukya King Vishnuvardhana IV. The Kailasanatha Temple in Ellora was commissioned during his time as described by the Alas inscription of 770. He was responsible for building 18 Shiva temples. 1800 coins of his, discovered recently, have the legend *Parama Maheshvara* which indicates his strong Shaiva faith. His eldest son, Govinda II came to power after him.

Govinda II (774-780)

The eldest son of Krishna I, Govinda II left the administration to his younger brother Dhruva Dharavarsha, also known as Nirupama.

Apart from his invasion of Vengi and the defeat of Eastern Chalukya king Vishnuvardhana IV, when his father Krishna I was still the king, not much is known about Govinda II, apart from his dedication to sensual pleasures. It seems that his younger brother Dhruva did most of the conquering as the kingdom had reached three times the size it was during the time of Krishna I. It appears from the Paithan copper plate inscription that an attempt by Govinda II to regain his lost control over the kingdom with the help of neighbouring Kings of Malwa, Kanchi and Vengi failed and that Dhruva Dharavarsha brought the kingdom firmly under his control.

Dhruva Dharavarsha (780-793)

Dhruva (780-793) C.E. was one of the ablest of the Rashtrakuta rulers and had ascended the throne after replacing his elder brother Govinda II. Govinda II had become unpopular among his subjects on account of his various misconducts and demeanors as a ruler, including excessive indulgence in sensual pleasure.

This is evident from the Karhad plates of Krishna III. The Dhulia grant of 779 and Garugadahalli inscription of 782 proclaim Dhruva the emperor. Though some historians claim that Dhruva revolted and grabbed the throne, other historians feel the transition of the throne from Govinda II to Dhruva was peaceful and may have happened willingly. He earned the titles like *Kalivallabha, Srivallabha, Dharavarsha, Maharajadhiraja* and *Parameshvara.*

Success in North and East

Dhruva Dharavarsha had a high level of political aspiration and he actively pursued the goal of expanding the frontiers of Rashtrakuta domination. In north India, he subjugated the might of the rulers of Kannauj.

In central India, he defeated the Gurjara Prathihara and also Dharmapala of the Pala Dynasty of Bengal (who was eager to rule Kannauj) in a battle in the Ganga-Yamuna doab. However, these great victories brought him no permanent land gains but only a lot of material gain and fame. However another historian has claimed that Dhruva's empire streatched from Ayodhya in the north to Rameshvaram in the south.

Victories in the Deccan and South

He humbled Vishnuvardhana IV, an Eastern or Vengi Chalukyan king in 784 and forged an alliance by marrying his daughter named Silabhattarika as per the Jetvai grant of 786. Thereafter, he defeated Shivamara II, the Western Ganga Dynasty ruler of Gangavadi, and imprisoned him and appointed his own son, Prince Kambarasa as the governor. He also forced Pallava Nandivarman to accept the suzerainty of Rashtrakuta who paid him handsomely with many elephants. He undertook campaigns to Kanchi in 785 and again against the Western Ganga Dynasty in 788.

All India Power

During his reign, Rashtrakutas emerged a true all-India power, controlling large regions across the Indian subcontinent.

Govinda III (793-814)

Govinda III (793-814) C.E. was a famous Rashtrakuta king who succeeded his illustrious father Dhruva Dharavarsha. He was militarily the most successful King of the dynasty with successful conquests from Cape Comorin in the south to Kannauj in the north, from Banaras in the east to Broach (Bharuch) in the west. He held titles such as *Prabhutavarsha, Jagattunga, Anupama, Kirthinarayana, Prithvivallabha, Shrivallabha, Vimaladitya, Atishayadhavala* and *Tribhuvanadhavala*. From the Someshvara inscription of 804 it is known that Gamundabbe was his chief queen.

Early Feud

Though Govinda III became the emperor it was not before having to face some internal family feuds. His elder brother Kambarasa (also known as Stambha) who coveted the throne went to war having formed an alliance of twelve chiefs as written in the Navasari record. Other records like the Sisvayi and Sanjan records mention support to Govinda III from brother Indra and victory against the combined forces of Kambarasa. Shivamara II of Ganga Dynasty of Talakad had joined Kambarasa but after the defeat was imprisoned for a second time while Kambarasa was pardoned and allowed to govern from Gangavadi.

Capture of Kannauj

From his capital in Mayurkhandi in Bidar district Govinda III conducted his northern campaign in 800. He successfully obtained the submission of Gurjara Pratihara Nagabhata II, Dharmapala of Pala Dynasty and the incumbent puppet ruler of Kannauj, Chakrayudha. It is said Nagabhata II ran away from the battle field. The Sanjan plates of Govinda III mentions that the horse of Govinda III drank the icy liquid bubbling in the Himalayan stream and his war elephants tasted the holy waters of the Ganga. The rulers of Magadha and Banga also submitted to him. A inscription of 813 states the Govinda III conquered Lata (southern and central Gujarat) and made his brother Indra the ruler of the territory. This in effect became a branch of the Rashtrakuta empire. However, another opinion is Govinda III had control over the regions between Vindhyas and Malwa in the north to Kanchi in the south, while the heart of his empire extended from the Narmada to Tungabhadra rivers.

Southern Conquests

The Eastern Chalukyas who had taken an antagonistic stand against the Rashtrakutas again had to face the wrath of Govinda III, who defeated Chalukya Vijayaditya II and installed Bhima Salki as its ruler. He further defeated the king of Kaushal (Kosala) and occupied parts of Andhra and defeated Pallava Dantivarman in 803 at Kanchi. He even obtained the submission of the King of Ceylon without even going to battle. The King of Ceylon is said to have sent him two statues, one of himself and another of his minister as an act of submission. The Nasari record states that now all the kingdoms of Tamil country, the Cholas, Pandyas and the Keralas paid their tribute to Govinda III.

Never had the Rashtrakuta empire reach such levels of military success and zenith of glory. Govinda III died in 814. His brother Indra during this time founded the Gujarat (Lata) branch kingdom.

Amoghavarsha I (814-878)

Amoghavarsha I. C.E. was a Rashtrakuta king, the greatest ruler of the Rashtrakuta dynasty, and one of the great kings of India. Historians have compared him to the legendary Emperor Ashoka for his religious temperament and love of peace. Many Kannada and Sanskrit scholars prospered during his rule, including, Mahaviracharya who wrote *Ganita-sara-samgraha,* Jinasena, Virasena, Shakatayan and Sri Vijaya (the Kannada language theorist). Amoghavarsha I was an accomplished poet and scholar. He wrote the *Kavirajamarga,* the earliest extant literary work in Kannada, and *Prashnottara Ratnamalika,* a religious work in Sanskrit. During his rule he held such titles as *Nripatunga, Atishadhavala, Veeranarayana, Rattamarthanda* and *Srivallabha.* He moved the Rashtrakuta regal capital from Mayurkhandi in the Bidar district to Manyakheta in the Gulbarga district in the modern Karnataka state. He is said to have built the regal city to "match that of Lord Indra". The capital city was planned to include elaborately designed buildings for the royalty using the finest of workmanship.

Early Years

Amoghavarsha I (whose birth name was Sharva) was born in 800 in Sribhavan on the banks of the river Narmada during the return journey of his father, King Govinda III, from his successful campaigns in northern India. This information is available from the Manne records of 803 and the Sanjan plates of 871, both important sources of information about Amoghavarsha I. The Sirur plates further clarify that Amoghavarsha I ascended to the throne in 814 at the age of 14 after the death of his father. All his inscriptions thereafter refer to him as Amoghavarsha I. His guardian during his early years as king was his cousin, Karka Suvarnavarsha of the Gujarat branch of the empire.

A revolt led by some of his relatives together with feudatories of the kingdom temporarily unseated Amoghavarsha I who, with the help of his guardian and cousin (Karka) also called Patamalla, re-established himself as the king of the empire by 821. This information comes from the Surat records and the Baroda plates of 835. The first to revolt was the Western Ganga feudatory led by King Shivamara II. In the series of battles that followed, Shivamara II was killed in 816 and Amoghavarsha I's commander and confidant, Bankesha, was defeated in Rajaramadu by the next Ganga king, Rachamalla. Due to the resilience of the Gangas, Amoghavarsha I was forced to follow a conciliatory policy. He married his daughter, Chandrabbalabbe, to the Ganga king Buthuga and another daughter, Revakanimmadi, to the Ganga prince Ereganga. More revolts occurred between 818 and 820, but by 821 Amoghavarsha I had overcome all resistance and established a stable kingdom to rule.

Wars in the South

Vijayaditya II of the Eastern Chalukya family overthrew Bhima Salki, the ruling Rashtrakuta feudatory at Vengi, took possession of the throne and continued his hostilities against the Rashtrakutas. He captured Sthambha (modern Kammamettu), a Rashtrakuta stronghold. From the Cambay and Sangli plates it is known that Amoghavarsha I overwhelmingly defeated the Vengi Chalukyas and drove them out of their strongholds in the battle of Vingavalli. The Bagumra records mention a "Sea of Chalukyas" invading the Ratta kingdom which Amoghavarsha I successfully defended. After these victories he assumed the title *Veeranarayana.*

Tranquility was restored temporarily by a marriage between Vijayaditya II's son, Vishnuvardhana V, and the Ratta princess Shilamahadevi, a sister of Karka of the Gujarat branch. However, Vishnuvardhana V attacked the northern Kalachuri feudatory of the Rashtrakutas in Tripuri, central India, and captured Elichpur near Nasik. Amoghavarsha I killed Vishnuvardhana V in 846 but continued a friendly relationship with the next Chalukya ruler, Gunaga Vijayaditya III, and suppressed the recalcitrant Alupas of South Canara under prince Vimaladitya in 870. Likewise, Amoghavarsha I maintained friendly interactions with the Pallava who were busy keeping the Pandyas at bay. The Pallavas had marital ties with the Rashtrakutas as well. Nandivarman was married to a Ratta princess, Sankha, and their son was also called Nripatunga. This has prompted historians to suggest that the

Pallava king must have married Amoghavarsha I's daughter. The Sanjan inscriptions of 871 claim Amoghavarsha I made a great effort to overthrow the kingdom of the Dravidas and that the mobilization of his armies struck terror in the hearts of the kings of Kerala, Pandya, Chola, Kalinga, Magadha, Gujarat and Pallava. The record also states that Amoghavarsha I imprisoned for life the *Gangavamshi* ruler and also those in his own court who had carried out plots against him.

Religion and Culture

Amoghavarsha I preferred to remain friendly with all his neighbours and feudatories and avoided taking an aggressive posture against them. It is still debated whether he abdicated his throne at times to fulfill religious pursuits. He deeply cared for his subjects and once when a calamity threatened to harm them, he offered his finger as a sacrifice to the goddess Mahalakshmi of Kholapur. For this act he has been compared to *puranic* heroes such as Bali, Shibi and Jimutavahana. It is written that the rulers of Vanga, Anga, Magadha, Malwa and Vengi worshipped him.

Amoghavarsha I was a disciple of Jinasenacharya. Proof for this comes from the writing, *Mahapurana* (also known as *Uttara Purana*), by Gunabhadra in which the author states "blissful for the world is the existence of Jinasenacharya, by bowing to whom Amoghavarsha considered himself to be purified". The same writing proves that Amoghavarsha I was a follower of the "Digambara" branch of Jainism. His own writing Kavirajamarga is a landmark literary work in Kannada language and became a guide book for future poets and scholars for centuries to come. The Sanskrit writing *Prashnottara Ratnamalika* is said to have been written by Amoghavarsha I in his old age when he had distanced himself from the affairs of the state. However others argue that it was written by Adi Shankara or by Vimalacharya.

Amoghavarsha I patronised both Jainism and Hinduism. His empire was one among the four great contemporary empires of the world and because of his peaceful and loving nature, he has been compared to Emperor Ashoka as noted above. The Jain Narayana temple of Pattadakal, (a UNESCO World Heritage Site) the basadi at Konnur and the Neminatha basadi at Manyakheta were build during his rule. His queen was Asagavve. Writings such as *Mahapurana* by Gunabhadra, *Prashnottara Ratnamalika* and

Mahaviracharya's *Ganita sara sangraha* are evidence that Amoghavarsha I had taken up Jainsim in his old age. Famous scholars of his time were Shakatayan, Mahaveera, Virasena, Jinasena, Gunabhadra and Sri Vijaya.

Krishna II (878-914)

Krishna II (878-914) C.E. ascended the Rashtrakuta throne after the demise of his famous father Amoghavarsha I. His Kannada name was Kannara. His queen was a Haihaya princess of Chedi called Mahadevi. From the chronology of inscriptions that mention the name of this king, it seems Krishna II may have started to rule even during the lifetime of his father. The fact that Amoghavarsha in his last years renounced the affairs of the state in religious pursuits supports this claim. The rule of Krishna II saw significant advances in literature, though in the affairs of expansion of the empire, his reign was mixed.

Vengi Affairs

His rule was one of mixed fortunes. He suffered some reversals against the Eastern Chalukyas ruled by King Gunaga Vijyaditya III whose commander pursued Krishna II to central India. After the death of Vijayaditya III, Krishna II continued hostilities against Chalukya Bhima I in 892 and succeeded in defeating him and taking him prisoner. However, Bhima I later freed himself and pushed back the Rashtrakutas from Vengi and crowned himself king. A few years later, Krishna II suffered two more defeats at the hands of the Vengi Chalukyas at Niravadyapura and Peruvanguru. However other sources claim Krishna II conquered Andhra.

Deccan and Northern Affairs

Krishna II defeated the Gurjara Bhoja I of Prathihara dynasty of Gujarat, merging the Lata line (Gujarat) of Rashtrakutas to bring it under his direct rule from Manyakheta. He defeated the kingdoms of Banga, Kalinga, Magadha. It is claimed his kingdom extended from the Ganga river in the north to Cape Comorin in the south. He held titles such as *Akalavarsha* and *Shubatunga.*

Tamil Politics

His daughter had married the Chola king Aditya I. With this the king had hoped to achieve influence in Tamil country. When

Parantaka became the king after the death of Aditya I and his grandson Kannara did not, Krishna II invaded the Chola kingdom with the help of the Banas and Vaidumbas, hoping to force the issue. He failed to consolidate his influence on the Cholas. The Rashtrakutas suffered a defeat in the battle of Vallala at the hands of Cholas under Parantaka I 916.

Indra III (914-929)

Indra III (914-929)C.E. was the grandson of Rashtrakuta Krishna II and son of Chedi princess Lakshmi. He became the king of the empire due to the early demise of his father Jagattunga. He had many titles such as *Nithyavarsha, Rattakandarapa, Rajamarathanda* and *Kirthinarayana*. He patronised Kannada poet and commander SriVijaya and Sanskrit poet Trivikrama. Indra III was married to princess Vijamba of the Kalachuri dynasty of central India (Chedi).

Capture of Kannauj

Immediately after coming to power, Indra III had to fight the Paramara ruler Upendra, a feudatory of Gurjara Prathihara and routed him out of Govardhana near Nasik. Thereafter the Paramaras became feudatories of the Rashtrakutas. The Prathihara ruler Mahendrapala was experiencing some family feuds and this gave Indra III an opportunity to attack Kannauj in the Ganga-Yamuna doab. Kannauj at this time was under the control of the Pratihara empire. From the writings of Kannada poet Adikavi Pampa it is known that Indra III sent his feudatory, Chalukya King Narasimha of Vemulavada (Andhra region) in pursuit of Mahipala I the incumbent ruler who fled the area. The northern campaign of Indra III produced more dramatic results then during the rule of Dhruva Dharavarsha and Govinda III as the Rashtrakutas were actually able to hold Kannauj until 916.

Trouble in Vengi

A civil war like situation prevailed in Vengi after the defeat of Eastern Chalukya Bhima at the hands of Baddega, a Rashtrakuta feudatory from Vemulavada. A period of intense politics continued when the Rashtrakutas tried to install the king of their choice in Vengi. Indra III's Jain general ShriVijaya who was also a poet won may wars for his king in the eastern Deccan and the bulk of Vengi was brought under the rule of Indra III for a few years.

Amoghavarsha II (929-930)

Govinda IV (930 – 936)

Govinda IV (930-935) C.E. was the younger brother of Amoghavarsha II who became the Rashtrakuta king in 930 as described in the Kalasa record of Chikmagalur. He was a very unpopular ruler who indulged in licentious acts. Control over Kannauj was lost during his rule. The Chalukyas of Vengi defeated him and much territory was lost. Finally, his own feudatories including King Arikesari of Vemulavada in Andhra revolted against him and placed Amoghavarsha III on the throne in 935. This is known from the records of Kannada Poet Adikavi Pampa, who was patronised by King Arikesari. Govinda IV had matrimonial relationship with the Cholas of Kanchi and finally found refuge with them when his feudatories revolted. Govinda IV patronised Kannada poet Ravinagabhatta.

Amoghavarsha III (936 – 939)

Amoghavarsha III (934-939) C.E. also known as Baddiga was in exile in Tripuri and was a younger brother of Indra III and uncle to Govinda IV. With the help of King Arikesari of Vemulavada in Andhra and other feudatories who revolted against Govinda IV he came to power. Not much is known about his uneventful reign. His advanced age and religious temperament did not allow him to show any interest in the governance of the kingdom, which was left to his son Krishna III. He was married to Kundakadevi, a princess from the Kalachuri dynasty of Tripuri. His daughter was married to Western Ganga Dynasty King Bhutuga II to whom a large territory was given as dowry.

Krishna III (939 – 967)

Krishna III whose Kannada name was Kannara (939 – 967 C.E.) was the last great warrior and able monarch of the Rashtrakuta Dynasty of Manyakheta. He was a shrewd administrator and skillful military campaigner. He waged many wars to bring back the glory of the Rashtrakutas and played an important role in rebuilding the Rashtrakuta empire. He patronised the famous Kannada poets Sri Ponna, who wrote *Shanti purana*, Gajankusha, also known as Narayana, who wrote on erotics, and the Apabhramsha poet Pushpadanta who wrote *Mahapurana* and other writings. His queen was a Chedi princess and his daughter Bijjabbe was married to a Western Ganga prince.

During his rule he held titles such as *Akalavarsha, Maharajadhiraja, Parameshvara, Paramamaheshvara, Shri Prithvivallabha* etc. At his peak, he ruled a vast empire stretching from the Narmada river in the north to the Kaveri river delta in the south. A copper grant of 993 issued by the Shilahara king of Thana claims the Rashtrakuta control extended from the Himalayas in the north to Ceylon in the south and from the eastern sea to the western seas. The grant states that when King Krishna III mobilised his armies, the kings of Chola, Bengal, Kannauj, Andhra and Pandya regions used to quiver.

Southern Invasion

He killed the Western Ganga ruler Rachamalla II and made his brother-in-law Butuga II the king of the Gangavadi territory. He invaded the territory of Gurjara Prathihara and captured Chitrakuta and Kalinjara regions. He even defeated his own family relations, the Chedi of Tripuri who had turned against the Rashtrakutas. Later he invaded the southern Deccan and recaptured Kolar and Dharmapuri from the Banas and Vaidumbas who had given shelter to Govinda IV due to his matrimonial relations with the Cholas. Though he initially may have experienced setbacks, Tondaimandalam (northern Tamil regions) was secured by 944.

He defeated the Cholas and captured Kanchi and Tanjore, according to the Siddalingamadam plates of 944. In 949 he defeated the Cholas decisively in a battle in Takkolam, North Arcot district. Krishna III was helped by his Western Ganga feudatory Buthuga II in these campaign. Rajaditya Chola was killed while seated on his elephant with a well-aimed arrow. Krishna III gave Buthuga II extensive Ratta territories near Banavasi in return for this victory. He later defeated the Pandyas, the rulers of Kerela region and obtained the submission of the King of Ceylon, extracted tributes from the Manadlika rulers, and erected a pillar of victory at Ramesvaram.

This victory is narrated in Somadeva's writing *Yashatilaka Champu* of 959 as well. However, from location of the inscriptions it is argued that Krishna III had full control only of Tondaimandalam (northern Tamil Nadu) as his inscriptions are not found further south in modern Tamil Nadu. After these victories he proclaimed himself "Conqueror of Kacci and Tanjai" (Kanchi and Tanjore). He exerted influence on the Vengi (modern Andhra Pradesh) by helping Badapa secure the throne against his competitor Amma II. Later, Danarnava of Vengi became his feudatory.

Northern Expedition

While Krishna III focussed on southern Deccan, the Chandelas had captured Chitrakuta and Kalinjar. This prompted Krishna III to send his Western Ganga feudatory Marasimha, son of Buthuga II, to retrieve the lost areas. Marasimha defeated the Gurjara Prathihara and the Paramara ruler Harsha Siyaka of Malwa. The northernmost Kannada inscription of the Rashtrakutas, dated about 964 is the Jura record (near Jabalpur) in present-day Madhya Pradesh. The details of these victories are inscribed in this inscription. At his peak, Krishna III ruled an empire that extended from Narmada river in the north and stretched south covering large parts of present-day northern Tamilnadu in the south. The Prathihara, the Paramara, the Seuna (ruled by Vaddiga) and the northern Kalachuri were his feudatories in the northern Deccan and central India.

His enemity towards the end of his rule with the northern Kalachuri of Tripuri proved fatal to the empire. Krishna III was also perhaps reckless in giving large *fiefs* (land grants) to his commanders. He gave the province of Tardavadi (present day Bijapur district) sometime before 965 to Tailapa II his Chalukya feudatory right in the heart of his empire. This later turned out to be to the Rashtrakutas' undoing.

Khottiga Amoghavarsha (967 – 972)

Khottiga Amoghavarsha (967-972) C.E. The decline in the Rashtrakuta empire had set in. The Paramara King Siyaka II plundered Manyakheta and Khottiga died fighting them. This fact is available from the Jain writing *Mahapurana* written by Pushpadanta. He was succeeded by Karka II who ruled for a few months.

Karka II (972 – 973)

Karka II (972-973) C.E. Karka II succeeded his uncle Kottigga Amoghavarsha to the Rashtrakuta throne. He had military successes against the Cholas, Gurjaras, Hunas and Pandyas and his feudatory, the Western Ganga Dynasty King Marasimha II defeated the Pallavas. But the weaknesses created by the earlier plunder of Manyakheta by Paramara King Siyaka II exposed the Rashtrakutas to further depredation who did not survive for long. During this time of confusion, Chalukya Tailapa II declared independence and killed Karka II.

Indra IV (973 – 982)

Indra IV (973-982) C.E. was the last Rashtrakuta king and a nephew of the feudatory king of Western Ganga Dynasty of Talakad. The Ganga king Marasimha II tried hard to keep the dwindling Rashtrakuta empire intact but in vain. Marasimha II committed Sallekhana in 975 and Indra IV followed him in 982. Thus this dynasty of Rashtrakutas vanished into history. However several related families had come to power in various parts of India during the imperial expansion of the Manyakheta Empire. These kingdoms continued to rule for several centuries. The Rajasthan branches continued to rule until emergence of India as a republic.

Tailapa II

The Early Chalukyas of Badami had been overrun by the rising power of Rashtrakutas. Tailapa II was a feudatory of the Rashtrakuta king Krishna III ruling from his *fief* territory called Taddevadi (Tardavadi-1000) in Indi taluk, Bijapur district which is known from his 957 and 965 inscriptions. The Rashtrakuta kingdom was invaded by the Malwa and their capital sacked in 972. Khottiga was killed in the raid and his nephew Karka II came to the Rashtrakuta throne. Tailapa, who had been biding his time, immediately overthrew Karka and established himself in Manyakheta.

Administration

Inscriptions and other literary records show the Rashtrakutas selected the crown prince based on heredity. The crown did not always pass on to the eldest son. Abilities were considered more important than age and chronology of birth, as exemplified by the crowning of Govinda III who was the third son of king Dhruva Dharavarsha. The most important position under the king was the Chief Minister (*Mahasandhivigrahi*) whose position came with five insignia commensurate with his position namely, a flag, a conch, a fan, a white umbrella, a large drum and five musical instruments called *Panchamahashabdas*. Under him was the commander (*Dandanayaka*), the foreign minister (*Mahakshapataladhikrita*) and a prime minister (*Mahamatya* or *Purnamathya*), all of whom were usually associated with one of the feudatory kings and must have held a position in government equivalent to a premier. A *Mahasamantha* was a feudatory or higher ranking regal officer. All cabinet ministers were well versed in political science (*Rajneeti*) and possessed military training. There were cases where woman supervised significant areas as when Revakanimaddi, daughter of Amoghavarsha I, administered Edathore *Vishaya*.

The kingdom was divided into *Mandala* or *Rashtras* (provinces). A *Rashtra* was ruled by a Rashtrapathi who on occasion was the emperor himself. Amoghavarsha I's empire had sixteen *Rashtras*. Under a *Rashtra* was a *Vishaya* (district) overseen by a Vishayapathi. Trusted ministers sometimes ruled more than a *Rashtra*. For example, Bankesha, a commander of Amoghavarsha I headed Banavasi-12000, Belvola-300, Puligere-300, Kunduru-500 and Kundarge-70, the suffix designating the number of villages in that territory. Below the *Vishaya* was the *Nadu* looked after by the Nadugowda or Nadugavunda; sometimes there were two such officials, one assuming the position through heredity and another appointed centrally. The lowest division was a *Grama* or village administered by a *Gramapathi* or *Prabhu Gavunda*.

The Rashtrakuta army consisted of a large infantry, numerous horseman, and many elephants. A standing army was always ready for war in a cantonment (*Sthirabhuta Kataka*) in the regal capital of Manyakheta. Large armies were also maintained by the feudatory kings who were expected to contribute to the defense of the empire in case of war. Chieftains and all the officials also served as commanders whose postings were transferable if the need arose. The Rashtrakutas issued coins (minted in an *Akkushale*) such as *Suvarna, Drammas* in silver and gold weighing 65 grains, *Kalanju* weighing 48 grains, *Gadyanaka* weighing 96 grains, *Kasu* weighing 15 grains, *Manjati* with 2.5 grains and *Akkam* of 1.25 grain.

Economy

The Rashtrakuta empire of Manyakheta came to power in South India in 753 and ruled for over two centuries. At its peak the Rashtrakutas of Manyakheta ruled a vast empire stretching from the Ganga River and Yamuna River doab in the north to Cape Comorin in the south, in a time of political expansion, architectural achievements and famous literary contributions.

The Rashtrakuta economy derived its funding from its natural and agricultural produce, its manufacturing revenues and moneys gained from its conquests. Cotton was the chief crop of the regions of southern Gujarat, Khandesh and Berar while cotton yarn and cloth was exported from Bharoch and incense and perfumes from the ports of Thana and Saimur. Minnagar, Gujarat, Ujjain, Paithan and Tagara were important centres of textile industry. White calicos were manufactured in Burhanpur and Berar and exported to Persia, Turkey, Poland, Arabia and Cairo. Jawarit Bajri was grown in some regions of modern Maharashtra and oil seeds in dry areas of northern Karnataka region. The Konkan region, ruled by the feudatory Silharas, produced large quantities of betel leaves, coconut and rice while the lush forests of Mysore, ruled by the feudtory Gangas, produced such woods as sandal, timber, teak and ebony. The Rashtrakuta empire controlled most of the western sea board of the subcontinent which facilitated its maritime trade.

The deccan soil, though not as fertile as that of the Gangetic plains, was rich in minerals. The copper mines of Cudappah, Bellary, Chanda, Buldhana, Narsingpur, Ahmadnagar, Bijapur and Dharwar were a source of income and played an important role in the economy. Diamonds were mined in Cudappah, Bellary, Kurnool and Golconda; the capital Manyakheta and Devagiri were important diamond and jewellery trading centres. Muslin cloth were manufactured in Paithan and Warangal and the leather industry and tanning flourished in Gujarat. Some regions of northern Maharashtra and Mysore, with its vast elephant herds, were important for the ivory industry. The Gujarat branch of the empire earned a significant income from the port of Bharoch, one of the most prominent ports in the world at that time.

Other important ports were Naosari, Sopara, Thana, Saimur, Dabhol, Jayagad, Kharepatan and Kalyan. The empire's chief exports were cotton yarn, cotton cloth, muslins, hides, mats, indigo, incense, perfumes, betel nuts, coconuts, sandal, teak, timber, sesame oil and ivory. Its major imports were pearls, gold, dates from Arabia, slaves, Italian wines, tin, lead, topaz, storax, sweet clover, flint glass, antimony, gold and silver coins, singing boys and girls (for the entertainment of the royalty) from other lands. Trading in horses was an important and profitable business, monopolised the Arabs and some local merchants.

Practicalities

Oxen and Bullock carts were used for business and leisure travel within the kingdom. While superior quality horses served the purpose for army cavalry, inferior horses were used as pack animals for moving commodities, especially in the hilly regions where cattle driven carts were too slow. Buying and selling land was not just the business of the two concerned parties but needed the consent of village elders and Mahajans (Brahmins). Artists and craftsman operated as corporations rather than as individual business. Inscriptions mention guilds of weavers, oilmen, artisans, basket and mat makers and fruit sellers. A Saundatti inscription refers to an assemblage of all the people of a district headed by the guilds of the region.

The weaver guild of Lakshmeshwar (in Gadag) had one executive head and the Mulgund guild had four executives with a membership of about two thousand artisans. The largest guilds were the Vira Balanju guilds of Belgamve (Balligavi) with nine heads and the Miraj inscription mentions another with nineteen executives. The number of executives depended directly on the membership in the guild. The Belgamve guild had five hundred inscriptions (*Shasana*) written outlining the rules and regulations by which all members had to adhere. Some guilds were considered superior to others, just as some corporations were, and received royal charters determining their powers and privileges. The Dambal inscription mentions its guild as the "lord of Aihole" and that its members owned their own royal umbrellas. Inscriptions suggest these guilds had their own militia to protect goods in transit and, like village assemblies, they operated banks that lent money to traders and businesses.

Taxation

Information on the kingdom's revenue system is now available from its copper plate grants, contemporaneous writings and inscriptions from neighbouring kingdoms. The accounts of Muslim writers of the time also provide insight into details. The government's income came from five principle sources: regular taxes, occasional taxes, fines, income taxes and tributes from feudatories. Regular taxes were called *Ujranga, Uparikara, Siddhaya* and *Visthi.* There were some miscellaneous taxes as well. Occasional taxes were called *chcitabhata pravesadavala* and *Rajasevakanam vasatidan.* An emergency tax was also imposed occasionally. Income tax included taxes on crown land, wasteland, specific types of trees considered valuable to economy, mines, salt, treasures unearthed by prospectors, and estates and moneys of persons who died without an heir.

Ujranga and *Uparikara* were universal produce taxes applied to items such as betel leaves, fruits, vegetables, flowers and grass. This may have included some additional taxes to pay for the salaries of government officials. The land owner or tenant paid a variety of taxes, including land taxes, produce taxes and payment of overheads for maintenance of the Gavunda. The theory that *Udranga* was applied to permanent landowners and *uparikara* to temporary land tenants has been proposed. Land taxes were varied, based on type of land, its produce and situation. A Banavasi inscription of 941 mentions reassessment of land tax due to the drying up of an old irrigation canal in the region. Various tax levels were determined ranging from 8% to 16%. The king determined the tax levels based on need and circumstances in the kingdom while ensuring that an undue burden was not placed on the peasants. A portion of all taxes earned by the government (usually 15%) was returned to the villages for maintenance. There is no mention of taxes on water, roads and other local facilities. The Rashtrakuta empire was frequently at war with the Palas and Gurjaras, a political situation that required significant expenditure to upgrade and maintain the army. The land tax therefore man have been as high as 20%.

Taxes on lands and property gifted to war heroes were lightly taxed while other lands were taxed in three installments. This type of taxation was called *Balagachchu.* The Ukkal inscription records that when land owners defaulted on taxes for three years in a row under normal circumstances, the lands were seized and sold by the village community. In most of the kingdom, land taxes were paid in goods and services and rarely was cash accepted. This was true in the domains of the feudatory Gangas and Cholas as well. From inscriptions it is known that government owned graneries and storehouses which ensured that grain and corn of the best quality was available at market rates, while old or low quality material was auctioned off at bargain prices or destroyed. A tax called *Bhutapattapratyaya* was levied on imported items called *upatta* while locally produced items were called *bhuta* and manufactured and stored items were called *sambhrta*. In addition, there were general excise and local taxes levied on villages. Taxes were levied on daily household items such as clarified butter and charcoal. Among non-agricultural rural people, herdsman and cattle breeders had to pay taxes also.

The Rashtrakuta government levied a shipping tax of one golden Gadyana on all foreign vessels embarking to any other ports and a fee of one silver Ctharna on vessels travelling locally. Taxes were levied on all types of artisans such as potters, sheep herders, weavers, oilmen, shopkeepers, stall owners, brewers and gardeners. Taxes on perishable items such as fish, meat, honey, medicine, fruits and essentials like fuel was as high as 16%. Under miscellaneous taxes were ferry and house taxes, only the Brahmins and their temple institutions being subjected at a lower rate. Some forms of taxation was occasional or uncommon, levied on villages only during encampment of the army or the police (*Bhafas*) on a march. Under such circumstances, the army (*Chata*) was allowed limited access to the village or township and that was only under special circumstances which ensured daily life in the communities continued unhindered. Customary presents were give to the king or royal officers on such festive occasions of as marriage or the birth of a son.

Emergency taxes are described in the writings of Somadeva and were applied under extraordinary circumstances when even Brahmins and temples were not excluded. These were applicable when the kingdom was under duress, facing natural calamities, or preparing for war or overcoming its ravages. Fines were charged on socially or politically alienated villages, the term used being *Sadandadas aparadhah* or *Pratishisiddhaya*. Since these taxes were uncommon, income to state from these sources was small overall. Income on government property included taxes on stray plots of cultivable land, forests, forest produce, waste lands, lands awaiting cultivation and specific trees such as sandal, Hirda, Mango and Madhuka, even when these were found growing on private property. The kingdom did not lay claim to the entire land inside its territory. A record of the feudatory Vaidumba king from southern deccan says the king had to purchase three veils of land from a local assembly in order to assign it to a temple in a village. Taxes on salt and minerals were mandatory although the empire did not claim sole ownership of mines, implying that private mineral prospecting and the quarrying business may have been active. The term used for these taxes was *Sahadhyantara Siddhi*. Treasures, even when discovered on private land, were included as taxable earnings as were the incomes and properties of persons who died without heirs. If there were no survivors in the family, the state claimed all the properties.

Culture

Religion: The Rashtrakutas kings supported the popular religions of the day in the traditional spirit of religious tolerance. Scholars have offered various arguments regarding which specific religion the Rashtrakutas favoured, basing their evidence on inscriptions, coins and contemporary literature. Some claim the Rashtrakutas were inclined towards Jainism since many of the scholars who flourished in their courts and wrote in Sanskrit, Kannada and a few in Apabhramsha and Prakrit were Jains. The Rashtrakutas built well known Jain temples at locations such as Lokapura in Bagalkot district and their loyal feudatory, the Western Ganga Dynasty, built Jain monuments at Shravanabelagola and Kambadahalli.

Scholars have suggested that Jainism was a principal religion at the very heart of the empire, modern Karnataka, accounting for a more than 30% of the population and dominating the culture of the region. King Amoghavarsha I was a disciple of the Jain Acuaria Jinasena and wrote in his religious writing, *Prashnottara Ratnamalika*, "having bowed to Varaddhamana (Mahavira), I write Prashnottara Ratnamalika". The mathematician Mahaviracharya wrote in his *Ganita Sarasangraha*, "The subjects under Amoghavarsha are happy and the land yields plenty of grain. May the kingdom of King Nripatunga Amoghavarsha, follower of Jainism ever increase far and wide." Amoghavarsha may have taken up Jainism in his old age.

However,few of the Rashtrakuta kings were Hindus, followers of the Shaiva, Vaishnava and Shakta faiths. Almost all of their inscriptions begin with an invocation to god Vishnu or god Shiva. The Sanjan inscriptions tell of King Amoghavarsha I sacrificing a finger from his left hand at the Lakshmi temple at Kolhapur to avert a calamity in his kingdom. King Dantidurga performed the *Hiranyagarbha* (horse sacrifice) and the Sanjan and Cambay plates of King Govinda IV mention Brahmins performing such rituals as *Rajasuya, Vajapeya* and *Agnishtoma*. An early copper plate grant of King Dantidurga (753) shows an image of god Shiva and the coins of his successor, King Krishna I (768), bear the legend *Parama Maheshwara* (another name for Shiva).

The kings' titles such as *Veeranarayana* showed their Vaishnava leanings Their flag had the sign of the Ganga and Yamuna rivers, perhaps copied from the Badami Chalukyas. The famous Kailasnatha temple at Ellora and other rock-cut caves attributed to them show that the Hinduism was flourishing. Their family deity was a goddess by name *Latana* (also known as *Rashtrashyena, Manasa Vindyavasini*) who took the form of a falcon to save the kingdom. They built temples with iconification and ornamentation that satisfied the needs of different faiths. The temple at Salotgi was meant for followers of Shiva and Vishnu and the temple at Kargudri was meant for worshipers of Shiva, Vishnu and Bhaskara (Surya, the sun god).

In short, the Rashtrakuta rule was tolerant to multiple popular religions, Jainism, Vaishnavaism and Shaivism. Buddhism too found support and was popular in places such as Dambal and Balligavi, although it had declined significantly by this time. The decline of Buddhism in South India began in the 8th century with the spread of Adi Shankara's Advaita philosophy. Islamic contact with South India began as early as the 7th century, a result of trade between the Southern kingdoms and Arab lands. Jumma Masjids existed in the Rashtrakuta empire by the 10th century and many Muslims lived and mosques flourished on the coasts, specifically in towns such as Kayalpattanam and Nagore. Muslim settlers married local women; their children were known as Mappilas (*Moplahs*) and were actively involved in horse trading and manning shipping fleets.

Society

Information regarding social life, the caste system, life style and recreational activities during the Rashtrakuta times comes from inscriptions and from the notes of Greek and Arab travellers to India at the time. These sources provide evidence that the

Hindu caste system was widespread. Chronicles mention more castes than the four basic castes in the Hindu social system known today, some as many as seven castes. One traveller's account mentions sixteen castes including the four basic castes of Brahmins, Kshatriya, Vaishya and Chandalas. One caste known as *Zakaya* or *Lahud* consisted of people belonging to communities specialising in dance and acrobatics. Intercaste marriages were uncommon except between highly placed Kshatriya girls and Brahmin boys. People belonging to such professions as sailing, hunting, weaving, cobblery, basket making and fishing were all accommodated into castes or subcastes. The *Antyajas* belonged to a caste the provided many menial services to the wealthy. Among people of upper castes only those Kshatriyas belonoging to the *Sat-Kshatriya* sub-caste (noble Kshatriyas) were considered higher in status than the Brahmins who otherwise enjoyed the highest status in Rashtrakuta society. A subcaste among Brahmins was the *istin* were solely specialised in the teaching the profession.

Brahmins were mostly involved in careers related to teaching, judiciary, astrology, mathematics, poetry and philosophy. However it was common for Brahmins to occupy hereditary administrative posts as well. In addition, such professions normally considered non-Brahminical; agriculture, trade in Betel nuts and martial posts were increasingly occupied by Brahmins. People of the medical profession were treated with regard and inscriptions mention some Brahmin doctors. Capital punishment though commonly practiced was not given to Brahmins who were found guilty of henious crimes and in this respect they enjoyed the same previleges as royal Kshatriya sub-castes. Instead, as an alternate punishment their right hand and left foot was severed leaving them disabled. The killing of a Brahmin in medieval Hindu India was considered as a henious crime and this alternate punishment served the purpose of enforcement of the law. The only caste of people considered above the Brahmins were the Kshatriyas belonging to royal and noble families. Not all Kshatriyas were considered upper caste and not all upper caste people were Kshatriyas.

By the 9th century, Kings from all the four castes had at one time or another occupied the highest seat in the monarchical system in Hindu India. Admitting Kshatriyas to Vedic schools along with Brahmins was common, although children of the Vaishya and Shudra castes were not allowed in these schools. Jains took up martial careers and landownership by people of all castes is recorded in inscriptions The Shudras had land rights in that any plot of land taken from one by fraud was restored back to them by the King himself. Brahmins, unlike the Vaishya and Shudra, were free to relocate from one province to another and even from one kingdom to another, where they were welcomed with gifts of land and housing. Special places of learning called *Brahmadeya* were constructed for them. The caste system was flexible to the extent that there are records of intercaste marriages although this was not common. However, toward the end of the Rashtrakuta rule, these intercaste marriages, especially those involving a Brahmin bride or groom, were becoming very rare while the practice remained relatively frequent among other castes. Brahmins were pure vegetarians and abstained from consuming alcohol of any kind while Kshatriyas indulged in both. Jainsim had become popular among traders and agriculturists who popularized vegetarianism. Intercaste functions were rare as dining together between people of various castes was avoided.

Joint families were the norm but legal separations between brothers and even father and son have been recorded in inscriptions. Women and daughters had rights over property and land, and there are inscriptions recording the sale of land by women. Moneys inheritable by women were called *Sthridhana*. The arranged marriage system ensured a strict policy of early marriage for women. Among Brahmins, boys married at or below 16 years of age and they chose brides of 12 or younger. This age policy was not as strictly followed by other castes. Inscriptions refer to numerous instances of the marriage of a man to his maternal cousin (daughter of a maternal uncle), prince Jagattunga, son of Krishna II being an example of this.

Women had the right to attend and the right to be in attendance in the court when it was occupied by the King. Sati was practiced but was voluntary. Very few examples of sati are noted in inscriptions and those that did occur were mostly in the royal families. The system of shaving the heads of widows was rarely practiced as epigraphs note that widows were allowed to grow their hair but decorating their hair was discouraged. The sentence "the cause of the cessation of the parting of the hairs of the damsels of enemies" (*ripuvilasiriisimantoddharanahetuh*) is repeated in many inscriptions. The remarriage of a widow was rare among the upper castes and common among the lower castes. Women who were dishonoured were admitted back into their families and caste.

Loans were granted in the presence of witnesses unless the receiver of the loan was of high social standing, in which case this requirement was waived. In the general population men wore two simple pieces of cloth, a loose garment on top and a garment worn like a *dhoti* for the lower part of the body. Only Kings could wear turbans, a practice that spread to the masses much later. Women's clothes were well stitched, and some wore petticoats. Names of Brahmin men consisted of the given name, the fathers name and the family *gotra* (lineage). The surnames popular today such as *Dvivedi, Upadhyaya, Dikshita* came into vogue only later. Dancing was a popular recreational activity and inscriptions speak of royal women being charmed by dancers, both male and female, in the king's palace. Devadasis were often present in temples.

Other recreational activities included attending animal fights of the same or different species. There has been found an Atkur hero stone (*virgal*) made for the favourite hound of feudatory Western Ganga King Butuga II that died fighting a wild boar in a sport. Game preserves for hunting by royalty are recorded in the inscriptions of Govinda III. Astronomy was well developed and so was astrology. Even Jains showed interest in astrological predictions and metaphysical beliefs. Superstitions were plentiful and catching a snake alive proved a woman's chastity. Old persons suffering from incurable diseases preferred to end their lives by drowning in the sacred waters of pilgrim site or by burning themselves.

Literature

Rashtrakuta literature is the body of work created during the rule of the Rastrakutas of Manyakheta, a dynasty that ruled the southern and central parts of the Deccan, India between the 8th and 10th centuries. The period of their rule was an important time in the history of South Indian literature in general and Kannada literature in particular. This era was practically the end of classical Prakrit and Sanskrit writings and a whole wealth of topics were available to be written in Kannada. Some of Kannada's most famous poets graced the courts of the Rashtrakuta kings. Court poets and royalty created eminent works in Kannada and Sanskrit that spanned such literary forms as prose, poetry, rhetoric, Hindu epics and Jain tirthankaras. Famous scholars wrote on secular subjects such as mathematics.

Kannada Writings

Kannada Poets and Writers in Rashtrakuta Empire (753-973 CE)

Amoghavarsha I	850
Srivijaya	850
Asaga	850
Shivakotiacharya	900
Ravinagabhatta	930
Adikavi Pampa	941
Jainachandra	950
Sri Ponna	950
Rudrabhatta	9th-10th c.
Kavi Rajaraja	9th-10th c.
Gajanakusha	10th century

Kavirajamarga is the earliest available writing on rhetoric, poetics and grammar in the Kannada language. It was written by the famous Rashtrakuta King "Nripatunga" Amoghavarsha I and is based partly on an earlier Sanskrit writing, *Kavyadarsa.* Some historians believe it may have been co-authored by a poet of the king's court, the Kannada language theorist, Sri Vijaya. The name means literally "Royal Path for Poets" and was used as a guide book for poets and scholars (*Kavishiksha*). From references made in this writing to earlier Kannada poetry and literature it is clear that a considerable body of work in prose and poetry must have existed in the preceding centuries.

Biography

The pre-coronation name of Amoghavarsha I was Sharva. He was born in Sribhavan in 800 to Rashtrakuta King Govinda III during the king's return from his successful northern campaigns in Kanauj. This is known from the Manne records (803), Sirur plates and Sanjan records (871) of Amoghavarsha I. Amoghavarsha I came to the throne in 814 at the age of 14 and took great interest in the Kannada language, culture, country and its people, and his writing *Kavirajamarga* goes into these details as well. The work describes the entire region between the Godavari river in the north and Kaveri river in the south as "Kannada country", which includes large territories in the north where now Marathi is spoken.

Early Writers and Literary Styles

Kavirajamarga makes important references not only to earlier Kannada writers and poets but also to early literary styles in vogue in the various written dialects of Kannada language. The aim of his writing was to standardise these written styles. The king mentions two styles of composition, the *Bedande* and the *Chattana,* and indicates that these styles were recognised by "earlier writers". Amoghavarsha I mentions several early Kannada writers who preceded him: Vimalachandra (777), Udaya, Nagarjuna, Jayabhandu and 6th century King Durvinita of the Western Ganga Dynasty as the best writers of Kannada prose; Srivijaya, Kavisvara, Pandita, Chandra and Lokapala as the best writers of Kannada poetry. But the works and compositions of these early authors are yet to be discovered. *Kavirajamarga* was formative in the literary growth of Kannada and is a guide book to the Kannada grammar that existed in that period. It laid the royal road of guiding many aspiring writers.

In his criticism, Amoghavarsha I mentions that old Kannada is appropriate in ancient poems but is insipid in works of the present time like an "association with an old woman". According to him, a mixture of Kannada with Sanskrit is harsh to the ear but a mixture of Kannada and Sama-Samskrita is pleasant to the ear like music, while a mixture of Kannada and Sanskrit in compounds is disagreeable like mixing drops of buttermilk (curdled milk) and boiling milk. He also condemned the usage of expletives such as *ante, matte,* and *Gadam,* etc.

Adikavi Pampa, widely regarded as one of the greatest Kannada writers, became famous for *Adipurana* (941). Written in champu style, it is the life history of the first Jain thirtankara Rishabhadeva. In this unique work of spiritual heroism, the soul moves through a series of births before attaining emancipation. The quest in this spiritual saga, as in many others, is the liberation of the soul from the cycle of life and death. Pampa's other classic *Vikramarjuna Vijaya* (or *Pampa Bharata,* 941), is the author's version of the Hindu epic the Mahabharata. The story differs from other earlier versions of the epic in that Arjuna alone is the hero, not the other Pandava brothers, and Draupadi is solely Arjuna's wife. The author underplays the role of the Hindu god Krishna and favourably compares his patron king Chalukya Arikesari (a Rashtrakuta feudatory) to Arjuna, while casting a lofty and noble image of Karna and the Kaurava prince Duryodhana. Pampa demonstrates such a command of classical Kannada that scholars over the centuries have written many interpretations of his work.

Another great writer in Kannada was Sri Ponna, patronised by King Krishna III and famed for his description of the life of the 16th Jain tirthankara Shantinatha entitled *Santipurana*. He earned the title *Ubhaya Kavichakravathi* (supreme poet in two languages) for his command over both Kannada and Sanskrit. His other writings in Kannada were *Bhuvanaika-karamabhyudaya, Jinaksaramale* and *Gatapratiagata*. Adikavi Pampa, Sri Ponna and Ranna (court poet of Western Chalukya King Tailapa II) are called the "three gems" of Kannada literature.

The earliest extant prose work in Kannada is *Vaddaradhane* (900) by Shivakotiacharya. The title means "worship of elders". The writing contains 19 stories mostly borrowed from the Sanskrit book *Brihatkatha-Kosha* and is about Jain tenets. The writing describes issues such as rebirth, *Karma*, plight of humans on earth, social issues of the time such as education, trade and commerce, magic, superstitions and condition of women in society. Other well known writers from this era were Rudrabhatta of Banahatti, Ravinagabhatta who was patronised by King Govinda IV, Kavi Rajaraja who wrote the Kalasa record, Gajanakusha (also known as Gajaga or Narayana) who wrote on erotics and was a minister in the court of King Krishna III.

Sri Vijaya, court poet of Amoghavarsha I wrote *Chandraprabha-purana* in early 9th century. Jinachandra, referred to by Sri Ponna as the author of *Pujyapada Charita* earned the honorific "modern Samantha bhadra", though his works have not been found. A contemporary of Amoghavarsha I was the Digambara Jain poet Asaga (or Asoka), who wrote the *Karnatakumarasambhava Kavya, Varadhamana Purana* and other writings which have been praised by later day poets such as Jayakirthi, but none of which are available today.

Asaga

Asaga was a mid-9th century Digambara Jain poet of Jain literature as well as early Kannada literature, as he wrote both in Sanskrit and Kannada languages. He is most known for his extant works in Sanskrit, including *Vardhaman Charitra* (Life of Vardhman Mahavir), an epic poetry work which runs in 18 cantos and written in 853 CE, the first Sanskrit language biography of 24th and last Thirthankara of Jainism, Mahavira; in all he has over eight works in Sanskrit to his credit. In Kannada none of his works including *Karnataka Kumarasambhava Kavya,* the Kannada language version of Kalidas's epic poem, *Kumarasambhava* have survived.

His works influenced Sri Ponna and other writers who wrote on the lives of Jain Tirthankaras; Kesiraja's work, *Shabdamanidarpana* written in 1260 CE, also cites his work as an authoritative example, along with other masters of early Kannada poetry.

Biography

His name probably is an *apbramsha* (corruption) of Sanskrit, Aœoka or Asanga. A contemporary of Rashtrakuta king, Amoghavarsha I (800–878) C.E, Asaga lived in Karnataka, and was an important author of Rashtrakuta literature in Kannada language created during the rule of the Rastrakutas of Manyakheta, a dynasty that ruled the southern and central parts of the Deccan, India between the 8th and 10th centuries, and Asaga, along with Gunavarma, are the only authors of repute who created works without direct royal patronage.

In his most important work written in 853 CE, *Vardhamacharita* (XVIII 105), he mentions writing eight works, making *Shanti purana* also in Sanskrit is a later work, though only two of his works have survived, and both in Sanskrit. Here he also mentions that he composed his works in Coda *visaya* (Coladesa) of the Kingdom of Srinatha, perhaps a vassal of Amoghavarsha, in the city of Virala (Dharala). Subsequently, in *Kaviprasastipradyani,* epilogue to his other extant work, *Shanti purana,* he talks about being born to Jain parents, and also mentions names of three Jain teachers, including Bhavakirti.

Today, not much is known about this poet, though references by his contemporaries and later poets give information about his works and its importance. Kannada poet Sri Ponna (c. 950), even used one of his narrative poems as a source, though he doesn't shy of calling his work superior to that of Asaga. His writings have been praised by later day poets and writers, such as Jayakirthi, who in his work, *Chchandanuphasana*, mentions, Asaga's *Kumarasambhava* in Kannada, and several of its verses have been quoted by later authors of Kannada literature. The 10th century Apabhramsha poet, Dhaval, praised his work the *Harivamsa-purana*. There is a mention about him being a path-breaking poet in the Munnudi of Shabdamanidarpana of Keshi Raja. His Kannada works were not found and are supposed to be lost. Nevertheless, his name is counted amongst noted poets Kannada literature, from his period, such as Gajaga, Aggala, Manasija, Srivardhadheva, Gunanandi.

Language of Asaga

Although such rare books by these ancient authors have not been found, the language used in them is *Poorva Halegannada* (Early Halegannada or Pre-old Kannada), which is extinct and not many people in today's Kannada literary world will be able to understand any of it. Even the later Halegannada (Old Kannada) and Nadugannada (Middle Kannada) versions have very few people understanding and deciphering them.

Works

- *Vardhamânacaritam: Hindi anuvada (Hindi translation), alocanatmaka prastavana (Critical Review), adi sahita*. Jain Sanskriti Samraksha Sangha. 1974.

Shivakotiacharya

Shivakotiacharya (also Shivakoti), a writer of the 9th-10th century, is considered the author of didactic Kannada language Jain text *Vaddaradhane*. A prose narrative written in pre-Old-Kannada (*Purva Halegannada*), *Vaddaradhane* is considered the earliest extant work in the prose genre in the Kannada language. Scholars are however still divided about when exactly the text was written, with claims ranging from pre-6th century to 10th century.

Controversies

The dating of the work and its authorship has been debated. According to the scholar R.S. Mugali, experts are not unanimous whether the prose piece was written before *Kavirajamarga* (c. 850) or after. According to modern Kannada poet and scholar Govinda Pai, the *Vaddaradhane* dates much further back. Based on his studies of the text and some pre-2nd century inscriptions from Shravanabelagola, Pai authored two scholarly publications in 1960: *Kannada Sahityada Halame* ("Antiquity of Kannada literature") and *Kannada Sahityada Prachinate* (also meaning "Antiquity of Kannada literature"), in which he argued the writing more accurately dates to the pre-6th century period. However, the scholar D.L. Narasimhachar opines that the writing is from around c. 920. Professor Upadhye dates the writing to the post-9th century period while A.R. Naronakar dates it to the 9th century.

There is an opinion that Shivakoti was not the author of the work, and that his Prakrit work *Bhagavati Aaradhane* may have been the inspiration for this Kannada writing. However, it has been pointed out that the author's name appears in the concluding section of every story in the writing, and that the Prakrit writer, also named Shivakoti, lived in the 2nd or 3rd century A.D. and was a disciple of the saint Samantha Bhadra. Another name, Revakotiacharya, also appears in some places in the Kannada text. Historian Jyotsna Kamat is of the opinion that the didactic work comprising 19 stories dates to the 10th century and was inspired by the Sanskrit writing *Brihatkatha-Khosa*.

Content

According to the scholar R.S. Mugali, *Vaddaradhane* is one of the finest pieces of Jain literature, which stands out by itself in all of Kannada literature. In addition to religious content describing the lives of Jain saints (*Jainas*), it treats on Jain tenets regarding the torments of flesh and spirit, interpretations of fate (*karma*), rebirth and the plight of humans on earth. The text gives useful information about contemporary society including education, trade and commerce, magic and superstitions, the caste system and untouchability, and position of women in society. The text provides details on contemporary urban and rural society: towns with majestic buildings and multi-storied houses; temples (*devalaya*); a street for the courtesans (*sulegeri*); palaces; streets with people, horses and elephants; homes of cloth merchants (*dusigar*); homes of diamond merchants (*baccara*); feudatories (*samanta*); royal officials (*niyogi*); grain markets and traders; and various types of settlements such as villages (*grama*) and towns (*nagara*). The text dwells on the evils of *Kali Yuga* including miscegenation and takes a critical look at contemporary Brahmin practices. It mentions fierce warriors, royal retainers (*velevali*) who were under oath to lay down their life for the king and royalty.

Adikavi Pampa

Pampa, also known as Adikavi Pampa, is one of the greatest Kannada poets of all time. He was born either in Annigeri or Banavasi, in modern Karnataka state, or in Vemulavada, Karimnagar District in modern Andhra Pradesh, and was the court poet of Chalukya King Arikesari, a Rashtrakuta feudatory. There is also a story that the Adikavi belongs to Bodhan in Nizamabad district. Dr. C. Narayanareddy in a function in Indur(Nizamabad) revealed this.

Early Life

Very little is known about Pampa's early life. Whatever is known has been obtained from inscriptions, references by other poets, Pampa's own accounts in some of his poems and a few other such meager sources. It is believed that he was born in Annigeri near Gadag to a Jaina family of Brahmin ancestry. His father was Abhiramaradevaraya (also Bheemappayya as per Pampa's younger brother Jinavallabha's Gangadharam inscription) and mother Abbanabbe.

They have been basically Kannada speaking and must have migrated to the Kannada speaking country of Banavasi when Pampa was a young boy. In fact, Pampa's mother hailed from Annigeri which was a part of the Kannada country. The beautiful Banavasi, located in the Western Ghats of Karnataka, with thick forests, mountains, streams and waterfalls, must have made a great impact on this poet at a very young age. Through the lines 'aarankusamittodam nenevudenna manam banvaasi deshamam' and 'maridumbiyaagi men kogileyaagi puttuvudu nandanadol banavaasideshadol' he has expressed his deep attachment towards Banavasi.

It is very evident from his works that he had mastered Sanskrit and Prakrit and that he must have had a good all-round education including Vedic literature and Jain philosophy. He may have studied and mastered various subjects like music, philosophy, dance, economics, medicine, kamashastra (the science of sensual pleasure). He is said to have studied under a guru by name Devendra Muni of Sharvanabelagola.

Sensitive, modest and imaginative, Pampa has earned a veritable place in the world of Kannada literature, which has remained unquestioned even today.

Poetic Life

A well-traveled man, he settled down as the court poet of King Arikesari II, a Chalukya king and a Rashtrakuta feudatory. Flattered by his knowledge and poetic abilities Arikesari (who possessed the title Gunarnava) conferred on him the title 'Kavita Gunarnava'. At the age of 39 he wrote his first masterpiece, Adipurana in 941 and a little later he completed Vikramarjuna Vijaya popularly known as Pampa Bharata. These two works have remained unparalleled works of classic Kannada composition.

Though there were several Kannada poets centuries prior to him, the quality of their works does not seem to have matched his. Such was the greatness of his literature that Pampa himself proudly proclaims that his works stamped and crushed all the other existing literature in Kannada. Rightly so, he is called the 'Adikavi' (first poet) of Kannada literature. He is also first of 'the three pearls' of Kannada poetry. A later poet Nagaraja says of him: "pasaripa kannadakkodayanorvane satkavi pampan' (the virtuous poet Pampa is the lone master of the famed Kannada).

Adipurana

Adipurana written in Champu style, a mixed form of prose and verse is a Kannada version of the Sanskrit work by Jinasena and details the life of Adinatha (*Vrishabhadeva*) in sixteen cantos, the first Jain Tirthankar. The work focusses in his own unique style the pilgrimage of a soul to perfection and attainment of *mukti*. In the work, Pampa describes the struggle for power and control over the entire world of two brothers Bharata and Bahubali, sons of Vrishabhadeva. While Bahubali wins, he renounces the worldly pursuits in favour of his brother. Many Jaina *puranas* of Middle Ages found a role model in this work.

Vikramarjuna Vijaya

Vikramarjuna Vijaya, also known as Pampa Bharata, is a Kannada version of the Mahabharata, which was originally written by Vyasa. It seems several poets prior to Pampa had composed poetry based on parts of the epic but not in its entirety. But Pampa prides in calling himself the first to narrate the 'Samasta Bharata'. The work was written in praise of his patron king Arikesari. He compares the king with Arjuna's character in the epic and centres his work around Arjuna. He says this himself in the 51st verse of the first chapter, thus '... kathaanaayakam maadi sandarjunanol polvi kathaabhittiyananunayadim pelal'. Vyasa's original work, however, does not portray any particular character as the hero of the epic.

To suit his needs Pampa has made several modifications to the original story of the epic. While some of his modifications seem absurd and even erroneous, some others seem to blend perfectly and add shine to the original story. In Pampa's version, Arjuna is the only husband of Draupadi. As polyandry is not considered a virtue this goes well with the story. On the other hand, to please his king, he refers to Arjuna with the titles of Arikesari at some places. The titles 'Chalukya Vamshodbhavam' (of the Chalukya clan) and 'Samanta Choodamani' (jewel among the feudatories) among others to the greatest archer of the world from the Kuru clan does not seem to go well. After the war of Kurukshetra, it is not Yudhishtira who is crowned king but Arjuna and his wife Subhadra becomes the queen royal. It is said that Bhima who played such a big role in Vyasa's epic and Draupadi who suffered much humiliation are not given much credit in Pampa's work.

Sri Ponna

Sri Ponna was a Kannada poet in the court of Rashtrakuta Dynasty king Krishna III (939–968 CE). The emperor honoured Ponna with the title "emperor among poets" (*Kavichakravarthi*) for his domination of the Kannada literary circles of the time, and the title "imperial poet of two languages" (*Ubhayakavi Chakravarti*) for his command over Sanskrit as well. Ponna is often considered one among the "three gems of Kannada literature" (*Ratnatraya, lit* meaning "three gems"; Adikavi Pampa and Ranna being the other two) for ushering it in full panoply. According to the scholar R. Narasimhacharya, Ponna is known to have claimed superiority over all the poets of the time. According to scholars Nilakanta Shastri and E.P. Rice, Ponna belonged to Vengi, in modern Andhra Pradesh, but later migrated to Manyakheta (in modern Gulbarga district, Karnataka), the Rashtrakuta capital, after his conversion to the Jain religion.

Writings

His most famous extant works in Kannada are *Shantipurana*, written in *champu* style (mixed prose-verse classical composition style inherited from Sanskrit), *Bhuvanaika-Ramabhyudaya*, a eulogical writing, and *Jinaksharamale*, a Jain *Purana* and an acrostic poem written in praise of noted Jain saints and Tirthankars (*Jainas*) in 39 chapetrs (*kandas*). It is uncertian whether his fourth writing, the extinct *Gatapratiagata*, was in Kannada or Sanskrit.

Shantipurana is an important Jain purana, and a eulogy of the 16th Jain Tirthankar and emperor of Jainism, Shantinatha. It was written to commomorate the attainment of *nirvana* ("salvation") of a Jain guru called Jainachandra Deva. The writing comprises twelve sections (*ashwasas*) of which nine sections focus on Shantinatha's eleven previous births, and the remaining three sections give biographical details of the protagonist. In this writing, Ponna borrowed significantly from previous works of the Sanskrit poet Kalidasa though he does rise to great heights in his narration justifying his claim to scholarship (*Vidwat Kavi*). Ponna also seems to have used as a source, a narrative poem written by a Kannada poet called Asaga, whose works are now extinct. Ponna's claim that his work is superior to that of Asaga gives us information that the latter must have been considered an important poet of that era.

Scholars were divided about Ponna's protagonist in *Bhuvanaika-Ramabhyudaya*. The scholar D.L. Narasimhachar had opined that Ponna had eulogised Shankaraganda, a vassal king under emperor Krishna III. This opinion was based on the fact that Shankaraganda held the honorific *Bhuvanaikarama*. However, modern Kannada poet Govinda Pai argued in his 1936 article, *Ponnana Bhuvanaikaramanu yaru* ("Who was Ponna's Bhuvanaikarama"?), that king Shankaraganda being a Jain by faith could not have been the central figure in a secular writing and that emperor Krishna III also held the same title. Later, D.L. Narasimhachar himself confirmed the validity of Govinda Pai's findings.

Influence and Style

Ponna was one of the most-notable writers of the classical age of Kannada literature, a period usually categorised as starting from the middle of 10th century and lasting for about a hundred and fifty years thereafter. During this era, Ponna and two other poets, Adikavi Pampa and Ranna, produced works of lasting merit, writings that set a standard in poetic form and composition that would influence future poets for centuries. So adept were these poets that their style of *champu* brought together the best of the earlier masters of Sanskrit literature in various proportions, giving their narration an artificiality:

Poet Bana's prose, Kalidasa's graceful verses, Bhatta Narayana's dramaticism and Megaduta's lyrical flavour are seen used deftly giving naturalised and assimilated Sanskrit words in the Kannada language priority over native (*desi*) expressions. Despite adherence to strict classical Sanskritic models (*margam*), the native composition styles of Kannada language, such as the *tripadi* (three-line verse), are found distributed in the narratives poems of these poets. Just as Ponna eulogised his patron king Krishna III as *Bhuvanaikarama,* so did the other Jain poets of the classical age.

Kannada writings by them used impressive Sanskrit-derived verses interspersed with prose to extol the virtues of their protagonists, who were often compared to heroes from the Hindu epics. While Adikavi Pampa (*Pampa Bharata,* c. 941) compared his patron, the feudatory Chalukya King Arikesari, to Pandava prince Arjuna, in his version of the Hindu epic Mahabharata, Ranna (c. 983) found it suitable to compare his patron, Chalukya King Satyasraya, to Pandava prince Bhima.

Sanskrit Writings

Many enduring works on religion and secular subjects were written in Sanskrit. In mathematics, ground breaking theories on Algebra, Arithmetic and Geometry were postulated by Mahaviracharya, a native of Gulbarga who belonged to the Karnataka mathematical tradition.

He was patronised by King Amoghavarsha I. His greatest contribution was *Ganitasarasangraha,* a writing in 9 chapters that defined important axioms. These axioms state that a proper fraction is a sum of improper fractions, a negative number is not a square number and hence does not have a square root. He also defined formulae to calculate the sum of complex progressions and a measurement unit for the size of an atom.

Trivikrama Bhatta was a noted scholar in the court of King Indra III. His classics were *Nalachampu* (915), the earliest in champu style in Sanskrit, *Damayanti Katha, Madalasachampu* and Begumra plates. Legend has it that Goddess Saraswati helped him in his effort to compete with a rival in the kings court. Jinasena was the spiritual preceptor and guru of Amoghavarsha I. A theologian, his contributions are *Dhavala* and *Jayadhavala* (written with another theologian Virasena). These writings are named after their patron king who was also called Athishayadhavala. Other contributions from Jinasena were *Adipurana* (later completed by his disciple Gunabhadracharya who also wrote *Atmanushasana*), *Harivamsha* and *Parshvabhyudaya*. Halayudha patronised by King Krishna III wrote *Kavirahasya*, a list of verbs with their meanings written in verse and a work on prosody called *Mritasanjivini*.

Somadevasuri of 950 wrote in the court of Arikesari II, a feudatory of Rashtrakuta Krishna III in Vemulavada. He was the author of *Yasastilaka champu, Nitivakyamrita* and other writings. The main aim of the *champu* writing was to propagate Jain tenets and ethics.

The second writing reviews the subject matter of *Arthasastra* from the standpoint of Jain morals in a clear and pithy manner. Well known Advaita philosophers from present day Karnataka region were Padmapada and Sureshvara (also known as Visvarupa) who wrote commentaries such as *Balakrida* upholding the Advaita beliefs. Pushpadanta who was patronised by a minister of King Krishna III wrote *Mahapurana, Nagakumara charita* and *Yashodhara charita*. King Amoghavarsha I himself a noted poet wrote *Prashnottara Ratnamalika*, a book of high value on religion, later translated into Tibetian language. Other well known scholars were logicians such as Manikyanandin, Mallavadin and Prabhachandra. Sakatayana patronised by Amoghavarsha I wrote *Sabdanusasana* and *Amoghavritti* and Chavundaraya wrote *Charitrasara*. Akalanka Bhatta wrote *Rajavarthika, Nyayavinishchaya, Ashtashati* and the *Laghiyastraya*, Lakshmidhara compiled *Vyavahara Kalpataru, Khandana Khanda Khadya* and others.

The Sanskrit writing on medicine *Kalyanakaraka* by a court poet, Ugraditya, relates that the king requested the poet give the court a discourse on the evils of a non-vegetarian diet and the need to avoid such a diet to treat illnesses.

Prakrit

Pushpadanta's contributions in Prakrit were *Jasauracharriu* and *Nayakumaracharriu*.

Architecture

The Rashtrakutas contributed much to the architectural heritage of the Deccan. The Rashtrakuta contributions to art and architecture are reflected in the splendid rock-cut cave temples at Ellora and Elephanta, located in present day Maharashtra. The Ellora site was originally part of a complex of 34 Buddhist caves probably created in the first half of the sixth century in rocky areas also occupied by Jains monks whose structural details show Pandyan influence. Cave temples occupied by Hindus only became feasible later.

The Rashtrakutas renovated these Buddhist caves and re-dedicated the rock-cut shrines. Amoghavarsha I espoused Jainism and there are five Jain cave temples at Ellora ascribed to his period. The most extensive and sumptuous of the Rashtrakutas work at Ellora is their creation of the monolithic Kailasanath Temple, a splendid achievement confirming the "Balhara" status as "one among the four principle Kings of the world". The walls of the temple have marvellous sculptures from Hindu mythology including Ravana, Shiva and Parvathi while the ceilings have paintings.

The Kailasanath Temple project was commissioned by King Krishna I after the Rashtrakuta rule had spread into South India from the Deccan. The architectural style used was Dravidian. It does not contain any of the *Shikharas* common to the *Nagara* style and was built on the same lines as the Virupaksha temple at Pattadakal in Karnataka. The achievement at the Kailasanath temple is considered an architectural consummation of the monolithic rock-cut temple and deserves be considered one of the wonders of the world. As an accomplishment of art, the Kailasnatha temple is considered an unrivalled work of rock architecture, a monument that has always excited and astonished travellers.

While some scholars have claimed the architecture at Elephanta is attributable to the Kalachuri, others claim that it was built during the Rashtrakuta period. Some of the sculptures such as *Nataraja* and *Sadashiva* excel in beauty and craftmanship even that of the Ellora sculptures. Famous sculptures at Elephanta include

Ardhanarishvara and *Maheshamurthy*. The latter, a three faced bust of Lord Shiva, is 25 feet (8 m) tall and considered one of the finest pieces of sculpture in India. It is said that, in the world of sculpture, few works of art depicting a divinity are as balanced. Other famous rock-cut temples in the Maharashtra region are the Dhumer Lena and Dashvatara cave temples in Ellora (famous for its sculptures of Vishnu and Shivaleela) and the Jogeshvari temple near Mumbai.

In Karnataka their most famous temples are the *Kashivishvanatha* temple and the Jain Narayana temple at Pattadakal, a UNESCO World Heritage site. Other well known temples are the *Parameshwara* temple at Konnur, *Brahmadeva* temple at Savadi, the *Settavva, Kontigudi II, Jadaragudi* and *Ambigeragudi* temples at Aihole, *Mallikarjuna* temple at Ron, *Andhakeshwara* temple at Huli (Hooli), *Someshwara* temple at Sogal, Jain temples at Lokapura, *Navalinga* temple at Kuknur, *Kumaraswamy* temple at Sandur, at Shirival in Gulbarga and the *Trikuteshwara* temple at Gadag which was later expanded by Kalyani Chalukyas. Archeological study of these temples show some have the stellar (multigonal) plan later to be used profusely by the Hoysalas of Belur and Halebidu. One of the richest traditions in Indian architecture took shape in the Deccan during this time and one writer calls it *Karnata dravida* style as opposed to traditional Dravida style.

Ellora Caves

Ellora is an archaeological site, 30 km (19 mi) from the city of Aurangabad in the Indian state of Maharashtra built by the Rashtrakuta rulers. Well-known for its monumental caves, Ellora is a World Heritage Site. Ellora represents the epitome of Indian rock-cut architecture. The 34 "caves" – actually structures excavated out of the vertical face of the Charanandri hills – being Buddhist, Hindu and Jain rock cut temples and monasteries, were built between the 5th century and 10th century. The 12 Buddhist (caves 1–12), 17 Hindu (caves 13–29) and 5 Jain (caves 30–34) caves, built in proximity, demonstrate the religious harmony prevalent during this period of Indian history.

The Buddhist Caves

The Buddhist caves were one of the earliest structures, created between the fifth and seventh centuries. These consist mostly of *viharas* or monasteries: large, multi-storeyed buildings carved into the mountain face, including living quarters, sleeping quarters, kitchens, and other rooms. Some of these monastery caves have shrines including carvings of Buddha, bodhisattvas and saints. In many of these caves, sculptors have endeavoured to give the stone the look of wood.

Most famous of the Buddhist caves is cave 10, a chaitya hall (chandrashala) or 'Vishwakarma cave', popularly known as the "Carpenter's Cave". Beyond its multi-storeyed entry is a cathedral-like stupa hall also known as chaitya, whose ceiling has been carved to give the impression of wooden beams. At the heart of this cave is a 15-foot statue of Buddha seated in a preaching pose. Amongst other Buddhist caves, all of the first nine (caves 1–9) are monasteries. The last two caves, Do Tal (cave 11) and Tin Tal (cave 12) have three stories.

The Hindu Caves

The Hindu caves were constructed between 500 CE and 1000 CE and represent a different style of creative vision and execution skills. Some were of such complexity that they required several generations of planning and co-ordination to complete. The early caves (caves 17–29) were constructed during the Kalachuri period, while the caves 15 and 16 were constructed during Rashtrakuta period.

Kailash Temple

Kailash Temple(Kailashnath Temple), also Kailasanatha Temple is one of the 34 monasteries and temples, extending over more than 2 km, that were dug side by side in the wall of a high basalt cliff in the complex located at Ellora, Maharashtra, India, and represents the epitome of Indian rock-cut architecture. It is designed to recall Mount Kailash, the abode of Lord Shiva. While it exhibits typical Dravidian features, it was carved out of one single rock. It was built in the 8th century by the Rashtrakuta king Krishna I.

The Kailash Temple is notable for its *vertical* excavation – carvers started at the top of the original rock, and excavated downward, exhuming the temple out of the existing rock. The traditional methods were rigidly followed by the master architect which could not have been achieved by excavating from the front. The architects found to design this temple were from the southern Pallava kingdom.

It is estimated that about 200,000 tons of rocks was scooped out over hundreds of years to construct this monolithic structure. From the chisel marks on walls of this temple, archeologists could conclude that three types of chisels were used to carve this temple.

All the carvings are done in more than one level. A two-storeyed gateway opens to reveal a U-shaped courtyard. The courtyard is edged by a columned arcade three stories high. The arcades are punctuated by huge sculpted panels, and alcoves containing enormous sculptures of a variety of deities. Originally flying bridges of stone connected these galleries to central temple structures, but these have fallen.

Within the courtyard are two structures. As is traditional in Shiva temples, an image of the sacred bull Nandi fronts the central temple housing the lingam. In Cave 16, the Nandi Mandap and main Shiva temple are each about 7 meters high, and built on two stories. The lower stories of the Nandi Mandap are both solid structures, decorated with elaborate illustrative carvings. The base of the temple has been carved to suggest that elephants are holding the structure aloft.

A living rock bridge connects the Nandi Mandap to the porch of the temple. The temple itself is tall pyramidic structure reminiscent of a South Indian temple. The shrine – complete with pillars, windows, inner and outer rooms, gathering halls, and an enormous lingam at its heart – carved from stone, is carved with niches, plasters, windows as well as images of deities, *mithuna*s and other figures. Most of the deities at the left of the entrance are Shaivaite (followers of Lord Shiva) while on the right hand side the deities are Vaishnavaites (followers of Lord Vishnu).

There are two Dhvajastambhas (pillars with the flagstaff) in the courtyard. The grand sculpture of Ravana attempting to lift Mount Kailasa, the abode of Lord Shiva, with his full might is a landmark in Indian art.

The Dashavatara

The Dashavatara cave (cave 15) was begun as a Buddhist monastery. It has an open court with a free-standing monolithic *mandapa* at the middle and a two-storeyed excavated temple at the rear. The layout of the temple is closely related to caves 11 and 12. Large sculptural panels between the wall columns on the upper floor illustrate a wide range of themes, which include the ten avataras of Vishnu. An inscription of grant of Dantidurga is found on the back wall of the front *mandapa*. According to Coomaraswamy, the finest relief of this cave is the one depicting the death of Hiranyakashipu, where Vishnu in man-lion (Narasimha) form, emerges from a pillar to lay a fatal hand upon the shoulder of Hiranyakashipu.

Other Hindu Caves

Other notable Hindu caves are the Ramesvara cave (cave 21), which has figurines of river goddesses Ganga and Yamuna at the entrance and the Dhumar Lena (cave 29) whose design is similar to the cave temple on Elephanta Island near Mumbai. Two other caves, the Ravan ki Khai (cave 14) and the Nilkantha (cave 22) also have several sculptures. The rest of the Hindu caves, which include the Kumbharvada (cave 25) and the Gopilena (cave 27) have no significant sculptures.

The Jain Caves

Jain caves reveal specific dimensions of Jain philosophy and tradition. They reflect a strict sense of asceticism – they are not relatively large as compared to others, but they present exceptionally detailed art works. The most remarkable Jain shrines are the *Chhota Kailash* (cave 30), the *Indra Sabha* (cave 32) and the *Jagannath Sabha* (cave 33). The *Indra Sabha* is a two storeyed shrine with a very fine carving of the lotus flower on the ceiling. In another cave, an imposing image of Ambika, the Yakshi (dedicated attendant deity) of Neminatha is found seated on her lion under a mango tree, laden with fruits. All other Jain caves are also characterized by intricate detailing. Many of the structures had rich paintings in the ceilings – fragments of which are still visible.

Elephanta Caves

The Elephanta are caves located on Elephanta Island in the Arabian Sea near Mumbai, Maharashtra, India that contain Shaivistic high reliefs in stone of Hindu deities important to worshipers of Shiva. The sculptures were created beginning in the late Gupta Empire, or some time after, and at later dates. Elephanta Island was designated a UNESCO World Heritage Site in 1987 to preserve the artwork.

The original name of this epitome of temple art is Agraharpuri. Agrahar is the necklace or most important neck ornament. The Agraharpuri slowly became Gharapuri; still retaining the original meaning as the focal point of Gharapuri Island, which was renamed Elephanta Island by the Portuguese and is located in Mumbai harbour off the coast of Mumbai (formerly known as Bombay), India.

The caves are thought to date back to the Silhara kings of the 9th through 13th centuries (810–1260). Some of the sculptures of this site are also attributed to the imperial Rashtrakutas of Manyakheta (in present day Karnataka). the *Trimurti* of Elephanta showing the three faces of Shiva almost akin to the Trinity of Brahma, Vishnu, and Mahesh. This was also the royal insignia of the Rashtrakutas. Other Rashtrakuta sculptures here are the reliefs of Nataraja and Sadashiva and the splendid sculptures of Ardhanarishvara.

The rock-cut temple complex cover an area of 60,000 sq ft (5,600 m) consisting of a main chamber, 2 lateral ones, courtyards and subsidiary shrines. The site of these magnificent caves contained beautiful reliefs, sculptures, and a temple to the Hindu god Œiva. The caves are hewn from solid rock. The temple complex is said to be the abode of Shiva.

Trimurti-Sadashiva Statue

The most important sculpture is that of Trimurti Sadasiva, carved in relief at the end of the N-S axis. The image, 20 ft (6.1 m) in height is of the three headed-Shiva, representing Panchamukha Shiva. The right half-face shows him as a young person with sensuous lips, embodying life and its vitality. In his hand he holds something that resembles a rose bud—again with the promise of life and creativity.

It is this face that is closest to that of Brahma, the creator or Uma or Vamadeva,the feminine side of Shiva. The left half-face face on the side is that of a young man. It is moustached, and displays anger. This is Shiva as Aghora Bhairava, as the one whose anger can engulf the entire world in flames leaving only ashes behind. This is Shiva, the Destroyer. The central face, benign, meditative, as the preserver Vishnu. This is Shiva as the yogi—Yogeshwar—in deep meditation praying for the 'preservation' of humanity.

Language

With the ending of the Gupta Dynasty in northern India in the early sixth century, major changes began taking place in the Deccan south of the Vindyas and in the southern regions of India. These changes were not only political but also linguistic and cultural. The royal courts of peninsular India (outside of Tamilakam) interfaced between the increasing use of the local Kannada language and the expanding Sanskritic culture. Inscriptions, including those that were bilingual, demonstrate the use of Kannada as the primary administrative language in conjunction with Sanskrit. Government archives used Kannada for recording pragmatic information relating to grants of land. The local language formed the *desi* (popular) literature while literature in Sanskrit was more *marga* (formal). Educational institutions and places of higher learning (*ghatikas*) taught in Sanskrit, the language of the learned Brahmins, while Kannada increasingly became the speech of personal expression of devotional closeness of a worshipper to a private deity. The patronage Kannada received from rich and literate Jains eventually led to its use in the devotional movements of later centuries.

Contemporaneous literature and inscriptions show that Kannada was not only popular in the modern Karnataka region but the linguistic change had spread further north into present day southern Maharashtra and to the northern Deccan by the eighth century. Kavirajamarga, the work on poetics, refers to the entire region between the Kaveri River and the Godavari River as "Kannada country". Higher education in Sanskrit included the subjects of Veda, *Vyakarana* (grammar), *Jyotisha* (astronomy and astrology), *Sahitya* (literature), *Mimansa* (Exegesis), *Dharmashastra* (law), *Puranas* (ritual), and *Nyaya* (logic).

An examination of inscriptions from this period shows that the *Kavya* (classical) style of writing was popular. The awareness of the merits and defects in inscriptions by the archivists indicates that even they, though mediocre poets, had studied standard classical literature in Sanskrit. An inscription in Kannada by King Krishna III, written in a poetic Kanda metre, has been found as far away as Jabalpur in modern Madhya Pradesh. Kavirajamarga, a work on poetics in Kannada by Amoghavarsha I, shows that the study of poetry was popular in the Deccan during this time.

Trivikrama's Sanskrit writing, *Nalachampu*, is perhaps the earliest in the *champu* style from the Deccan.

Mahaviracharya (AD 850)

Mahaviracharya, the great Jaina mathematician, probably hailed from the Kanarese-speaking areas fo south India and flourished during the reign of the Rastrakuta King Amoghavarsa Nrpatunga (814-877). In keeping with the Jaina tradition he studied mathemnatics, for its own sake and not in association with astronomy as was the vogue with the Brahmana mathematicians. His Ganita-sara-samgraha does not, therefore, form part of any astronomical treatise, but treats fo mathematical problems in a more simple and direct manner. The copious illustrations characterizing his work also bear this impress. But he seems to be fully conversant with Brahmana mathematics and, in particular, with the works of Brahmagupta whose reputation as an authority was far and wide.

In fact, he dealt with several of the problems which had engaged the attention of his illustrious predecessor and tried to improve upon them, often times with success which shows that he was neither a mere compiler nor a commentator but an original investigator. From the fact that the manuscripts of his work and its commentaries have come down to us in Kanarese and in Telugu translations, Bhaskara II and other scholars in northern and central India do not refer to his work and it is not even mentioned in Sudhakara Dvivedi's Ganakatarangini, it is reasonable to infer that his work was in circulation only in the south.

Ganita-sara-samgraha is a work in nine chapters, dealing with operations with numbers excluding those o f addition and subtraction which are taken for granted, squaring and cubing, determination of square and cube roots, summation of arithmetic and geometric series, fractions, rule fo three, mensuration and algebra, including quadratic and indeterminate equations. His arithmetical operations are based on decimal place-value numeration. He mentions 24 notational places and uses word numerals as had been the established practice.

He gives operating with zero, but erroneously states thsat a number divided by zero remains unchanged. Negative numbers are used. The process of summation of a series from which the first few terms are omitted is called by him vyutkalita. In his treatment of fractions he was the first among the Indian mathematicians to have used the method of lowest commong multiple, called by him niruddha, in order to shorten the process. In mensuration, Mahavira's treatment is similar in spirit with that of either Brahmagupta or Bhaskara II, but much fuller and in certain cases a little more advanced. Like Brahmagupta he gives the area of a quadrilateral as square root of but does not mention that it holds good only for a cyclic one.

The only known book by Mahavira is Ganita Sara Samgraha, dated 850 AD, which was designed as an updating of Brahmagupta's book. Filliozat writes:-

This book deals with the teaching of Brahmagupta but contains both simplifications and additional information.... Although like all Indian versified texts, it is extremely condensed, this work, from a pedagogical point of view, has a significant advantage over earlier texts.

It consisted of nine chapters and included all mathematical knowledge of mid-ninth century India. It provides us with the bulk of knowledge which we have of Jaina mathematics and it can be seen as in some sense providing an account of the work of those who developed this mathematics. There were many Indian mathematicians before the time of Mahavira but, perhaps surprisingly, their work on mathematics is always contained in texts which discuss other topics such as astronomy. The Ganita Sara Samgraha by Mahavira is the earliest Indian text which we possess which is devoted entirely to mathematics.

In the introduction to the work Mahavira paid tribute to the mathematicians whose work formed the basis of his book. These mathematicians included Aryabhata I, Bhaskara I, and Brahmagupta. Mahavira writes:-

With the help of the accomplished holy sages, who are worthy to be worshipped by the lords of the world... I glean from the great ocean of the knowledge of numbers a little of its essence, in the manner in which gems are picked from the sea, gold from the stony rock and the pearl from the oyster shell; and I give out according to the power of my intelligence, the Sara Samgraha, a small work on arithmetic, which is however not small in importance.

The nine chapters of the Ganita Sara Samgraha are:

1. Terminology
2. Arithmetical operations
3. Operations involving fractions
4. Miscellaneous operations
5. Operations involving the rule of three
6. Mixed operations
7. Operations relating to the calculations of areas
8. Operations relating to excavations
9. Operations relating to shadows.

Throughout the work a place-value system with nine numerals is used or sometimes Sanskrit numeral symbols are used. Of interest in Chapter 1 regarding the development of a place-value number system is Mahavira's description of the number 12345654321 which he obtains after a calculation. He describes the number as:-

... beginning with one which then grows until it reaches six, then decreases in reverse order.

Notice that this wording makes sense to us using a place-value system but would not make sense in other systems. It is a clear indication that Mahavira is at home with the place-value number system. Among topics Mahavira discussed in his treatise was operations with fractions including methods to decompose integers and fractions into unit fractions. For example

2/17 = 1/12 + 1/51 + 1/68.

He examined methods of squaring numbers which, although a special case of multiplying two numbers, can be computed using special methods. He also discussed integer solutions of first degree indeterminate equation by a method called kuttaka. The kuttaka (or the "pulveriser") method is based on the use of the Euclidean algorithm but the method of solution also resembles the continued fraction process of Euler given in 1764. The work kuttaka, which occurs in many of the treatises of Indian mathematicians of the classical period, has taken on the more general meaning of "algebra".

An example of a problem given in the Ganita Sara Samgraha which leads to indeterminate linear equations is the following:

Three merchants find a purse lying in the road. One merchant says "If I keep the purse, I shall have twice as much money as the two of you together". "Give me the purse and I shall have three times as much" said the second merchant. The third merchant said "I shall be much better off than either of you if I keep the purse, I shall have five times as much as the two of you together". How much money is in the purse? How much money does each merchant have?

If the first merchant has x, the second y, the third z and p is the amount in the purse then

$p + x = 2(y + z)$, $p + y = 3(x + z)$, $p + z = 5(x + y)$.

There is no unique solution but the smallest solution in positive integers is $p = 15$, $x = 1$, $y = 3$, $z = 5$. Any solution in positive integers is a multiple of this solution as Mahavira claims.

Mahavira gave special rules for the use of permutations and combinations which was a topic of special interest in Jaina mathematics. He also described a process for calculating the volume of a sphere and one for calculating the cube root of a number. He looked at some geometrical results including right-angled triangles with rational sides.

Mahavira also attempts to solve certain mathematical problems which had not been studied by other Indian mathematicians. For example, he gave an approximate formula for the area and the perimeter of an ellipse. In [8] Hayashi writes:-

The formulas for a conch-like figure have so far been found only in the works of Mahavira and Narayana.

It is reasonable to ask what a "conch-like figure" is. It is two unequal semicircles (with diameters AB and BC) stuck together along their diameters. Although it might be reasonable to suppose that the perimeter might be obtained by considering the semicircles, Hayashi claims that the formulae obtained:-

... were most probably obtained not from the two semicircles AB and BC.

Virsena, Jinsena and Gunbhadra

A remarkable feature of Jaina Saint authors of the South is the direct succession of highly qualified and equally capable teachers and their disciples. The classic example of this rare type is that of Acuaria Virasena, his disciple Acuaria Jinasena, and Jinasena's disciple Acuaria Gunabhadra, who flourished in the 9th and 10th centuries A.D. during the reign of the Rashtrakuta monarchs.

Acuaria Virasena is supposed to have written "Siddha-bhupaddhatitika" a learned treatise on the measurement of land as he was a great mathematician also. But this treatise has not been traced as yet. He composed his famous "Dhavala-Tika" consisting of 72,000 stanzas in Prakrit and Sanskrit language. It is a commentary on the renowned work "Shatkhandagama Sutra". Acuaria Virasena also undertook to write "Jayadhavala-Tika" as a commentary on "Kashaya-Prabhruta" of Acuaria Gunabhadra. Acuaria Virasena died after composing 20,000 stanzas of the "Jayadhavala-Tika" which was to consist of 60,000 stanzas.

The remaining 40,000 stanzas of the "Jayadhavala-Tika" Acuaria Jinasena composed "Vardhamana-Purana", the distinctive poetic work "Parshva-bhyudya". In his "Parshvabhyudya" Jinasena has performed the wonderful feat of utilising each line of the love poem "Meghaduta" of Kalidasa for narrating the life of the 23rd Tirthankara Lord Parshvanatha. The concluding line of each verse in Jinasena's poem has been borrowed from the successive stanzas of Meghaduta. Thus poetic work "Parshvabhyudaya" consisting of 334 stanzas in unparalleled in Sanskrit literature. Later on Acuaria Jinasena started to write a great poetic work to be known as "Mahapurana" depicting the life-history of 63 Great Ones in Jainism. But unfortunately he could not finish the work. After composing 1 to 42 Parvas or Chapters and 3 stanzas of 43rd Parva, i.e. in all 10, 380 stanzas, Jinasena died. This portion of "Mahapurana" known as "Adi-Purana" was ably completed by Acuaria Gunabhadra the disciple of Acuaria Jinasena. Gunabhadra composed 43rd to 47th Parvas (i.e. In all 1620 stanzas) and completed the "Adipurana" the unfinished work of his teacher. In the same strain Gunabhadra also composed "Uttara-Purana" consisting of 8000 stanzas.

In this manner Gunabhadra very satisfactorily completed the literary project of "Mahapurana" commenced by his teacher, Jinasena. In addition, Gunabhadra composed "Atmanushasana" a poem of 272 stanzas and 3 Sargas or Chapters of "Jinadatta Charitra". Thus in a very significant manner the continuity of literary activities was ably maintained by the Jaina Saints.

8

Paramara Dynasty

The Paramara dynasty was an early medieval Indian dynasty who ruled over Malwa region in central India. This dynasty was founded by Upendra in c.800. The most significant ruler of this dynasty was Bhoja I.

The seat of the Paramara kingdom was *Dhara Nagari* (the present day Dhar city in Madhya Pradesh state). The main sources for the history of the Paramara dynasty are the *Navasahasankacharita* of Padmagupta and the *Udaypur Prashasti* found in Vidisha district of Madhya Pradesh.

Origin

The Paramaras were a rajput clan, who began as feudatories of the Rashtrakutas, but revolted against their overlords at the end of the 10th century. Although the earlier tradition relates them with the Rashtrakutas, later tradition provides an interesting narrative regarding the origin of the name, Paramara. According to this tradition, the *Kamadhenu* (a cow which grants all wishes of one) of the sage Vasishtha was stolen by another sage Vishvamitra. Vasishtha therefore made an offering to the sacrificial fire at Mount Abu. A hero sprang out from the sacrificial fire and brought back the cow to the sage Vasishtha, who bestowed the name Paramara (slayer of the enemy) on him.

Upendra

Upendra was the first known ruler of this dynasty. He had two sons, Vairisimha and Dambarasimha. His elder son, Vairisimha succeeded his father.

Siyaka II

Siyaka II succeeded his father Vairisimha II. He was also known as Harsha. He had two sons by his queen Vadaja, Vakpatiraja and Sindhuraja. His elder son Vakpatiraja succeeded him.

Vakpatiraja II

Munja, also known as Utpala or Vakpatiraja II succeeded his father Siyaka II. He assumed the titles, *Shrivallabha, Prithvivallabha* and *Amoghavarsha.* He defeated the Kalachuri king Yuvaraja II and captured his capital Tripuri. He also defeated the Guhilas of Medapata (Mewar) and plundered the capital Aghata (Ahar). He defeated the Chalukya ruler Mularaja of Anahilapataka.

Sindhuraja

Sindhuraja succeeded his elder brother Vakpatiraja II. He assumed the titles, *Kumaranarayana* and *Navasahasanka.* The *Navasahasankacharita* provides information about his reign. It describes how he helped a Naga king, Shankhapala of the Barsur in the present-day Dantewada district in Chhattisgarh state against Vajrankusha, a ruler of Vairagad in the present-day Chandrapur district in Maharashtra state and married his daughter Shashiprabha. He was succeeded by his son Bhoja I.

Bhoja I

Bhoja was a philosopher king and polymath of medieval India. He belonged to the Parmara dynasty and ruled the kingdom of Malwa in central India from about 1010 to 1060. The name means "bountiful, liberal" and appears as the name of a tribe, the descendants of *Mahabhoja,* in the Mahabharata.

Biography

Bhoja was from the Paramara dynasty of Arya, who ruled Malwa from the mid-tenth century to about 1200. His extensive writings cover philosophy, poetry, medicine, veterinary science, phonetics, yoga, and archery.

Under his rule, Malwa and its capital Dhar became one of the chief intellectual centres of India. King Bhoj, together with the Solanki king Bhima of Gujarat (Anhilwara), rebuilt the temple at Somnath between 1026 and 1042 after it was sacked by Mahmud of Ghazni in 1024. Bhoj also founded the city of Bhopal, which is named after him, to secure the eastern frontier of his kingdom. He was also referred to as "Juzr/Gujar" by a poet.

Career

The Paramaras were a subsidiary branch of the Rashtrakuta Dynasty, who were appointed as governors of central India in Malwa province by the main ruling branch. The Paramara dynasty founded the notable city of Dhar in central India, which remained their capital until its ultimate conquest. It was here that their greatest king and a remarkable genius, Bhoja Raja came to power by 1000 AD and ruled for more than half a century. He was the son of Sindhuraja, who was a notable conqueror, who defeated the Chalukyas, Hunas and Shilaharas of the Konkan region. Bhoja's path was similar to other great Hindu rulers of the time engaged in wasteful internecine struggles for supremacy. We get some glimpses of his remarkable life from the apocryphal biography Bhoja Prabandham.

Early in his career, just before he came to power, Bhoja was afflicted by a tumor in his brain which used to cause him intense headaches. Two learned Brahmin brothers from the school of Ujjain, who were pre-eminent surgeons of the era, performed a surgery on his brain and relieved him of his tumor. The description of the surgery that survives suggests that they artificially induced a coma with a special preparation known as the sammohini and then opened his skull to remove the tumor. He was then brought back to consciousness with another drug.

Bhoja survived this surgery remarkably well and had an illustrious reign both as a military commander and encylopaedic scholar. Bhoja long desired to reduce his arch-rivals the Chalukyas of the Deccan and initiated several successful campaigns again them. Then he tried a remarkable political game to destroy the Chalukyas: by forming an alliance with the ChoLa king Rajendra, Bhoja induced him to attack the Chalukyas from the south.

Likewise he induced the Kalachuri king Kumara Gangeyadeva (who claimed descent from the Haihayas who had survived the ancient assault of the Bhargavas) to attack the Chalukyas from the east. Bhoja himself pressed on them from the north. For this purpose he erected the mighty fortifications of mandu and initially put the Chalukyas on the retreat.

But the Chalukyas, suddenly reviving the glory that Pulakeshin-II had taken them to, remained firm in the 3-front war, eventually causing Bhoja's allies to give up.

Someshvara, the Chalukya subsequently invaded the paramara kingdom and stormed the fort of Mandu after a long siege, then took Ujjain, and finally captured Dhara the capital of Bhoja from him. Bhoja unfazed retreated north and with the help of Rajendra Chola who kept the pressure from the south, took back Dhara and Ujjain. Then Bhoja conquered Chitrakuta (Chittor) and Medhapatha (Mewar) from the Shishodias and established his sway over the Arbuda fort (Mount Abu).

Raja Bhoja then organized his armies to attack Mahmud Ghaznavi who had invaded Somnath. Ghaznavi fearing the powerful army of Bhoja retreated via the desert of Sindh to avoid a clash (reported by Turkic author Gardizi as Hindu padishaw Parmar Dev) with the Hindu king and lost many of his men.

Bhoja repulsed the Ghaznavid Masu'd who lead a huge army into India to attack the rich inner cities which his father had failed to raid. Then Bhoja realizing the national threat from Islam, organized a confedration of Hindu kings including the Kalachuri Lakshmi-Karna, the Chahamana and other Rajputs to fight the Ghaznavid Maliq Salar Masud.

In the great battle of Bahraich the Hindu confedracy fought a pitched battle for about a month with the Moslems and completely defeated them killing, Salar Masud in the process.

They then went on to liberate Hansi, Thaneshvar, Nagarkot and other cities taken by the Ghaznavids and marched against Lahore and besieged it. Just at the point Lahore was about to fall to them, the Hindu kings had a disagreement over who would own the liberated territories and their armies disbanded and dispersed in a huff. Bhoja started fighting his erstwhile allies in the war against the Moslems.

Bhoja first defeated the Chahamanas of Shakambhari, but the Chahamanas of Naddula repulsed his attempt to take their kingdom. Bhoja next tried to seize the kingdom of the Chandellas, but they formed an alliance with the Rashtrakutas of Kannauj and Kachchapaghatas of Gwalior and repulsed him.

Bhoja however, did keep the Ghaznavids in check with help from his Shishodia feudatories. Bhoja then seized the territory of the western Chalukya Bhima of Gujarat. Bhima unfazed by this formed an alliance with the Haihaya, Lakshmi-Karna to attack Bhoja in a two-front war on both east and west. Bhoja was caught in the pincer grip, and while fighting his two enemies he was shot down by an arrow on the battle field. Thus, the great Raja Bhoja having spent his career in numerous campaigns had fallen like a true Kshatriya in the defense of his capital.

Hence its said that when he was alive the poets would say:

"adya dhara sadadhara sadalamba sarasvati | panditah manditah sarve bhojarAje bhuvam gate ||"

Today Dhara is ever supported, and the Goddess Sarasvati is ever propped up. All the pundits are adorned with the coming of king Bhoja on this earth.

Bhoja the Genius

An analysis of Bhoja's military campaigns show that he was undoubtedly a good general in war and was studded with many major victories over rival Rajas and Islamic marauders.

His military career was however, hardly any greater than his equally warlike and militarily successful contemporaries such as Rajendra Chola or Lakshmi-Karna Kalachuri or Someshvara Chalukya. Yet Raja Bhoja is remembered much more than any of these contemporaries of his and is often compared with the illustrious Vikramaditya of the golden Gupta era. His name is a household one amongst all brought up in the Sanskritic culture. Why is this so?

The main reason for this is that Hindus have always remembered philosophers, poets and scholars much more than kings merely decorated with military success. A king who did good to the people was much more embedded in the collective memory of the Hindus than a king who conquered vast territories. Raja Bhoja definitely stood out in this regard as one of historical India's most remarkable intellectuals with an astonishing variety of interests and oceanic knowledge.

Bhoja Raja constructed several spectacular temples, one of the most dramatic of which is seen in the form of the great temple of Shiva termed Bhojeshvara at Bhojapura at some distance from the modern city of Bhopal.

Another notable construction, which is a historical civil engineering masterpiece, is the Bhoja lake which was built by daming and channelizing the Betwa river. He is also supposed to have paid great attention to the education of his people, so much so that even humble weavers in kingdom are supposed to have composed metrical Sanskrit kavyas.

Works

Raja Bhoja wrote 84 books during his life of which several survive. We shall summarize a few below to illustrate the remarkable breadth of his knowledge and originality:

Sarasvatika Gmhabhara Ga: a treatise on Sanskrit grammar for poetic and rhetorical compositions. Some of the poetic examples provided by him in this work are still appreciated as the highest cream of Sanskrit poetry.

Rajamartanda (Patanjali yoga sutra bhashya): Major commentary on the Yoga Sutras of Patanjali, wherein the Raja clearly explains various forms of meditations such as savitarka, savichAra, sAnanda and sAsmita, which are critical for understanding the nature of cognition from the view point of yoga.

Samarangana Sutradhara

Samarangana Sutradhara is an encyclopedic work on classical Indian architecture (Vastu Shastra) written by Paramara King Bhoja of Dhar (1000-1055 AD).

In 83 chapters, subjects treated are town planning, house architecture, temple architecture and sculptural arts together with Mudras (the different hand poses and the poses of the body as well as the postures of legs), the canons of painting, and a chapter on the art of mechanical contrivances, the yantras.

This chapter on yantras has attracted the attention of pseudoscience and ufology in particular. Verses 95-100 mentions bird-shaped aerial cars (Vimanas), and verses 101-107 mention a sort of robots acting as guards.

Here are some verses from Samarangana Sutradhara, which describes characteristics a "sthapati" i.e. architect (based on translation by Punya Mishra).

- The architect should be well-versed in the science involving the significance of objects to be created and their specificationss. He should know the theory and the practice; he should have the insight and the skill accompanied with procedure.
- That person is said to be an expert in workmanship who knows how to sketch the ground plan, draftsmanship, the horizontal and vertical measurements, the details of ground work of the plot, the 14 kinds of sketch lines, the cutting of the logs and stones etc., and seven kinds of circular sections; well finished joinings of the joints and proper demarcation of upper, lower and outer lines.
- An sthapati should know eight-fold workmanship, the draftsmanship and sketches of various kinds, and variety of carpentery, stone-masonry and gold-smithy. The engineer equipped with these merits invokes respect. One who knows the fourfold engineering with its eight constituents and who is pure in his mind gets status in the assembly of engineers, and is endowed with a long life.

tattva-prakAsha: A remarkable siddhAnta tantra work providing a synthesis of the entire ancient and voluminous literature of the siddhanta tantras of shiva. It was the basis of all subsequent developments of the siddhantic pAshupata streams that followed.

Rasa-raja-mriganka: A treatise on chemistry, especially dealing with the extraction of metals from ores, and production of various drugs.

Jyoti sha-raja-mriganka: A treatise on astronomy and construction of instruments for astronomical observations.

Udayaditya

Udayaditya (reigned c.1060-1087) was a Paramara dynasty ruler of Malwa region of central India, who succeeded Jayasimha I. He was succeeded by his son, Lakshmanadeva.

Situation after Bhoja I's Death

The Udaipur Prashasti says that at Bhoja's death " Dhara was filled with a dense darkness by his foes and his hereditary warriors become infirm in body.

Then arose king Udayaditya, another sun as it were, destroying the dense darkness......and gladdening the sight of his people by his splendour". According to the Nagpur inscription, "when he(Bhoja) had become Indra's companion, when the realm was overrun by floods in which its sovereign was submerged, his relative Udayaditya become king delivering the earth which was troubled by kings and taken possession oı by Karna...... joined by Karnatas."

Merutunga in his *Prabandha Chintamani* confirms this fact, stating that at Bhoja's death Karna and Bhimadeva of Gujarat were allies.

The friendship and alliances between these two did not last long as the same author tells us that Bhima, not long last after, threatened karna who came to terms and presented Bhimadeva with a golden litter which he had taken from Bhoja.

The Karnata mentioned as an ally of Karna would appear to be the Hoysala Yadava price Ereyanga. A record of this house states that Ereyanga in a conquest of the north, took Dhara the stronghold of Lords of Malwa, which had made prosperous by king Bhoja.

Reign

The fame of Udayaaditya as delivering Dhar and Malwa generally from a foreign yoke has given him a position of exaggerated importance. In his deliverance Dhar, this king was assisted by the Chalukya Vikramaditya VI of Kalyana. In the *Vikramankadevacharita* of Bilhana, Vikramaditya is said to have lent his assistance to the Malwa king, while his father Somesvara I was still ruling.

"He (Vikramaditya VI) placed the suppliant king (of Dhar) on his throne, free of all fear from enemies."

This shows that ancient feud that existed between rulers of Dhar abd Kalyana was then in abeyance.

Personal Life

Udayaditya appears to have had the hereditary fondness for literature and art, and to have brought up his sons as scholars, and his second son Naravarman is believed to have been the author of more than one Prashasti.

While Jayasimha is said to have been a son, Udayaditya is only spoken of as relation of Bhoja, but the exact relationship is never given.

It may thus be surmised that the direct line ended with Jayasimha, Udayaditya starting a collateral branch as holders of the throne.

Udayaditya had three sons Lakshmanadeva, Naravarman, Jagadeva, and one daughter. The elder sons in turn succeeded their father while the daughter, Shyamaladevi, was married to the Gohi prince Vijaysinha and become the mother of Alhandevi afterwards wife of the Chedi king Gayakarnadeva.

Coinage

The gold coins issued by Udayaditya are of 4.05 g weight. On the obverse of these coins the image of seated Lakshmi is depicted. On the reverse, the Devanagari legend, *Shrimad Udayadeva* is inscribed in three lines.

The rulers of Paramara dynasty :

1. Upendra (c. 800 – c. 818)
2. Vairisimha I (c. 818 – c. 843)
3. Siyaka I (c. 843 – c. 893)
4. Vakpatiraja I (c. 893 – c. 918)
5. Vairisimha II (c. 918 – c. 948)
6. Siyaka II (c. 948 – c. 974)
7. Vakpatiraja II (c. 974 – c. 995)
8. Sindhuraja (c. 995 – c. 1010)
9. Bhoja I (c. 1010 – c. 1055)
10. Jayasimha I (c. 1055 – c. 1060)
11. Udayaditya (c. 1060 – c. 1087)
12. Lakshmanadeva (c. 1087 – c. 1097)

13. Naravarman (c. 1097 – c. 1134)
14. Yasovarman (c. 1134 – c. 1142)
15. Jayavarman I (c. 1142 – c. 1160)
16. Vindhyavarman (c. 1160 – c. 1193)
17. Subhatavarman (c. 1193 – c. 1210)
18. Arjunavarman I (c. 1210 – c. 1218)
19. Devapala (c. 1218 – c. 1239)
20. Jaitugideva (c. 1239 – c. 1256)
21. Jayavarman II (c. 1256 – c. 1269)
22. Jayasimha II (c. 1269 – c. 1274)
23. Arjunavarman II (c. 1274 – c. 1283)
24. Bhoja II (c. 1283 – ?)
25. Mahlakadeva (c. ? – c. 1305).

9

Hoysala Empire

The Hoysala Empire was a prominent South Indian Kannadiga empire that ruled most of the modern day state of Karnataka between the 10th and the 14th centuries. The capital of the Hoysalas was initially located at Belur but was later moved to Halebidu.

The Hoysala rulers were originally hill people of Malnad Karnataka, an elevated region in the Western Ghats range. In the 12th century, taking advantage of the internecine warfare between the then ruling Western Chalukyas and Kalachuri kingdoms, they annexed areas of present day Karnataka and the fertile areas north of the Kaveri River delta in present day Tamil Nadu. By the 13th century, they governed most of present-day Karnataka, parts of Tamil Nadu and parts of western Andhra Pradesh in Deccan India.

The Hoysala era was an important period in the development of art, architecture, and religion in South India. The empire is remembered today primarily for its temple architecture. Over a hundred surviving temples are scattered across Karnataka, including the well known Chennakesava Temple at Belur, the Hoysaleswara Temple at Halebidu, and the Kesava Temple at Somanathapura. The Hoysala rulers also patronised the fine arts, encouraging literature to flourish in Kannada and Sanskrit.

History

Kannada folklore tells of a young man, Sala, who saved his Jain guru Sudatta by striking dead a tiger he encountered near the temple of the Goddess Vasantika at Sosevur. The word "strike" literally translates to "Hoy" in Hale Kannada (Old Kannada), hence the name "Hoy-sala". This legend first appeared in the Belur inscription of Vishnuvardhana (1117), but owing to several inconsistencies in the Sala story it remains in the realm of folklore. The legend may have come into existence or gained popularity after King Vishnuvardhana's victory over the Cholas at Talakad as the Hoysala emblem depicts the fight between the mythical Sala and a tiger, the emblem of the Cholas.

Early inscriptions, dated 1078 and 1090, have implied that the Hoysalas were descendants of the Yadava by referring to the Yadava *vamsa* (clan) as Hoysala *vamśa*. But there are no early records directly linking the Hoysalas to the Yadavas of North India.

Historians refer to the founders of the dynasty as natives of Malnad Karnataka, based on numerous inscriptions calling them *Maleparolganda* or "Lord of the Male (hills) chiefs" (*Malepas*). This title in the Kannada language was proudly used by the Hoysala kings as their royal signature in their inscriptions. Literary sources from that time in Kannada (*Jatakatilaka*) and Sanskrit (*Gadyakarnamrita*) have also helped confirm they were natives of the region known today as Karnataka. The first Hoysala family record is dated 950 and names Arekalla as the chieftain, followed by Maruga and Nripa Kama I (976). The next ruler, Munda (1006–1026), was succeeded by Nripa Kama II who held such titles as *Permanadi* that show an early alliance with the Western Ganga dynasty. From these modest beginnings, the Hoysala dynasty began its transformation into a strong subordinate of the Western Chalukyas. Through Vishnuvardhana's expansive military conquests, the Hoysalas achieved the status of a real kingdom for the first time. He wrested Gangavadi from the Cholas in 1116 and moved the capital from Belur to Halebidu.

Vishnuvardhana's ambition of creating an independent empire was fulfilled by his grandson Veera Ballala II, who freed the Hoysalas from subordination in 1187–1193. Thus the Hoysalas began as subordinates of the Western Chalukyas and gradually established their own empire in Karnataka with such strong Hoysala kings as Vishnuvardhana, Veera Ballala II and later Veera Ballala III. During this time, peninsular India saw a four way struggle for hegemony-Pandya, Kakatiya and Seuna Yadavas of Devagiri being the other kingdoms. Veera Ballala II defeated the aggressive Pandya when they invaded the Chola kingdom. He assumed the title "Establisher of the Chola Kingdom" (*Cholarajyapratishtacharya*), "Emperor of the south" (*Dakshina*

Chakravarthi) and "Hoysala emperor" (*Hoysala Chakravarthi*). He founded the city of Bangalore according to Kannada folklore.

The Hoysalas extended their foothold in areas known today as Tamil Nadu around 1225, making the city of Kannanur Kuppam near Srirangam a provincial capital and giving them control over South Indian politics that began a period of Hoysala hegemony in the southern Deccan.. Vira Narasimha II's son Vira Someshwara earned the honorific "uncle" (*Mamadi*) from the Pandyas and Cholas. The Hoysala influence spread over Pandya kingdom also. Toward the end of 13th century, Veera Ballala III recaptured territory in the Tamil country which had been lost to the Pandya uprising, thus uniting the northern and southern portions of the kingdom.

Major political changes were taking place in the Deccan region in the early 14th century when significant areas of northern India were under Muslim rule. Alla-ud-din Khilji, the Sultan of Delhi, was determined to bring isolated South India under his domain and sent his commander, Malik Kafur, on a southern expedition to plunder the Seuna capital Devagiri in 1311. The Seuna empire was subjugated by 1318 and the Hoysala capital Halebidu (also called Dorasamudra or Dwarasamudra) was sacked twice, in 1311 and 1327.

By 1336, the Sultan had conquered the Pandyas of Madurai, the Kakatiyas of Warangal and the tiny kingdom of Kampili. The Hoysalas were the only remaining Hindu empire who resisted the invading armies. Veera Ballala III stationed himself at Tiruvannamalai and offered stiff resistance to invasions from the north and the Sultanate of Madurai to the south. Then, after nearly three decades of resistance, Veera Ballala III was killed at the battle of Madurai in 1343, and the sovereign territories of the Hoysala empire were merged with the areas administered by Harihara I in the Tungabhadra region. This new Hindu kingdom resisted the northern invasions and would later prosper and come to be known as the Vijayanagara Empire.

Nripa Kama II (1026–1047)

Nripa Kama II (1026-1047 CE) was an early king of the Hoysala Empire from the malnad region of Karnataka and was possibly a feudatory of the Western Ganga Dynasty and fought many wars against the Cholas. Thought unable to rout the Cholas from southern regions of present day Karnataka, he successfully ruled some regions in the malnad area.

Hoysala Vinayaditya (1047–1098)

Vinayaditya (1047-1098 CE) an able king of the Hoysala Empire distinguished himself as an able feudatory of the Kalyani Chalukya during his long reign. He helped bring many small Malnad chiefs like the Kongalvas, Chengalvas, Santharas of Humcha Shimoga and the Kadambas of Bayalnadu (Vainadu) under control. After the complete disappearance of the Gangas during Chola occupation of Gangavadi, Vinayaditya brought some small portions of Gangavadi under his control. He was either a brother-in-law or father-in-law of Chalukya Somesvara I.

Ereyanga (1098–1102)

Ereyanga (1098-1102 CE) was the son of Hoysala Vinayaditya and distinguished himself as a Chalukya feudatory during their campaigns against Dhara of Malwa. Though his rule as a monarch of Hoysala Empire was short, he served his father brilliantly as the *Yuvaraja*.

Veera Ballala I (1102–1108)

Veera Ballala I (?1102-1108 CE) was king of the Hoysala Empire. His rule was short and uneventful other than subduing the Chengalvas and the Santharas. It is claimed he made some unsuccessful attempts to overthrow the overlordship of the Western Chalukyas but was brought under control by Chalukya Vikramaditya VI.

Vishnuvardhana (1108–1152)

Vishnuvardhana (1108-1152 CE), was a king of the Hoysala Empire in present day Indian state of Karnataka. Vishnuvardhana took the first step in consolidating the Hoysala Empire in South India through a series of battles against the Cholas and is overlords, the Western Chalukya empire. It is said that The Hoysala feudatory gained the dignity of a Kingdom starting from his rule onwards.

Conquests

Vishnuvardhana worked closely with his elder brother Veera Ballala I in matters of administration and military campaigns.

Vishnuvardhana's first major conquest was the Cholan territory of Gangavadi in 1116, which is now a major portion of south Karnataka. Vishnuvardhana's general Gangaraja wrested the territory from the Cholas.

Vishnuvardhana now assumed the title *Talakadugonda* and *Veera Ganga,* minted coins with these legends and in celebration built the Kirthinarayana temple at Talakad. Chola commanders like Adigaiman may have helped Vishnuvardhana in his conquest. Being Vaishnava Hindu by faith, the Chola commander may not have been treated well by Kulothunga Chola I. One Hoysalan epitaph notes that Vishnuvardhana burned the Gangavadi city of Talakad and polluted the waters of river Kaveri by throwing the corpses of his enemies into it.

After his victory against the Cholas, Vishnuvardhana proceeded southeast to Kolar and captured the town. Some records indicate that he travelled further east into Tamil territory defeating the Kongalvas, the Chengalvas and the Nidugal Chola ruler Irungola. He married the Kongalva princes Chandaladevi and conquered Kanchi and Rameshwaram from the Pandyas in the battle of Dumme. He now assumed the title *Nolambavadigonda* in 1117 and minted coins with his title.

The Hoysalas defeated Chalukyan king Vikramaditya VI at Kennagala in 1118, and at Hallur in 1120. Vishnuvardhana captured the fort of Hanagal, subdued the Kadambas of Banavasi. However Vishnuvardhana suffered reversals at the hands of Chalukya commander Achugi of Gulbarga and had to submit to the Chalukya overlordship. After the death of Vikramaditya VI in 1126 Vishnuvardhana recaptured Hanagal, Uchchangi, Bankapura and Banavasi-12000 province and marched up to Lakkundi in Gadag district.

Towards the end of his life, Vishnuvardhana had wrested many territories that were hitherto under the control of other ruling dynasties. Though not fully able to conquer South India from the Chalukyas, Vishnuvardhana was able to rise the territory to the dignity of a real kingdom and laid the foundations for the conquests that were to follow by his successors Veera Ballala II and III.

There is controversy regarding the year in which Vishnuvardhana died. Though some historians claim he lived up to 1152. the proof from Yalladahalli inscription shows that his younger son Narasimha I was already the king in 1145. The demise of Vishnuvardhana is fixed at 1141 by other scholars.

Art & Religion

Scholars believe that Vishnuvardhana was originally a Jain known as Bittideva. Under the influence of the Hindu philosopher Ramanujacharya, Vishnuvardhana converted to Hinduism and practiced Vaishnavism. Numerous Vishnu temples were built during his reign at Belur, Talakad and Melkote. However, Vishnuvardhana's chief queen, Shantala Devi remained a devout Jain, and set a precedent of religious tolerance in the kingdom. Many of Vishnuvardhana's generals, including Gangaraja, were Jains.

The Famous Chennakesava Temple at Belur is attributed to him. He built this temple to commemorate his victory against the Cholas of Tamil country. The famous Hoysaleswara temple at Halebidu was also built during his time.

According to research scholar M. S. Mate of the Deccan College, the devotee Pundalik—who is assumed to be a historical figure—was instrumental in persuading Vishnuvardhana alias Bittidev to build the Pandharpur temple dedicated to Vishnu. The deity was subsequently named as Vitthala, a derivative of Bittidev, by the builder-king.

Upon Vishnuvardhana's death in 1152, his son Narasimha I ascended to the Hoysala throne.

Narasimha I (1152–1173)

Narasimha I. was a ruler of the Hoysala Empire. Apart from his victory over his overlord Chalukya Tailapa III which paved way for declaration of independence by his successor, his importance to historians is considered little.

Tailapa III was killed by Narasimha I. He however failed to meet the challenge of their Kalachuri feudatory Bijjala II. He was overthrown by his son Veera Ballala II.

Veera Ballala II (1173–1220)

Veera Ballala II. was the greatest monarch of the Hoysala Empire. This is proven by his successes against the Seuna, Southern

Kalachuri, Pandya and the waning Kalyani Chalukya and Chola dynasties. His period also saw prolific literary activity in Kannada. He patronised Ranna and Rudrabhatta. During his forty seven years of rule, the Hoysala kingdom consolidated to the extent of being called an independent empire. The Kedareshwara temple at Halebidu and Amritheswara temple in Chikmagalur were some important temples built by him.

Ballala's Revolt

Ballala II was unhappy with the shrinking size of the Hoysala kingdom during the rule of his not too popular father Narasimha I. With the help of some malnad chiefs, Ballala II overthrew his father and assumed control of the kingdom. He later ensured the same Malnad chiefs could not rise against him.

Wars against Kalachuri, Chalukya and Seuna

During his early rule in 1178 Ballala II captured Hanagal and tried to reach Belvola where he faced defeat against the Kalachuri. But in the subsequent years with the weakening of the Kalachuri after the assassination of Bijjala II and the waning of the Kalyani Chalukya power, Veera Ballala II once again pressed his claims over these northern territories.

He captured Balligavi from the Kalachuri and defeated Chalukya Somesvara IV in 1187. He won a comprehensive victory against the Seuna Bhillama V at Soraturu in 1190 and gained much material and land gains from the victory. An inscription dated 1196 claims he had reached as far north as Kaliburgi (Gulbarga). He certainly had full control over lands up to the Krishna River. However by 1212 it seems some of his gains were lost due to southern incursions of Senua Singhana II.

Relations ship with Cholas

Ballala II was married to a daughter of Kulothunga Chola III and vice versa. When the Pandyas attacked the Cholas, Ballala's sent crown prince Vira Narasimha II who fought successfully to maintain the Chola kingdom and drive back the Pandyas. By virtue of this, Ballala II gained the title *Cholarajyapratishtacharya* or "Establisher of the Chola kingdom". In 1206-1218 Hoysalas invaded Magadai Mandalam. His overlordship over the Cholas gained him some territories in Tamil country as well.

Vira Narasimha II (1220–1235)

Vira Narasimha II. was a king of the Hoysala Empire. During his reign the Hoysalas gained much influence in the affairs of the Ancient Tamil country. He defeated the Kadavas and Pandyas and levied a tribute. He acted as a support to Chola king Rajaraja Chola III, who possibly his son-in-law, against Pandya incursions. During his rule, Vira Narasimha made Kannanur Kuppam near Srirangam his second capital, with an intent to maintain close watch and control over affairs in Tamil country. Later he fought for the Chola cause again and marched all the way to Rameswaram. Kannada poet Sumanobana was the court poet of King Vira Narasimha II

Wars with Pandyas

During the rule of Vera Narasimha II, a Hoysala army was stationed at Kanchi possibly to avert any incursion from the Telugu Chodas of Nellore, the Kakatiya dynasty of Warangal and the Pandyas of Madurai. The Chola monarch Rajaraja III defied the Pandyas by not paying their annual tribute. Sundara Pandya went on the offensive and routed the Cholas in the battle of Tellaru. Vira Narasimha II rushed to the aid of the Cholas, defeated the South Arcot chiefs and captured Srirangam. Magadai Mandalam was invaded again in 1220–1238. The Hoysala commanders Appanna and Gopayya then reached Chidambaram, routing on their way the Kopperunjinga chiefs who were a Pandya ally in the battle of Perumbalur. Finally, receiving news that the Kopperunjinga chiefs were willing to set free the Chola monarch Rajaraja III and consider the Cholas a free kingdom, the Hoysalas escorted the Chola monarch back to Kanchi in 1231. At the same time, Vira Narasimha II himself had defeated Sundara Pandya in the battle of Mahendramangalam.

Vira Someshwara (1235–1254)

Vira Someshwara. was a king of the Hoysala Empire. The preoccupation of Vira Narasimha II in the affairs of Tamil country resulted in neglect of northern territories and Vira Someshwara had to face Seuna incursion south of the Tungabhadra river.

Tamil Country Politics

During the time period 1225-1250, the Hoysalas consolidated their domination over the South Deccan by asserting complete influence on the Cholas and the Pandyas. Someshwara was actually called *Mamadi* or "uncle" by the kings of Tamil country.

Magadai Mandalam was conquered by Veera Somesvara in1236. He allied himself with Chola Rajendra III but made friendship with the Pandyas when the Chola king tried to invade Pandya territory in 1238. Later having defeated Rajendra III, Someshwara again fought for the cause of the Cholas against the Pandyas.

In 1254 Someshwara divided his kingdom between his two sons, Ramanatha who ruled from Kannanur and Narasimha III who ruled from Halebidu. Like his father Narasimha II, Someshwara stayed back at Kannanur with Ramanatha where he was killed in a war with the Pandyas.

Narasimha III (1254–1291)

Narasimha III. (1254-1291 CE). During his rule over the Hoysala Empire, internal feud between the king and his brother Ramanatha ruling from Kannanur came to the forefront. He also had to face invasions from the Seuna who attacked his regal capital. However, Narasimha III was able to inflict defeat on these incursions and safeguard his kingdom. He was succeeded by his son Veera Ballala III.

Veera Ballala III (1292–1343)

Veera Ballala III. (1291-1343 CE), was the last great king of the Hoysala Empire that ruled over what is now the South Indian state of Karnataka. Veera Ballala's commanders, Harihara (popularly known as Hakka) and Bukkaraya (popularly known as Bukka) are perhaps better known in Kannada folklore as the founders of the Vijayanagar empire. He ruled during a time of tremendous political and cultural uncertainty, when all other major Hindu kingdoms of the Deccan and South India had fallen to the Muslim invasion from the north.

Northern Success

Veera Ballala successfully repulsed the Seuna invasion and also combined the divided Hoysala empire after the death of Vishvanata, the Hoysala king ruling from Kannanur. He defeated the Kadambas of Hangal and extended his kingdom up to Lakkundi, north of the Tungabhadra River.

Pandya Affairs

Ballala III successfully arbitered in the affairs of Tamil country by appointing Sundara Pandya as the Pandya king as opposed to his competitor, Vira Pandya. This was during 1311. However his focus on Tamil affairs laid open the northern boundaries of his territories to the invasion of Malik Kafur, commander of Sultan of Delhi, All-ud-din-Khilji. Halebidu was attacked and plundered. Veera Ballala had to accept defeat to the Delhi Sulthan and his son Veera Virupaksha Ballala was sent to Delhi as an act of peace. His son returned in 1313.

Invasion from Delhi

By 1318, the Seuna kingdom had been completely destroyed and Devagiri occupied by the Delhi Sultan. The tiny kingdom of Kampili, on the banks of Tungabhadra with its capital at Kummata (close to present day Hampi) became the focus of attention. Veera Ballala III fought to bring Kampili under control but with no gains. Ballala III had also withdrawn support to the Delhi Sultan, who with an intent of teaching Ballala III a lesson launched a campaign against Halebidu in 1327. By 1336 all Hindu kingdoms of the south with the exception of the Hoysala kingdom had been defeated and large areas annexed by the Sultan of Delhi. The Madurai Sultanate was also formed. With Tiruvannamalai as his new capital, Veera Ballala III summoned his last reserves of strength to launch an offensive against the rule of a foreign power over the Hindu south India. With an intention of meeting the Muslim invasion, Ballala III founded a second capital Hosapattna on the banks of Tungabhadra river, later to be renamed Vijayanagara.

Veera Ballala was said to have been ably assisted by his chief council, Sangama. Sangama was custodian of parts of the Hoysala empire in the proximity of the town of Hampi on the banks of river Tungabhadra. The eldest of Sangama's sons, Harihara I, was appointed a "Mahamandaleshwara", a chief of several smaller rulers, in the northern part of the Hoysala empire.

In 1336, the Hoysala Empire, under the military leadership of Hakka and Bukka were able to repulse the attacks and encroachments of the Sultan of Delhi, to the north of the kingdom. Veera Ballala himself lead a military expedition to Madhurai to attack the Sultan's assets in that region. After the Hoysala victory over the Sultanate of Delhi, Bukka was appointed Crown Prince of the Reunited Kingdom.

Vijayanagar

The Hoysala empire, along with the new territories conquered during battle in 1336, came to be known as the Vijayanagara Empire. A century later, the Vijayanagara empire would gain prominence for its political, military, musical and literary progress under the reign of King Krishnadevaraya. After the founding of the kingdom of Vijayanagar, Veera Ballala III returned to Madhurai to counter attempts of invasion by the Sultan of Delhi. Veera Ballala was killed in one of the series of skirmishes that ensued against the Sultanate in 1343. Thus ended the life of the last great Hoysala king.

Harihara Raya (Vijayanagara Empire) (1342–1355)

Economy

Economy of Hoysala empire was primarily based on agriculture though business within India as well as foreign trade flourished to some extent.

Agriculture

The administration sustained itself through agriculture. Land grants were made by the kings to religious beneficiaries like Brahmins, Jains and persons rewarded for services rendered to the king. The type of land grant was generally wetland which was already under cultivation. This was popular in the fertile river valleys of the Tungabhadra and Kaveri. In addition, clearing of forests for cultivation was viewed favourably as it not only brought new sources of revenue but also created job opportunities for the landless and introduced forest dwellers to a more agrarian life style. Whenever land was cleared for cultivation, it was on a large scale.

Knowledge of agriculture included assessing irrigation systems like tanks, reservoirs with sluices, canals and wells which were built and maintained at the expense of local villagers. The more impressive irrigation tanks such as *Vishnusagara, Shantisagara, Ballalarayasagara* were created at the expense of the state. Irrespective of whether the expense and control came from local or state bodies, organizing labour to till the land was taken up at the village and across village levels and the job of cultivation was largely that of the landless. The highlands (*malnad* regions) with its favorable climate was suitable for cattle farming, orchards and spices.

Paddy and corn were staple crops in the plains (*Bailnad*). In Kannada country, key figures in rural areas were the rich land owners called *gavunda* or *Gauda* and *heggade*. They are mentioned in inscriptions relating to land transactions, maintenance of irrigation, collection of taxes and works of village council. The *gavunda* of people (*praja gavunda*) was lower in status than the wealthy lord of *gavundas* (*prabhu gavunda*). The *gavundas* sometimes had a dual role as village representatives and appointees of the state. Some judicial responsibilities were also included like raising a militia if required.

Imports and Exports

Import of horses on the western seaboard was a flourishing business and inscriptions speak of Brahmin merchants who were active. Arabs made wealth from the unending need for horses from Indian kingdoms. Rich forest produce like Teak was exported through ports of present day Kerela. Merchants from this region settled down in Arasikere and Halebidu in addition to Jain traders. *Virgal* (hero stone) in the coastal areas depict ships indicating active sea trade with shipping fleets. Piracy was common and *Virgals* made for fallen heroes have been found. Inscriptions mention a flourishing textile industry.

Trade with overseas kingdoms reached unprecedented levels. Sung dynasty records from China mention Indian merchants in ports of South China. Chinese interest in Indian astrology and Alchemy is well known. South India exported textiles, spices, medicinal plants, precious stones, pottery, salt made from salt pans, jewels, gold, ivory, Rhino horn, ebony and camphor to China. The same products reached ports like Dhofar, Aden. In addition, aloe wood, perfumes, Sandalwood and condiments reached western ports like Siraf which was the entrypot to Egypt, Arabia and Persia. Cairo and Alexandria were in active trade across the Arabian Sea. Architects (*Vishwakarmas*), sculptors, quarry workers, goldsmiths and others whose trade directly or indirectly related to construction of temples were also prosperous due to the vigorous temple building activities undertaken.

Tax System

Tax assessment was done by the village assembly who were responsible for collecting for the government. Land revenue was called *Siddhaya* and included original assessment (*Kula*) and various cesses. Cesses were collected in proportion to *Kula*. Taxes were levied on professions, marriage, goods in transit on chariots, carriages, domesticated animals. Taxes on commodities like gold, precious stones, perfumes, Sandalwood, ropes, yarn, residence, hearth, shops, cattle pans, sugarcane presses and produce like black pepper, betel leaves, ghee, paddy, spices, palm leaves, coconuts and sugar are mentioned in records. Cattle tax was called *balavana* and loom tax was called *maggadere*. Fines for violating laws were also collected. The village assembly could levy tax for a specific purpose like construction of a water tanks.

Administration

Hoysala administration was influenced by the Western Ganga Dynasty whom the Hoysalas replaced in present day South Karnataka and their early overlords, the Western Chalukyas.

The Hoysala administrative machinery had many similarities with that of the Western Chalukya and Western Ganga Dynasties in matters of cabinet and command, local governing bodies and division of territory into provinces and districts. Some historians state that in the highly centralised Hoysala empire the king sought the advice of five major ministers (*Pancha Pradhanas*) while others claim a higher number. As the empire grew in the 13th century, the number of ministers also grew with each having limited authority. Inscriptions mention many names with responsibilities tied to such areas as foreign affairs (*Sandhivigrahi*), treasurer (*Mahabhandari* or *Hiranyabhandari*), personal secretary (*Paramavishvasi*), chief master of robes (*Mahapasayita*), justice (*Dharmadhikari*), central register (*Kaditha*), and head of the State Secretariat (*Srikaranadhikari*). Some ministers also oversaw clusters of departments (*Sarvadhikari*). Army commanders were called *Dandanayaka* (or *Senadhipati*).

The kingdom was divided into provinces (*Nadu* and *Vishayas*). Further division of land was into *Kampanas* and *Deshas*. Under the caretaker commander were minister (*Mahapradhana*), treasurer (*Bhandari*), clerk (*Senabove*) and junior officers (*Heggades*). Feudatory families such as Alupas, Santharas, Chengalvas, Kongalvas, Sindas were allowed to continue to govern their respective territories. The Hoysalas minted gold coins with Kannada and Devanagari legends. King Vishnuvardhana's coins had the legends "victor at Nolambavadi" (*Nolambavadigonda*), "victor at Talakad" (*Talakadugonda*), "victor of the hills" (*Malaparolgonda*). Their gold coin was called *Honnu* or *Gadyana* and weighed 62 grains of gold. *Pana* or *Hana* was 1/10th of the *Honnu*. *Haga* was ¼th of the *Pana*. *Visa* was ¼th of *Haga*. There were coins called *Bele* and *Kani* as well. It must be noted that some of these terms *Hana, Bele* are still used in Kannada language and mean "money" and "cost" respectively.

The *Garudas* were the elite bodyguards of kings and queens. They were known as *lenkas* (heroes) or *jolavalis* (indebted to the king for food) and *velavalis* (those who stood by the king at all times). They served the king the way the mythical eagle Garuda served Lord Vishnu and committed suicide upon the demise of their master. Hero stones (*virgal*) erected in memory of such heroes are called Garuda pillars. The Garuda pillar at the Hoysaleswara temple in Halebidu depicts heroes brandishing knives and others cutting their own heads. Kuvara Lakshma, a minister and bodyguard of king Veera Ballala II took his own life and that of his wife and other bodyguards upon the death of his master. The details of his loyalty are etched on this inscription (*Shasana*).

Culture

Religion: The defeat of the Jain Western Ganga Dynasty by the Cholas in early 11th century and the rising numbers of followers of Vaishnava Hinduism and Virashaivism in the 12th century was mirrored by a decreased interest in Jainism. Two notable locations of Jain worship in the Hoysala territory were Shravanabelagola and Kambadahalli. The decline of Buddhism in South India began in the 8th century with the spread of Adi Shankara's Advaita philosophy.

The only places of Buddhist worship during the Hoysala time were at Dambal and Balligavi. Shantala Devi, queen of Vishnuvardhana was a Jain but nevertheless commissioned the Hindu Kappe Chennigaraya temple in Belur, evidence that the royal family was tolerant of all religions. During the rule of the Hoysalas, three important religious developments took place in present day Karnataka inspired by three philosophers, Basavanna, Madhvacharya and Ramanujacharya.

While the origin of Virashaiva faith is debated, the movement grew through its association with Basavanna in the 12th century. Basavanna and other Virashaiva saints preached of a faith without a caste system. In his Vachanas he appealed to the masses in simple Kannada and wrote "work is worship" (*Kayakave Kailasa*). Madhvacharya was critical of the teachings of Shankaracharya and argued the world is real and not an illusion. His philosophy gained popularity enabling him to establish eight Mathas (monastery) in Udupi. Ramanujacharya, the head of the Vaishnava monastery in Srirangam, preached the way of devotion (*bhakti marga*) and wrote *Sribhashya,* a critique on the Advaita philosophy of Adi Shankara.

The impact of these religious developments on culture, literature, poetry and architecture in South India was profound. Important works of literature and poetry based on the teachings of these philosophers were written during the coming centuries. The Saluva, Tuluva and Aravidu dynasties of Vijayanagar empire were followers of Vaishnavism and a Vaishnava temple with an image of Ramanujacharya exists in the Vitthalapura area of Vijayanagara. Scholars in later Mysore Kingdom wrote Vaishnavite works upholding the teachings of Ramanujacharya. King Vishnuvardhana built many temples after his conversion from Jainism to Vaishnavism. The later saints of Madhvacharya's order, Jayatirtha, Vyasatirtha, Sripadaraya, Vadirajatirtha and devotees (*dasa*) such as Vijaya Dasa, Gopaladasa and others from the Karnataka region spread his teachings far and wide. His teachings inspired later day philosophers like Vallabhacharya in Gujarat and Chaitanya in Bengal. Another wave of devotion (*bhakti*) in the 17th century–18th century found inspiration in his teachings.

Society

Hoysala society in many ways reflected the emerging religious, political and cultural developments of those times. A notable feature of the Hoysala kingdom was the involvement of women, especially of royalty, in administrative matters. Queen Umadevi governed Halebidu in the absence of Veera Ballala II and is known to have fought wars against antagonistic feudatories. Women participated in music, dance, literature, poetry, politics and administration. Queen Shantala Devi was well versed in dance and music and rendered public performances. Akka Mahadevi, a Vachana poet who renounced the temporal world in favour of one of devotion became an example for woman of the day. The practice of sati, though voluntary was prevalent and prostitution was socially acceptable. Temple dancers (*Devadasi*) were common in temples and some were well educated and accomplished in arts. These qualifications gave them more freedom than other urban and rural women who were restricted to daily mundane tasks. Like in most of India, the Indian caste system was conspicuously present.

Trade on the west coast brought many foreigners to India including Arabs, Jews, Persians, Chinese and people from the Malay Peninsula. Large scale migration of people from present day Karnataka to Tamil Nadu happened during this time. With the expansion of Hoysala territory in Tamil country, these immigrants went as officers and soldiers of the empire and were given land concessions.

Migration of Tamil sculptors to Belur and Halebidu is also apparent from the presence of some Chola style sculptures in a few Hoysala temples. The marketplace was the nuclei of urban centres. This is where materials and produce was brought and exchanged hands. These were the location of recurring festivals and fairs.

In South India, towns were called *Pattana* or *Pattanam* and the marketplace, *Nagara* or *Nagaram*. Important marketplaces gradually grew into townships and so did famous pilgrim places. Shravanabelagola in Hassan district developed from a place of religion in the 7th century to an important settlement by the 12th century when rich Jain merchants were established here. The market place was also closely tied with temple administration.

The prolific temple construction was not entirely for religious reasons. Temples acted as local courts or as surrogate courts, especially when built from royal endowments. They were seen as palaces and the rituals marking the daily routine of the deity imitated those of the king. Some temples also received local patronage from rich landlords. Temples built from royal patronage took on an aura of a leading ceremonial center. When king Vishnuvardhana built the Chennakesava Temple (a Vaishnava temple) at Belur, the town was transformed into a famous city. Competition from the Shaiva merchants of Halebidu resulted in the construction of the Hoysaleswara temple which gave the town prominence. Often temples built in rural areas were not supported by royal patronage.

They evolved into complex institutions related to fiscal, political, cultural and religious needs. Irrespective of patronage, temples were also establishments that provided employment to hundreds of people. Temple funds maintained families of priests, record keepers, administrators, guards, garland makers, dancers, *devadasis*, sculptors, carpenters and craftsmen. They were also a source of loans. Inscriptions mention 12%-15% interest on loans. In short, Hindu temples began to take on the shape of wealthy Buddhist monasteries.

Literature

The Hoysala Empire (1025–1343), in what is now southern India, produced a large body of literature in the Kannada and Sanskrit languages. The empire was established by Nripa Kama II, came into political prominence during the rule of King Vishnuvardhana (1108–1152), and declined gradually after its defeat by the Khilji dynasty invaders in 1311.

Kannada literature during this period consisted of writings relating to the socio-religious developments of the Jain and Veerashaiva faiths, and to a lesser extent that of the Vaishnava faith. The earliest well-known brahmin writers in Kannada were from the Hoysala court. While most of the courtly textual production was in Kannada, an important corpus of monastic Vaishnava literature relating to *Dvaita* (dualistic) philosophy was written by the renowned philosopher Madhvacharya in Sanskrit.

Writing Kannada literature in native metres was first popularised by the court poets. These metres were the *sangatya*, compositions sung to the accompaniment of a musical instrument; *shatpadi*, six-line verses; *ragale*, lyrical compositions in blank verse; and *tripadi*, three-line verses. However, Jain writers continued to use the traditional *champu*, composed of prose and verse. Important literary contributions in Kannada were made not only by court poets but also by noblemen, commanders, ministers, ascetics and saints associated with monasteries.

Kannada Writings

Overview: Kannada poets and writers in Hoysala Empire (1100-1343 CE).

Nagachandra	1105
Kanti	1108
Rajaditya	12th. c
Harihara	1160–1200
Udayaditya	1150
Vritta Vilasa	1160
Kereya Padmarasa	1165
Nemichandra	1170
Sumanobana	1175
Rudrabhatta	1180
Aggala	1189
Palkuriki Somanatha	1195
Sujanottamsa	12th c.
Kavi Kama	12th c.
Devakavi	1200
Raghavanka	1200–1225
Bhanduvarma	1200
Parsva Pandita	1205
Maghanandycharya	1209
Janna	1209–1230
Puligere Somanatha	13th c.
Hastimalla	13th c.
Somaraja	1222
Gunavarma II	1235
Polalvadandanatha	1224
Andayya	1217–1235
Sisumayana	1232
Mallikarjuna	1245
Naraharitirtha	1281
Kumara Padmarasa	13th c.
Mahabala Kavi	1254
Keshiraja	1260
Kumudendu	1275
Ratta Kavi	1300
Nagaraja	1331

Beginning with the 12th century, important socio-political changes took place in the Deccan, south of the Krishna river. During this period, the Hoysalas, native Kannadigas from the Malnad region (hill country in modern Karnataka) were on the ascendant as a political power. They are known to have existed as chieftains from the mid-10th century when they distinguished themselves as subordinates of the Western Chalukyas of Kalyani. In 1116, Hoysala King Vishnuvardhana defeated the Cholas of Tanjore and annexed Gangavadi (modern southern Karnataka), thus bringing the region back under native rule. In the following decades, with the waning of the Chalukya power, the Hoysalas proclaimed independence and grew into one of most powerful ruling families of southern India.

Consequently, literature in Kannada, the local language, flourished in the Hoysala empire. This literature can be broadly subdivided as follows: works dominated by the themes of Jain writings, contrasting works by Veerashaiva writers not belonging to the vachana poetic tradition, rebuttals to Shaiva writings from Jain writers, early brahminical works (Vaishnava), works from the birth of the Bhakti (devotional) movement in the Kannada-speaking region, writings on secular topics, and the first writings in native metres (*ragale, sangatya* and *shatpadi*).

As in earlier centuries, Jain authors wrote about tirthankars (saints), princes and other personages important to the Jain religion. Jain versions of the Hindu epics such as the Ramayana and Bhagavata (tales of Hindu god Krishna) were also written. According to R. Narasimhacharya, a noted scholar on Kannada literature, more Jain writers wrote in Kannada than in any other Dravidian language during the "Augustan age" of Kannada literature, from the earliest known works to the 12th century. The Veerashaiva writers, devotees of the Hindu god Shiva, wrote about his 25 forms in their expositions of Shaivism.

Vaishnava authors wrote treatments of the Hindu epics, the Ramayana, the Mahabharata and the Bhagavata. Breaking away from the old Jain tradition of using the *champu* metre for writing Kannada literature, Harihara penned poems in the *ragale* metre in *Siva-ganada-ragalegalu* (1160).

His nephew Raghavanka established the *shatpadi* tradition by writing a unique version of the story of King Harishchandra in

Harishchandra Kavya (1200). Sisumayana introduced the *sangatya* metre in his *Anjanacharita* and *Tripuradahana* (1235). However, some scholars continued to employ Sanskritic metres such as *champu* (*Ramachandra Charitapurana*), *shataka* (100-line verses, *Pampa sataka*) and *ashtaka* (eight-line verses, *Mudige ashtaka*).

The exact beginnings of the haridasa movement in the Kannada-speaking region have been disputed. Belur Keshavadasa, a noted *Harikatha* scholar, claimed in his book *Karnataka Bhaktavijaya* that the movement was inspired by saint Achalananda Dasa of Turvekere (in the modern Tumkur district) in the 9th century. However, neither the language used in Achalananda Dasa's compositions nor the discovery of a composition with the pen name "Achalanada Vitthala", which mentions the 13th-century philosopher Madhvacharya, lends support to the 9th-century theory. Naraharitirtha (1281), one of earliest disciples of Madhvacharya, is therefore considered the earliest haridasa to write Vaishnava compositions in Kannada. Secular topics were popular and included treatises on poetry (*Sringararatnakara*) and writings on natural sciences (*Rattasutra*), mathematics (*Vyavaharaganita*), fiction (*Lilavati*), grammar (*Shabdamanidarpana*), rhetoric (*Udayadityalankara*) and others.

Important contributions were made by some prominent literary families. One Jain family produced several authors, including Mallikarjuna, the noted anthologist (1245); his brother-in-law Janna (1209), the court poet of King Veera Ballala II; Mallikarjuna's son Keshiraja (1260), considered by D. R. Nagaraj, a scholar on literary cultures in history, to be the greatest theorist of Kannada grammar; and Sumanobana, who was in the court of King Narasimha I and was the maternal grandfather of Keshiraja. Harihara (1160) and his nephew Raghavanka (1200), poets who set the trend for using native metres, came from a Shaiva family (devotees of the god Shiva).

The support of the Hoysala rulers for the Kannada language was strong, and this is seen even in their epigraphs, often written in polished and poetic language, rather than prose, with illustrations of floral designs in the margins. In addition to the Hoysala patronage, royal support was enjoyed by Kannada poets and writers during this period in the courts of neighbouring kingdoms of the western Deccan. The Western Chalukyas, the southern Kalachuris, the Seuna Yadavas of Devagiri and the Silharas of Kolhapur are some of the ruling families who enthusiastically used Kannada in inscriptions and promoted its literature.

Writers bilingual in Kannada and Telugu gained popularity which caused interaction between the two languages, a trend that continued into modern times. The Veerashiva canon of the Kannada language was translated or adapted into Telugu from this time period. Palkuriki Somanatha (1195), a devotee of social reformer Basavanna, is the most well-known of these bilingual poets. The Chola chieftain Nannechoda (c. 1150) used many Kannada words in his Telugu writings. After the decline of the Hoysala empire, the Vijayanagara empire kings further supported writers in both languages. In 1369, inspired by Palkuriki Somanatha, Bhima Kavi translated the Telugu *Basavapurana* to Kannada, and King Deva Raya II (c. 1425) had Chamarasa's landmark writing *Prabhulingalile* translated into Telugu and Tamil. Many Veerashaiva writers in the court of the 17th century Kingdom of Mysore were multilingual in Kannada, Telugu and Sanskrit while the Srivaishnava (a sect of Vaishnavism) Kannada writers of the court were in competition with the Telugu and Sanskrit writers.

Information regarding several writers from this period whose works are considered lost are available from contemporary records. They include Maghanandi (probable author of *Rama Kathe* and guru of Kamalabhava of 1235), Balachandra (guru of Nagachandra of 1105), Nachi Raja (*Nachiraji*, a commentary on the *Amara Khosha*, 1158), Srutakirti (guru of Aggala of 1189 and author of *Raghava Pandaviya* and possibly a *Jina-stuti*), Sambha Varma (mentioned by Nagavarma of 1145), Vira Nandi (*Chandraprabha Kavyamala*), Dharani Pandita (*Bijjala Raya Charita* and *Varangana Charita*), Amrita Nandi (*Dhanvantari Nighantu*), Vidyanatha (*Prataparudriya*), Ganeshvara (*Sahitya Sanjivana*), Harabhakta, a Veerashaiva mendicant (*Vedabhashya*, 1300), and Siva Kavi (author of *Basava Purana* in 1330).

Jain Epics

During the early 12th-century ascendancy of the Hoysalas, the kings of the dynasty entertained imperial ambitions. King Vishnuvardhana wanted to perform Vedic sacrifices befitting an emperor, and surpass his overlords, the Western Chalukyas, in military and architectural achievements. This led to his conversion from Jainism to Vaishnavism. Around the same time, the well-known philosopher Ramanujacharya sought refuge from the Cholas in Hoysala territory and popularised the Sri Vaishnava faith, a sect of Vaishnavism. Although Jains continued to dominate culturally in what is now the southern Karnataka region for a while, these social changes would later contribute to the decline of Jain literary output. The growing political clout of the Hoysalas attracted many bards and scholars to their court, who in turn wrote panegyrics on their patrons.

Nagachandra, a scholar and the builder of the Mallinatha Jinalaya (a Jain temple in honour of the 19th Jain tirthankar, Mallinatha, in Bijapur, Karnataka), wrote *Mallinathapurana* (1105), an account of the evolution of the soul of the Jain saint. According to some historians, King Veera Ballala I was his patron. Later, he wrote his *magnum opus*, a Jain version of the Hindu epic Ramayana called *Ramachandra Charitapurana* (or *Pampa Ramayana*). Written in the traditional *champu* metre and in the *Pauma charia* tradition of Vimalasuri, it is the earliest extant version of the epic in the Kannada language.

The work contains 16 sections and deviates significantly from the original epic by Valmiki. Nagachandra represents King Ravana, the villain of the Hindu epic, as a tragic hero, who in a moment of weakness commits the sin of abducting Sita (wife of the Hindu god Rama) but is eventually purified by her devotion to Rama. In a further deviation, Rama's loyal brother Lakshmana (instead of Rama) kills Ravana in the final battle. Eventually, Rama takes *jainadiksha* (converts to Jainism), becomes an ascetic and attains *nirvana* (enlightenment). Considered a complementary work to the *Pampa Bharatha* of Adikavi Pampa (941, a Jain version of the epic Mahabharata), the work earned Nagachandra the honorific "Abhinava Pampa" ("new Pampa"). Only in the Kannada language do Jain versions exist of the Hindu epics, the Mahabharata and Ramayana, in addition to their brahminical version.

Kanti (1108), known for her wit and humour, was one of the earliest female poets of the Kannada language and a contemporary of Nagachandra, with whom she indulged in debates and repartees. Rajaditya, a native of either Puvinabage or Raibhag (the modern Belgaum district), was in the Hoysala court during the days of King Veera Ballala I and King Vishnuvardhana. He wrote in easy verse on arithmetic and other mathematical topics and is credited with three of the earliest writings on mathematics in the Kannada language: *Vyavaharaganita, Kshetraganita* and *Lilavati.* Udayaditya, a Chola prince, authored a piece on rhetoric called *Udayadityalankara* (1150). It was based on Dandin's Sanskrit *Kavyadarsa.*

Age of Harihara

Harihara (or Harisvara) was a noted Kannada poet and writer in the 12th century. A native of Halebidu in modern Hassan district, he came from a family of accountants (*Karnikas*) and initially served in that capacity in the court of Hoysala King Narasimha I (1152–1173 CE). Later, he moved to Hampi and authored many classics. Among his important writings, the *Girijakalyana* written in *champu* metre (mixed prose-verse) is considered one of the classics of Kannada language.

Famous Writings

Magnum Opus

Harihara, although one of the earliest Veerashaiva writers, was not part of the famous *Vachana* literary tradition. He wrote under the patronage of King Narasimha I. He wrote his *magnum opus,* the *Girijakalyana* ("Marriage of the mountain born Goddess") in the Kalidasa tradition, though employing the old Jain *champu* style, with the story leading to the marriage of God Shiva and his consort Parvati in ten sections. Harihara brings out his ability for narration while describing the lamentation of Rati for Kama, and the intense love and devotion of Parvati for Shiva.

Though known for his *magnum opus,* his poetic talent found complete expression in his lyrical and narrative *ragale* poems. It was Harihara who popularised the *ragale* (couplets in blank verse), a metre native to Kannada language. In a deviation from the norm of the day, Harihara avoided glorifying famous mortals and continued the Jain tradition of "glorifying the spirit" and the "conquest of evil within oneself". So against eulogising earthly mortals was Harihara, legend has it that he physically abused his protege Raghavanka for writing about King Harishchandra in the work *Harishchandra Kavya* (c. 1200).

Ragale Writings

Shivaganada Ragale

Harihara is credited with more than one hundred poems in

the *Ragale* metre and is called the *Nambiyanana ragale* (also called *Shivaganada ragale* or *Saranacharitamanasa*–"The holy lake of the lives of the devotees", c. 1160) after the saint Nambiyana. In this writing, which is a eulogy of the 63 saints of early Shaivism (devotion to God Shiva), of the later social reformers such as Basavanna, Allama Prabhu and Akka Mahadevi, and of God Virupaksha (a form of Hindu god Shiva), Harihara express emotions as few poets could. Referenced in this writing is the Tamil epic *Periyapuranam*.

Basavarajadevara Ragale

Another important writing, though partially available, in the same metre was *Basavarajadevara ragale*, on the life of Basavanna emphasising the protagonist's compassion for devotees of God Shiva. This work is the earliest biography of Basavanna from which 13 out of 25 sections are available and are considered important because the author was a near contemporary of his protagonist and set the trend for future biographers. Harihara thus became the earliest poetic biographer in the Kannada language. Interesting details of Basavanna's life are narrated by Harihara, some of which contradict commonly held beliefs.

The author, who does not appear to be personally acquainted with his protagonist, mixed facts with some mythtological details. While popular theory holds that Basavanna left his native place over a difference of opinion with his father regarding the brahminical initiation ritual (sacred thread ceremony), Harihara's account states Basavanna lost his parents early in life and was cared for by his grandmother.

Later he discarded his thread and left for Sangama, indicating he was already initiated. Regarding Basavanna's employment under King Bijjala II, while popular theory holds that Basavanna succeeded his deceased maternal uncle (whose daughter he was married to) as the treasurer of the King, according to Harihara, Basavanna's introduction to the king was made by the incumbent treasurer Sidhdandadhisa, whom he later succeeeded to the post.

Harihara's other writings were *Pushpa ragale, Marichanana ragale* and *Pampa sataka* (in the *shataka* metre, string of 100 verses), in praise of lord Virupaksha of Hampi. For his poetic talent, he has earned the honorific "poet of exuberance" (*utsava kavi*).

Ashtaka Writing

Mudigeya ashtaka (1200) is an important *ashtaka* (eight line verse) by Harihara. Legend has it that once when Harihara bowed down in prayer to his God (Shiva), the "Rudraksha" flowers in his headgear (a *mudige*) fell on the floor. Seeing this, the devotees who had gathered there derided Harihara for wearing the headgear. In response, Harihara composed the *ashtaka* extempore in honour of his deity and included a challenging phrase "I have laid the *mudige* on the floor, let me see who can pick it up".

Famous among Vaishnava writers and the first brahmin writer (of the Smartha sect) of repute, Rudrabhatta wrote *Jagannatha Vijaya* (1180) in a style considered a transition between ancient and medieval Kannada. Chandramouli, a minister in the court of King Veera Ballala II, was his patron. The writing, in *champu* metre, is about the life of the god Krishna. Leading to the god's fight with Banasura, it is based on an earlier writing, *Vishnupurana*.

Nemichandra, court poet of King Veera Ballala II and the Silhara King Lakshmana of Kholapur, wrote *Lilavati Prabandham* (1170), the earliest available true fiction (and hence a novel) in Kannada, with an erotic bent. Written in the *champu* metre, with the ancient town Banavasi as the background, it narrates the love story of a Kadamba prince and a princess who eventually marry after facing many obstacles. The story is based on a c. 610 Sanskrit original called *Vasavadatta* by Subhandu. His other work, *Neminathapurana*, unfinished on account of his death (and hence called *Ardhanemi* or "incomplete Nemi"), details the life of the 22nd Jain tirthankar Neminatha while treating the life of the god Krishna from a Jain angle.

Palkuriki Somanatha, a native of modern Karnataka or Andhra Pradesh, is considered one of the foremost multi-lingual Shaiva (or Shiva-following) poets of the 12th and 13th centuries. Historians are divided about the time and place of his birth and death and his original faith. He was adept in the Sanskrit, Telugu and Kannada languages. He was a devotee of Basavanna (the founder of the Veerashaiva movement), and all his writings propagate that faith. It is generally accepted that he was born a brahmin and later adopted the Shaiva faith, although according to the scholar Bandaru Tammayya he was born a *Jangama* (follower of the Shaiva faith). His time of birth has been identified as either the 12th century or late 13th century. In Kannada, his most important writings are *Silasampadane, Sahasragananama* and *Pancharatna*. His well-known poems, written in the *ragale* metre, are *Basava ragale, Basavadhya ragale* and *Sadguru ragale*. He is known to have humbled many Vaishnava poets in debates.

Other well-known personalities from the 12th century included several Jain writers. These include Aggala, who authored *Chandraprabhapurana* (1189), an account of the life of the eighth Jain tirthankar Chandraprabha; Sujanottamsa, who wrote a panegyric on Gomateshwara of Shravanabelagola; and Vritta Vilasa, who authored *Sastra sara* and *Dharmaparikshe* (1160). The latter was Vilasa's version of the Sanskrit original of the same name written by Amitagati c. 1014. In this *champu* writing, the author narrates the story of two Kshatriya princess who went to Benares and exposed the vices of the gods after discussions with the brahmins there.

The author questions the credibility of Hanuman (the Hindu monkey god) and the Vanaras (monkey-like humanoids in the Hindu epic Ramayana). Although controversial, the work sheds useful information on contemporary religious beliefs. Kereya Padmarasa, a Veerashaiva poet patronised by King Narasimha I, wrote *Dikshabodhe* in the *ragale* metre in 1165. He would later become the protagonist of a biographical work called *Padmarajapurana* written by his descendant Padmanaka in c. 1400. The brahmin poet Deva Kavi authored a romance piece called *Kusumavali* (1200), and brahmin poet Kavi Kama (12th century) authored a treatise called *Sringara-ratnakara* on the *rasa* (flavor) of poetical sentiment. Sumanobana (1170) was a poet-grammarian and the *Katakacharya* ("military teacher") under King Narasimha I. He was also a priest in Devagiri, the Seuna Yadava capital.

Jain–Veerashaiva Conflict

Harihara's nephew and protege, the dramatic poet Raghavanka of Hampi, whose style is compared to that of 10th-century poet Ranna, was the first to establish the *shatpadi* metre in Kannada literature in the epic *Harishchandra Kavya* (1200). According to L. S. Seshagiri Rao, it is believed that in no other language has the story of King Harishchandra been interpreted in this way. The writing is an original in tradition and inspiration that fully develops the potential of the *shatpadi* metre. The narration has many noteworthy elegiac verses such as the mourning of Chandramati over the death of her young son Lohitashva from snake bite.

The very writing that made Raghavanka famous was rejected by his guru, Harihara. His other well-known writings, adhering to strict Shaiva principles and written to appease his guru, are the *Siddharama charitra* (or *Siddharama Purana*), a larger than life stylistic eulogy of the compassionate 12th-century Veerashaiva saint, Siddharama of Sonnalige; the *Somanatha charitra*, a propagandist work that describes the life of saint Somayya (or Adaiah) of Puligere (modern Lakshmeshwar), his humiliation by a Jain girl and his revenge; the *Viresvara charita*, a dramatic story of the blind wrath of a Shaiva warrior, Virabhadra; the *Hariharamahatva*, an account of the life of Harisvara of Hampi; and *Sarabha charitra*. The last two classics are considered lost.

In 1209, the Jain scholar, minister, builder of temples and army commander Janna wrote, among other classics, *Yashodhara Charite*, a unique set of stories in 310 verses dealing with sadomasochism, transmigration of the soul, passion gone awry and cautionary morals for human conduct. The writing, although inspired by Vadiraja's Sanskrit classic of the same name, is noted for its original interpretation, imagery and style. In one story, the poet tells of the infatuation of a man for his friend's wife. Having killed his friend, the man abducts the wife, who dies of grief. Overcome by repentance, he burns himself on the funeral pyre of the woman. The stories of infatuation reach a peak when Janna writes about the attraction of Amrutamati, the queen, to the ugly mahout Ashtavakra, who pleases the queen with kicks and whip lashes. This story has piqued the interest of modern researchers. In honour of this work, Janna received the title *Kavichakravarthi* ("Emperor among poets") from his patron, King Veera Ballala II. His other classic, *Anathanatha Purana* (1230), is an account of the life of the 14th tirthankar Ananthanatha.

Andayya, taking a non-conformist path that was never repeated in Kannada literature, wrote *Madana Vijaya* ("Triumph of cupid", 1217–1235) using only pure Kannada words (*desya*) and naturalised Sanskrit words (*tadbhava*) and totally avoiding assimilated Sanskrit words (*tatsamas*). This is seen by some as a rebuttal meant to prove that writing Kannada literature without borrowed Sanskrit words was possible. The poem narrates the story of the moon being imprisoned by the god Shiva in his abode in the Himalayas. In his anger, Kama (Cupid, the god of love, also called Manmata) assailed Shiva with his arrows only to be cursed by Shiva and separated from his beloved. Kama then contrived to rid himself of Shiva's curse. The work also goes by other names such as *Sobagina Suggi* ("Harvest of Beauty"), *Kavane Gella* ("Cupid's Conquest") and *Kabbigara-kava* ("Poets defender"). Kama has an important place in Jain writings even before Andayya. The possibility that this writing was yet another subtle weapon in the intensifying conflict between the dominant Jains and the Veerashaivas, whose popularity was on the rise, is not lost on historians.

Mallikarjuna, a Jain ascetic, compiled an anthology of poems called *Suktisudharnava* ("Gems from the poets") in 1245 in the court of King Vira Someshwara. Some interesting observations have been made by scholars about this important undertaking. While the anthology itself provides insight into poetic tastes of that period (and hence qualifies as a "history of Kannada literature"), it also performs the function of a "guide for poets", an assertive method of bridging the gap between courtly literary intelligentsia and folk poetry. Being a guide for "professional intellectuals", the work, true to its nature, often includes poems eulogising kings and royalty but completely ignoring poems of the 12th-century vachana canon (Veerashaiva folk literature). However, the selection of poems includes contributions from Harihara, the non-conformist Veerashaiva writer. This suggests a compromise by which the author attempts to include the "rebels".

Other notable writers of the early 13th century were Bhanduvarma, author of *Harivamsabhyudaya* and *Jiva sambhodana* (1200), the latter bearing on morals and renunciation, and written addressing the soul; Maghanandycharya, author of *Sastrasara Samuccaya-tiku* (1209); Hastimalla, who worte *Purvapurana;* Chandrama, author of *Karkala Gomateshvara charite*, and Sisumayana, who introduced a new form of composition called *sangatya* in 1232. He wrote an allegorical poem called *Tripuradahana* ("Burning of the triple fortress") and *Anjanacharita*. The latter work was inspired by Ravisena's Sanskrit *Padma charitra*. Somaraja, a Veerashaiva scholar, wrote a eulogy of Udbhata, the ruler of Gersoppa, and called it *Sringarasara* (or *Udbhatakavya*, 1222). Other Jain writers were Parsva Pandita, author of *Paravanathapurana*, and Gunavarma II, the author of the story of the ninth Jain tirthankar

Pushpadanta called *Pushpadanta purana* (both were patronised by the Ratta kings of Saundatti). Polalva Dandanatha, a commander, minister, and the builder of the Harihareshwara temple in Harihar, wrote *Haricharitra* in 1224. He was patronised by King Veera Ballala II and his successor, King Vira Narasimha II. Puligere Somanatha authored a book on morals called *Somesvarasataka*.

Consolidation of Grammar

Keshiraja was a notable writer and grammarian of the 13th century. He came from a family of famous poet-writers. Although five of Keshiraja's writings are not traceabie, his most enduring work on Kannada grammar, *Shabdamanidarpana* ("Mirror of Word Jewels", 1260), is available and testifies to his scholarly acumen and literary taste. True to his wish that his writing on grammar should "last as long as the sun, the moon, the oceans and the Meru mountain lasted", *Shabdamanidarpana* is popular even today and is considered a standard authority on old Kannada grammar. It is prescribed as a textbook for students of graduate and post-graduate studies in the Kannada language. Although Keshiraja followed the model of Sanskrit grammar (of the Katantra school) and that of earlier writings on Kannada grammar (by King Amoghavarsha I of the 9th century and grammarian Nagavarma II of 1145), his work has originality. Keshiraja's lost writings are *Cholapalaka Charitam, Sri Chitramale, Shubhadraharana, Prabodhachandra* and *Kiratam* (or *Kiratarjuniyam*).

A major development of this period that would have a profound impact on Kannada literature even into the modern age was the birth of the Haridasa ("servants of Hari or Vishnu") movement. This devotional movement, although reminiscent in some ways of the Veerashaiva movement of the 12th century (which produced Vachana poetry and taught devotion to the god Shiva), was in contrast intimately devoted to the Hindu god Vishnu as the supreme God. The inspiration behind this movement was the philosophy of Madhvacharya of Udupi. Naraharitirtha (1281) is considered the first well-known haridasa and composer of Vaishnava devotional songs in Kannada. Before his induction into the Madhva order, he had served as a minister in the court of Kalinga. The Vaishnava poetry however disappeared for about two centuries after Naraharitirtha's death before resurfacing as a popular form of folk literature during the rule of the Vijayanagara

Empire. Only three of Naraharitirtha's compositions are available today.

Other writers worthy of mention are Mahabala Kavi, the author of *Neminathapurana* (1254), an account of the 22nd Jain tirthankar Neminatha, and Kumudendu, author of a Jain version of the epic Ramayana in *shatpadi* metre in 1275. The effort was influenced by *Pampa Ramayana* of Nagachandra. Kumara Padmarasa, son of Kereya Padmarasa, wrote the *Sananda Charitre* in *shatpadi* metre. Ratta Kavi, a Jain noble, wrote a quasi-scientific piece called *Rattasutra* (or *Rattamala*) in 1300. The writing bears on natural phenomena such rain, earthquakes, lightning, planets and omens. Towards the end of the Hoysala rule, Nagaraja wrote *Punyasrava* in 1331 in *champu* style, a work that narrates the stories of puranic heroes in 52 tales and is said to be a translation from Sanskrit.

Sanskrit Writings

The Vaishnava movement in the Kannada-speaking regions found momentum after the arrival of the philosopher Ramanujacharya (1017–1137). Fleeing possible persecution from the Chola King (who was a Shaiva), Ramanujacharya sought refuge initially in Tondanur and later moved to Melkote. But this event had no impact on Vaishnava literature in Hoysala lands at that time. However, the teachings of Madhvacharya (1238–1317), propounder of the *Dvaita* philosophy, did have a direct impact on Vaishnava literature, in both the Sanskrit and Kannada languages. This body of writings is known as *haridasa sahitya* (haridasa literature).

Born as Vasudeva in Pajaka village near Udupi in 1238, he learnt the Vedas and Upanishads under his guru Achyutapreksha. He was initiated into *sanyasa* (asceticism) after which he earned the name Madhvacharya (or Anandatirtha). Later, he disagreed with the views of his guru and began to travel India. He successfully debated with many scholars and philosophers during this time and won over Naraharitirtha, a minister in Kalinga, who would later become Madhvacharya's first notable disciple.

Unlike Adi Shankaracharya (788–820) who preached Advaita philosophy (monism) and Ramanujacharya who propounded Vishishtadvaita philosophy (qualified monism), Madhvacharya taught the Dvaita philosophy (dualism). Madhvacharya taught complete devotion to the Hindu god Vishnu, emphasising

Jnanamarga or the "path of knowledge", and insisted that the path of devotion "can help a soul to attain elevation" (*Athmonathi*). He was however willing to accept devotion to other Hindu deities as well. He wrote 37 works in Sanskrit including *Dwadasha Sutra* (in which his devotion to the god Vishnu found full expression), *Gita Bhashya, Gita Tatparya Nirnaya, Mahabharata Tatparya Nirnaya, Bhagavata Tatparya Nirnaya, Mayavada Khandana* and *Vishnu Tattwa Nirnaya*. To propagate his teachings he established eight monasteries near Udupi, the Uttaradhi monastery, and the Raghavendra monastery in Mantralayam (in modern Andhra Pradesh) and Nanjanagud (near modern Mysore).

The writings of Madhvacharya and Vidyatirtha (author of *Rudraprshnabhashya*) may have been absorbed by Sayanacharya, brother of Vidyaranya, the patron saint of the founders of the Vijayanagara empire in the 14th century. Bharatasvamin (who was patronised by Hoysala King Ramanatha) wrote a commentary on *Samaveda*, Shadgurusishya wrote commentary on *Aitareya Brahmana* and *Aranyaka*, and Katyayana wrote *Sarvanukramani*. A family of hereditary poets whose names have not been identified held the title "Vidyacharkravarti" (poet laureate) in the Hoysala court. One of them wrote *Gadyakarnamrita*, a description of the war between Hoysala king Vira Narasimha II and the Pandyas, in the early 13th century. His grandson with the same title, in the court of king Veera Ballala III, composed a poem called *Rukminikalyana* in 16 *kandas* and wrote commentaries (on poetics) on the *Alankarasarvasva* and *Kavyaprakasa*. Kalyani Devi, a sister of Madhvacharya, and Trivikrama, his disciple, wrote commentaries on the Dvaita philosophy. To Trivikrama is ascribed a poem narrating the story of Usha and Aniruddha called *Ushaharana*. Narayana Pandita composed *Madhwavijaya, Manimanjari* and a poem called *Parijataharana*. The Jain writer Ramachandra Maladhari authored *Gurupanchasmriti*.

Literature after the Hoysalas

Literary developments during the Hoysala period had a marked influence on Kannada literature in the centuries to follow. These developments popularised folk metres which shifted the emphasis towards *desi* (native or folk) forms of literature. With the waning of Jain literary output, competition between the Veerashaiva and Vaishnava writers came to the fore. The Veerashaiva writer

Chamarasa (author of *Prabhulingalile*, 1425) and his Vaishnava competitor Kumaravyasa (*Karnata Bharata Kathamanjari*, 1450) popularised the *shatpadi* metric tradition initiated by Hoysala poet Raghavanka, in the court of Vijayanagara King Deva Raya II. Lakshmisa, the 16th–17th century writer of epic poems, continued the tradition in the *Jaimini Bharata*, a work that has remained popular even in the modern period. The *tripadi* metre, one of the oldest in the Kannada language (Kappe Arabhatta inscription of 700), which was used by Akka Mahadevi (*Yoganna trividhi*, 1160), was popularised in the 16th century by the mendicant poet Sarvajna. Even Jain writers, who had dominated courtly literature throughout the classical period with their Sanskritic *champu* style, began to use native metres. Among them, Ratnakaravarni is famous for successfully integrating an element of worldly pleasure into asceticism and for treating the topic of eroticism with discretion in a religious epic written in the native *sangatya* metre (a metre initiated by Hoysala poet Sisumayana), his *magnum opus*, the *Bharatadesa Vaibhava* (c. 1557).

Though the Vaishnava courtly writings in Kannada began with the Hoysala poet Rudrabhatta and the devotional song genre was initiated by Naraharitirtha, the Vaishnava movement began to exert a strong influence on Kannada literature only from the 15th century on. The Vaishnava writers consisted of two groups who seemed to have no interaction with each other: the Brahmin commentators who typically wrote under the patronage of royalty, and the Bhakti (devotion) writers (also known as haridasas) who played no role in courtly matters.

The Bhakti writers took the message of God to the people in the form of melodious songs composed using folk genres such as the *kirthane* (a musical composition with refrain, based on tune and rhythm), the *suladi* (a composition based on rhythm) and the *ugabhoga* (a composition based on melody). Kumara Vyasa and Timmanna Kavi were well-known among the Brahmin commentators, while Purandara Dasa and Kanaka Dasa were the most notable of the Bhakti writers. The philosophy of Madhvacharya, which originated in the Kannada-speaking region in the 13th century, spread beyond its borders over the next two centuries. The itinerant haridasas, best described as mystic saint-poets, spread the philosophy of Madhvacharya in simple Kannada, winning mass appeal by preaching devotion to God and extolling the virtues of *jnana* (enlightenment), *bhakti* (devotion) and *vairagya* (detachment).

Vachana poetry, developed in reaction to the rigid caste-based Hindu society, attained its peak in popularity among the under-privileged during the 12th century. Though these poems did not employ any regular metre or rhyme scheme, they are known to have originated from the earlier *tripadi* metrical form. The Veerashaivas, who wrote this poetry, had risen to influential positions by the Vijayanagara period (14th century). Court ministers and nobility belonging to the faith, such as Lakkanna Dandesa and Jakkanarya, not only wrote literature but also patronised talented writers and poets. Veerashaiva anthologists of the 15th and 16th centuries began to collect Shaiva writings and vachana poems, originally written on palm leaf manuscripts. Because of the cryptic nature of the poems, the anthologists added commentaries to them, thereby providing their hidden meaning and esoteric significance. An interesting aspect of this anthological work was the translation of the Shaiva canon into Sanskrit, bringing it into the sphere of the Sanskritic (*marga* or main stream as opposed to *desi* or folk) cultural order.

Architecture

Hoysala architecture is the building style developed under the rule of the Hoysala Empire between the 11th and 14th centuries, in the region known today as Karnataka, a state of India. Hoysala influence was at its peak in the 13th century, when it dominated the Southern Deccan Plateau region. Large and small temples built during this era remain as examples of the Hoysala architectural style, including the Chennakesava Temple at Belur, the Hoysaleswara Temple at Halebidu, and the Kesava Temple at Somanathapura. Other examples of fine Hoysala craftsmanship are the temples at Belavadi, Amruthapura, Hosaholalu, Arasikere and Nuggehalli. Study of the Hoysala architectural style has revealed a negligible Indo-Aryan influence while the impact of Southern Indian style is more distinct.

The vigorous temple building activity of the Hoysala Empire was due to the social, cultural and political events of the period. The stylistic transformation of the *Karnata* temple building tradition reflected religious trends popularized by the Vaishnava and Virashaiva philosophers as well as the growing military prowess of the Hoysala kings who desired to surpass their Western Chalukya overlords in artistic achievement. Temples built prior to Hoysala independence in the mid-12th century reflect significant Western Chalukya influences, while later temples retain some features salient to Chalukyan art but have additional inventive decoration and ornamentation, features unique to Hoysala artisans. About one hundred temples have survived in present-day Karnataka state, mostly in the Malnad (hill) districts, the native home of the Hoysala kings.

As popular tourist destinations in Karnataka, Hoysala temples offer an opportunity for pilgrims and students of architecture to examine medieval Hindu architecture in the *Karnata Dravida* tradition. This tradition began in the 7th century under the patronage of the Chalukya dynasty of Badami, developed further under the Western Chalukyas of Basavakalyan in the 11th century and finally transformed into an independent style by the 12th century during the reign of the Hoysalas. Medieval Kannada language inscriptions displayed prominently at temple locations give details of the temples and offer information about the history of the Hoysala dynasty.

Temple Deities

Hinduism is a combination of secular and sacred beliefs, rituals, daily practices and traditions that has evolved over the course of over two thousand years and embodies complex symbolism combining the natural world with philosophy. Hindu temples began as simple shrines housing a deity and by the time of the Hoysalas had evolved into well articulated edifices in which worshippers sought transcendence of the daily world. Hoysala temples were not limited to any specific organised tradition of Hinduism and encouraged pilgrims of different Hindu devotional movements. The Hoysalas usually dedicated their temples to Lord Shiva or to Lord Vishnu (two of the major Hindu gods), but they occasionally chose a different deity.

Worshippers of Shiva are called Shaivas or Lingayats and worshippers of Vishnu are called Vaishnavas. While King Vishnuvardhana and his descendants were Vaishnava by faith, records show that the Hoysalas maintained religious harmony by building as many temples dedicated to Shiva as they did to Vishnu. Most of these temples have secular features with broad themes depicted in their sculptures. This can be seen in the famous Chennakesava Temple at Belur dedicated to Vishnu and in the Hoysaleswara temple at Halebidu dedicated to Shiva. The Kesava temple at Somanathapura is different in that its ornamentation is strictly Vaishnavan. Generally Vaishnava temples are dedicated to Keshava (or to Chennakeshava, meaning "Beautiful Vishnu") while a small number are dedicated to Lakshminarayana and Lakshminarasimha (Narayana and Narasimha both being avatars, or physical manifestations, of Vishnu) with Lakshmi, consort of Vishnu, seated at his feet. Temples dedicated to Vishnu are always named after the deity. The Shaiva temples have a Shiva linga, symbol of fertility and the universal symbol of Shiva, in the shrine. The names of Shiva temples can end with the suffix *eshwara* meaning "Lord of". The name "Hoysaleswara", for instance, means "Lord of Hoysala".

The temple can also be named after the devotee who commissioned the construction of the temple, an example being the Bucesvara temple at Koravangala, named after the devotee Buci. The most striking sculptural decorations are the horizontal rows of exquisitely detailed, intricately carved images of gods, goddesses and their attendants on the outer temple wall panels. The Doddagaddavalli Lakshmi Devi ("Goddess of Wealth") Temple is an exception as it is dedicated to neither Vishnu nor Shiva. The defeat of the Jain Western Ganga Dynasty (of present-day south Karnataka) by the Cholas in the early 11th century and the rising numbers of followers of Vaishnava Hinduism and Virashaivism in the 12th century was mirrored by a decreased interest in Jainism. However, two notable locations of Jain worship in the Hoysala territory were Shravanabelagola and Kambadahalli. The Hoysalas built Jain temples to satisfy the needs of its Jain population, a few of which have survived in Halebidu containing icons of Jain tirthankaras. They constructed stepped wells called *Pushkarni* or *Kalyani*, the ornate tank at Hulikere being an example. The tank has twelve minor shrines containing Hindu deities.

The two main deities found in Hoysala temple sculpture are Lord Shiva and Lord Vishnu in their various forms and avatars (incarnations). Shiva is usually shown with four arms holding a trident and a small drum among other emblems that symbolise objects worshiped independently of the divine image with which they are associated. Any male icon portrayed in this way is Shiva although a female icon may sometimes be portrayed with these attributes as Shiva's consort, Parvati. Various depictions of Lord Shiva show him in action, such as slaying a demon or dancing on the head of an elephant. He is often accompanied by his consort Parvati or shown with Nandi the bull. He may be represented as Bhairava, another of Shiva's many manifestations.

A male figure depicted holding certain objects such as a conch (symbol of eternal, heavenly space) and a wheel (eternal time and destructive power) is Vishnu. If a female figure is depicted holding these objects, she is seen as his consort, Lakshmi. In all the depictions Vishnu is holding four objects: a conch, a wheel, a lotus and a mace.

These can be held in any of the icon's hands, making possible twenty-four different forms of Vishnu, each with a unique name. Apart from these, Vishnu is depicted in any of his ten *avataras*, which include Vishnu sitting on Anantha (the celestial snake and keeper of life energy), Vishnu with Lakshmi seated on his lap (Lakshminarayana), with the head of a lion disemboweling a demon on his lap (Lakshminarasimha), with head of a boar walking over a demon (Varaha), in the Krishna avatar (as Venugopala or the cow herder playing the Venu (flute}, dancing on the head of the snake Kaliya, lifting a hill such as Govardhana), with his feet over head of a small figure (*Vamana*), with Lakshmi seated on Garuda, and the eagle (stealing the parijata tree).

Temple Complex

A Hindu temple is a place of contact between the gods or deities and man. The focus of a temple is the centre or sanctum sanctorum (garbhagriha) where the image of the deity resides, so temple architecture is designed to move the devotee from outside to the garbhagriha through ambulatory passageways for circumambulation and halls or chambers (*mantapas*) that become increasingly sacred as the deity is approached. Hoysala temples have distinct parts that are merged to form a unified organic whole, in contrast to the temples of Tamil country where different parts of a temple stand independently. Although superficially unique, Hoysala temples resemble each other structurally. They are characterised by a complex profusion of sculpture decorating all the temple parts chiseled of soft soapstone (chloritic schist), a good material for intricate carving, executed mostly by local craftsmen, and exhibit architectural features that distinguish them from other temple architectures of South India.

Most Hoysala temples have a plain covered entrance porch supported by lathe turned (circular or bell-shaped) pillars which were sometimes further carved with deep fluting and moulded with decorative motifs. The temples may be built upon a platform raised by about a metre called a "jagati". The *jagati*, apart from giving a raised look to the temple, serves as a *pradakshinapatha* or "circumambulation path" for circumambulation around the temple, as the *garbagriha* (inner sanctum) provides no such feature. Such temples will have an additional set of steps leading to an open *mantapa* (open hall) with parapet walls. A good example of this style is the Kesava Temple at Somanathapura. The *jagati* which is in unity with the rest of the temple follows a star-shaped design and the walls of the temple follow a zig-zag pattern, a Hoysala innovation. A pair of small shrines, each with a deity and a miniature tower directly facing the entrance, could adorn either side of steps of the *jagati*. This would be repeated for all entrances leading to the *jagati*. Devotees can first complete a ritual circumambulation on the *jagati* starting from the main entrance by walking in a clockwise direction (towards the left) before entering the *mantapa*, following the sculptural clockwise-sequenced reliefs on the outer temple walls depicting a sequence of epic scenes from the Hindu epics. Temples that are not built on a *jagati* can have steps flanked by elephant balustrades (parapets) that lead to the *mantapa* from ground level. An example of a temple that does not exhibit the raised platform is the *Bucesvara* temple in Korvangla, Hassan District. In temples with two shrines (*dvikuta*), the *vimanas* (the shrines or cellae) may be placed either next to each other or on opposite sides. The Lakshmidevi temple at Doddagaddavalli has a minor shrine at each of the four corners of the walled temple complex in addition to five major shrines.

Hoysaleswara Temple

Hoysaleswara temple is a temple dedicated to Hindu God Shiva. It was built in Halebidu (in modern Karnataka state) during the Hoysala Empire rule in the 12th century by King Vishnuvardhana. The construction was completed in 1121 CE. During the early 14th century, Halebidu was sacked and looted by Muslim invaders from northern India and the temple fell into a state of ruin and neglect. Previously known as Dorasamudra or Dwarasamudra, Halebidu is 16 km from Belur, 31 km from Hassan and 149 km from Mysore, in the state of Karnataka, India.

From records it is known that the temple derives its name from the Hoysala ruler at that time, King Vishnuvardhana Hoysaleswara, though interestingly, the construction of the temple was initiated and financed by wealthy Shaiva citizens of the city, prominent among whom were Ketamalla and Kesarasetti. The temple building activity was taken up in competition to the construction of the Chennakesava Temple at Belur, a Vaishnava temple. The temple faces a large tank which was built in the middle of the 11th century and received water through channels from an ancient *anecut* (dam) built over the Yagachi river. The tank preceded the temple by nearly seventy five years. It is one of the largest temples dedicated to God Shiva in South India.

Temple Plan

The temple is a simple *dvikuta vimana* (two shrined), one for "Hoysaleswara" and the other for "Shantaleswara" (after Shantala Devi, queen of king Vishnuvardhana) and is built with chloritic chist (Soapstone, also known as potstone). The temple complex as a whole is elevated on a *jagati* (platform), a feature that became popular in contemporary Hoysala designs. The two shrines which are adjoining, face east and each have a *mantapa* (hall) in front. The two *mantapas* are connected giving a large and imposing view of the hall. Individually, each shrine is smaller than the one at the Chennakesava Temple at Belur and contains a simple *linga*, the universal symbol of Shiva.

The plan of the inside of the temple is simple but the exterior looks different because of the introduction of many projections and recesses in the walls. The towers of the shrines that are missing must have followed the star shape of the shrine, just as in many existing well-preserved towers in other Hoysala temples. The superstructure of the vestibule (which connects the shrine to the *mantapa*), called *sukanasi*, and the row of decorated miniature roofs above the eaves of the hall are all missing. The temple was built at a height that provided the architects sufficient horizontal and vertical space to depict large and small sculptures. The overall effect of the vertical and horizontal lines, the play of the outline, the effect of light and shade and the plan of the projections and recesses all amounts to a "marvellous exhibition of human labor to be found even in the patient east and surpasses anything in Gothic art". The outer walls of these temples contain an intricate array of stone sculptures. The temple of Halebidu, has been described as an "outstanding example of Hindu architecture" and as the "supreme climax of Indian architecture".

The temple has four porches for entry and the one normally used by visitors as main entry today is actually a lateral entrance (north). There is one entry on the south side and two on the east side, facing two large detached open pavilions whose ceiling is supported by lathe turned pillars. All entry porches have miniature shrines as flanking. In addition there is a sanctuary for the Sun God Surya, whose image stands 7 ft (2.1 m) tall. The pavilions enshrine large images of Nandi, the bull, an attendant of Shiva. The pavilions share the same *jagati* as the main temple. As in the Chennakesava temple, this temple originally had an open *mantapa* to which, outer walls with pierced window screens made with the same material were erected, making the *mantapa* a closed one. The window screens are devoid of any art work. The interior of the temple is quite plain except for the lathe turned pillars that run in rows between the north and south entrances. The four pillars in front of each shrine are the most ornate and the only ones that have *madanika* sculptures in their pillar brackets. There are no other *madanikas* in the temple.

Sculptures

The Hoysaleswara temple is most well-known for its wall sculptures that run all along the outer wall, starting with an image of dancing Ganesha on the left hand side of the south entrance and ending with another image of Ganesha on the right hand side of the north entrance. In all there are 240 such images. Perhaps no other Hoysala temple is as sculpturally articulate as this is and these sculptures are "second to none in all of India". The most intricate of all sculptures are found in the lintels over two of the doorways, one on the south side doorway and the other on one of the eastern doorways.

Horizontal Treatment

In this temple, the Hoysala architects have broken from the tradition of using five friezes as the base of the temple, below the large wall sculptures and the window screens. The outer walls have two eaves that run around the temple. The top eaves is at the roof of the temple and the second eaves about a meter below. In between there are decorated miniature towers (aedicule). Below the lower eaves are the wall sculptures and eight friezes. This type of relief work is called horizontal treatment.

Each of the eight friezes carries an array of decoration. Going from the bottom where the temple wall meets the platform, the lowest frieze depicts charging elephants which symbolise strength and stability, above which, in order, are friezes with lions which symbolise courage, floral scrolls as decoration, horses for speed, another band of floral scrolls, depiction of Hindu epics, *makara* (beasts) and finally a frieze with *hansas* (swans). No two animals are alike in a total frieze span of over 200 m. In the epic frieze, the epics are not continuous as they are mixed with other depictions. After the construction of this temple, Hoysala architects used this new kind of horizontal treatment only 50 years later, making it a standard style, but with six friezes.

Garuda Pillar

Another interesting object in the temple complex is the rare *Garuda Sthamba* (Garuda pillar). These are different from *virgals* (hero stones). Garudas were elite bodyguards of the kings and queens. They moved and lived with the royal family and their only purpose was to protect their master. Upon the death of their master, they committed suicide. The rare pillar on the south side depicts heroes brandishing knives and cutting their own heads. The inscription honors Kuruva Lakshma, a bodyguard of Veera Ballala II. A devoted officer, he took his life and that of his wife and other bodyguards after the death of his master. This event is narrated in an old Kannada inscription on the pillar. An 8 ft (2.4 m) tall sculpture of Ganesha including the platform rests at the South entrance.

Chennakesava Temple

The Chennakesava Temple originally called Vijayanarayana Templewas built on the banks of the Yagachi River in Belur, an early capital of the Hoysala Empire. Belur is 40 km from Hassan city and 220 km from Bangalore, in Hassan district of Karnataka state, India. Chennakesava literally means "handsome Kesava" and is a form of Hindu God Vishnu. Belur is well-known for its marvelous temples, built during the rule of Hoysala dynasty, making it and nearby Halebidu, a favored tourist destination in Karnataka.

The temple was commissioned by Hoysala King Vishnuvardhana in 1117 CE. Scholars are divided about the reason why King Vishnuvardhana commissioned the construction of the temple. The military successes of Vishnuvardhana is considered a probable reason. Some scholars believe Vishnuvardhana commissioned the temple to surpass his overlords, the Western Chalukya Empire (who ruled from Basavakalyan), after his military victories against them. According to another theory, Vishnuvardhana was celebrating his victory against the Cholas of Tamil country in the battle of Talakad, which resulted in the annexation of Gangavadi (modern southern Karnataka) by the Hoysalas.

Another explanation points to Vishnuvardhana's conversion from Jainism to Vaishnavism, considering this is predominantly a Vaishnava temple. The Hoysalas employed many noted architects and artisans who developed a new architectural tradition, which some historians call *Karnata Dravida* tradition. A total of 118 inscriptions have been recovered from the temple complex, covering the period between c. 1117 CE to 18th century, which give details of the artists employed, grants made to the temple and renovations.

The main entrance to the complex is crowned by a Rayagopura built during the days of Vijayanagar empire. Within the temple complex, the Chennakesava temple is in the centre, facing east and flanked by Kappe Channigraya temple and a small Lakshmi temple on its right. On its left and to its back is an Andal temple. Two main *Sthambha* (pillar) exist here. The pillar facing the main temple was erected in the Vijayanagar period while the pillar on the right dates from the Hoysala period. This is the first great Hoysala temple, though the artistic idiom is still Western Chalukyan. Hence, over decoration which is seen in later Hoysala temples (including the Hoysaleswara temple at Halebidu and the Keshava temple at Somanathapura) is not visible here.

During later years, the Hoysala art took an inclination towards craftsmanship, with a weakness for minutia. The Chennakesava temple has three entrances and the doorways have decorated sculptures called *dvarapalaka* (doorkeepers) on either side. While the Kappe Channigraya temple is smaller than the Chennakesava temple, it is architecturally significant, though it lacks any sculptural features. The Kappe Chennigraya temple became a *dvikuta* (two shrined temple) with the later addition of a shrine to its original plan. The original shrine has a star-shaped plan while the additional shrine is a simple square. The icon inside is also that of Kesava and was commissioned by Shantala Devi, queen of king Vishnuvardhana.

Temple Plan

The building material used in the Chennakesava temple is chloritic schist (soapstone) and is essentially a simple Hoysala plan built with extraordinary detail. What differentiates this temple from other Hoysala temples of the same plan is the unusually large size of the basic parts of the temple. The temple is a *ekakuta vimana* design (single shrine) of 10.5 m by 10.5 m size. A large vestibule connects the shrine to the *mandapa* (hall) which is one of the main attractions of the temple. The *mandapa* has 60 bays. The superstructure (tower) on top of the *vimana* has been lost over time. The temple is built on a *jagati* (platform).

There is one flight of steps leading to the *jagati* and another flight of steps to the *mantapa*. The *jagati* provides the devotee the opportunity to do a *pradakshina* (circumambulation) around the temple before entering it. The *jagati* carefully follows the staggered square design of the *mantapa* and the star shape of the shrine. The mantapa here was originally an open one. A visitor would have been able to see the ornate pillars of the open *mantapa* from the platform.

The *mantapa* is perhaps the most magnificent one in all of medieval India. The open mantapa was converted into a closed one after about 50 years, during the Hoysala rule. This was done by erecting walls with pierced window screens. The window screens are on top of 2 m high walls.

There are 28 such windows, with star-shaped perforations and bands of foliage, figures and mythological subjects. On one such screen, King Vishnuvardhana and his queen Shanatala Devi are depicted. Another icon depicts the king in a standing posture.

Shrine

The *vimana* (shrine) is at the back of the *mantapa*. Each side of the *vimana* measures 10.5 m and has five vertical sections. Each vertical section comprises a large double storeyed niche in the centre and two heavy pillar like sections on either side. The two pillar-like sections adjoining the niche are rotated about their vertical axis to produce a star-shaped plan for the shrine. The pillar-like section and the niche bear many ornate sculptures, belonging to an earlier style. There are some 60 large sculptures of deities from both Vaishnava and Shaiva faiths. From the shape of the *vimana* it has been inferred that the tower above it would have been of the *Bhumija* style and not the regular star shaped tower that followed the shape of the *vimana*. The *Bhumija* towers, which are intact on the miniature shrines at the entrance of the hall are actually a type of *nagara* (North Indian) tower, being curvilinear in shape. This shape of tower is quite uncommon in pure dravidian architecture. The shrine has a life size (about 6 ft) image of Kesava (a form of Vishnu) with four hands. Each hand holds an attribute; the discus (*chakra*), the mace (*gadha*), the lotus-flower (*Padma*) and the conch (*Shanka*), in clockwise direction. The entrance to the shrine is flanked by life size sculptures of door guardians (*dvarapalaka*).

Pillars and Sculptures

The pillars inside the hall are an attraction and the most popular one is the Narasimha pillar which at one time, it is said, could revolve on its ball bearings. There is a rich diversity about the pillar styles here. While all the 48 pillars and the many ceilings are well decorated, nothing surpasses the finish of the four central pillars and the ceiling they support. These pillars may have been hand chiselled while the others were lathe turned. All of these four pillars bear *madanikas* (*Salabhanjika*–celestial damsels) and there are 42 of them, 4 inside the hall and the rest outside, between the eaves on the outer walls of the hall. They are also called *madanakai*, *salabanjika* or *shilabalika* and epitomise the ideal female form. They are depicted in various forms, such as, dancers, musicians and drummers and are rarely erotic in nature. Some *madanikas* that are popular with tourists are the *Darpana Sundari* (beauty with mirror), "The lady with the parrot", "The huntress" and *Bhasma mohini*. Other interesting sculptures inside the *mantapa* are *Sthamba buttalika* (pillar image) which are more in the Chola style indicating that the Hoysalas may have employed Chola craftsman along with locals. These images have less decor than regular Hoysala sculptures, the *mohini* pillar being an example.

At the base of the outer walls are friezes of charging elephants (650 of them) which symbolise stability and strength, above which are lions which symbolise courage, and further up are horses which symbolise speed. Above the horses are panels with floral designs signifying beauty above which are sculptures depicting the Hindu epics, the Ramayana and the Mahabharata. This style of articulation is called horizontal treatment with friezes. Hoysala artistry preferred to be discreet about eroticism, mingling miniature erotic sculptures in not so conspicuous places such as recesses and niches. Sculptures depict daily life in a broad sense.

The doorways to the *mantapa* have on both sides an image of "Sala slaying a tiger". Though Sala is popularly known to be the founder of the Hoysala empire, there is no support for this theory from scholars. Normally this image is placed on the *sukanasi* (tower over the vestibule) adjoining the main tower. Legend has it that Sala killed the tiger which was about to pounce on the meditating *muni* (saint) who sought Sala's help. Some historians speculate that the legend may have gained importance after the victory of King Vishnuvardhana over the Cholas at Talakad, the tiger being the royal emblem of the Cholas.

Other important sculptures here are the Narasimha (a form of Vishnu) image in the south western corner, Shiva-Gajasura (Hindu God Shiva slaying demon in form of elephant) on the western side, the winged Garuda, a consort of God Vishnu standing facing the temple, dancing Kali, a seated Ganesha, a boy with an umbrella and a king (the Vamana *avatar* or incarnation of Vishnu), Ravana shaking Mount Kailash, Durga slaying demon Mahishasura, standing Brahma, Varaha (*avatar* of Vishnu), Shiva dancing on demon (Andhakasura), Bhairava (*avatar* of Shiva) and the Sun God Surya. The sculptural style of the wall images bear similarities with wall sculptures in contemporary temples of northern Karnataka and adjacent Maharashtra.

Artists

The Hoysala artists, unlike other medieval artists, preferred to sign their work in the form of inscriptions. In doing so, they sometimes revealed fascinating details about themselves, their families, guilds and place of origin. Stone inscriptions and copper plate inscriptions provide more information about them. Ruvari Mallitamma was a prolific artist to whom more than 40 sculptures are attributed. Dasoja and his son Chavana who were from Balligavi in modern Shimoga district made important contributions. Chavana is credited with the work on five *madanikas* and Dasoja with four. Malliyanna and Nagoja created birds and animals in their sculptures. Artists such as Chikkahampa and Malloja are credited with some of the sculptures in the *mantapa.*

Chennakesava Temple at Somanathapura

The Chennakesava Temple located at Somanathapura is one of the finest examples of Hoysala architecture. This temple was built by Soma, a *Dandanayaka* (commander) in 1268 under Hoysala king Narasimha III, when the Hoysala Empire was the major power in South India.

General Plan

The temple is housed inside an impressive high wall and the entrance to the complex is through a porch with tall lathe-turned pillars. The material used for the temple is chloritic schist or soapstone. The main reasons that make the Keshava temple standout amidst the large number of Hoysala monuments are its symmetrical architecture, fine sculptures on equally prominent shrines, and a temple that is surrounded by panels forming a cloister. While there are Hoysala temples with better sculpture and others with better architecture, this temples satisfies all requirements. It was built by the famous architect/sculptor Ruvari Malithamma who was well-known for his expertise in ornamentation.

The temple which is built on a *jagati* (platform) is a *trikuta* (triple shrined) and fully satisfies the terminology as all *vimanas* (shrines) have a superstructure (tower). Inside the temple, each *vimana* has a vestibule that connects it to the main rectangular *mantapa* (hall). Like the shrines, all three vestibules also have their own tower which is called the *sukanasi* (or nose), though it is shorter and hence looks like a low extension of the main superstructure over the shrine. The outer walls of all three shrines, their towers and nose are equally well decorated, making it overall a very well balanced design. The temple stands on a *jagati* (platform) and the three *vimanas* are located at the back and are connected by a common rectangular closed *mantapa*. The *jagati* closely follows the plan of the temple and there is a gallery with lathe-turned pillars all along the sides of the temple complex which adds to the effect. There is one flight of steps that leads to the *jagati* and one that leads from the *jagati* into the *mantapa*. The wide *jagati* invites devotees to follow the ritualistic clockwise circumambulation before entering the temple hall. The full effect of the rectangular hall is seen only when the temple profile is viewed. The hall has 16 bays. The outside wall of the hall is well decorated with relief friezes, and pierced windows screens above them. All the three shrines have a 16 pointed stellate (star-shaped) design and their towers follow the same pattern. Hence the whole structure looks like a rhythmic progression of well decorated projections and recesses. The number of points make the towers look circular

Horizontal Treatment

The temple is of later Hoysala style because it has two eaves running around the temple. The upper eaves is where the tower meets the wall of the shrine. The lower eaves is about a metre below the upper eaves. Between the two eaves are decorative miniature towers (aedicule). Below the lower eaves are a panel of Hindu deities and their attendants. There are nearly 200 such panels. Below these panels are six horizontal mouldings or friezes of equal size with ornate depictions. The six mouldings of the base is divided into two sections. In the lower section, where the *jagati* meets the temple wall, the orderly placement of friezes starts with sculpted procession of elephants, horsemen and a band of foliage. The upper section has depictions from the Hindu epics and puranic scenes executed with detail, *yalis* (or *makara*, an imaginary beast) and *hamsas* (swans). The Ramayana is depicted on the friezes on the south side wall, stories of Hindu God Krishna on the rear and the Mahabharata on the north side. The overall effect of the decorated towers, wall images, friezes is well balanced.

Deity and Sculptures

The ceiling of the hall is supported by lathe turned pillars. Between pillars, the ceiling is domed and intricately decorated.

These decorations include multi-petalled lotuses, banana bud motifs based on stepped ponds and *ananta* (snake) knots symbolising eternity. Of the three shrines, one is of Keshava, but the image is missing from the sanctum. The other two shrines house images of Janardhana and Venugopala (the three images are forms of Vishnu). This is strictly a Vaishnava temple and there is no depiction of any forms of Hindu God Shiva. Other sculptures are of depictions of affluence of that age including members of the royal family riding richly decorated chariots, soldiers and commoners riding horses, camel drawn vehicles, dancers, musicians, hunters armed with bows and arrows and accompanied by their dogs, and heading for a hunt. There are sculptures of palaces of kings protected by armed guards, jewellery such as pendants, necklaces, waistbands and rings and of woman with different hair styles as well.

The names of many architects and sculptors have been discovered from which it is evident that the artists were both local and from outside the region. The famous Ruvari Mallithamma, Masanithamma, Chameya, Rameya, Chaudeya and Nanjeya are considered locals while Pallavachari and Cholavachari are thought of as artists from Tamil country.

Lakshmi Devi temple, Doddagaddavalli

The Lakshimi Devi temple is located in Doddagaddavalli, a village in Hassan District of Karnataka state, India. It is located 16 km from Hassan and lies on the route to the famous temple town, Belur. The town's main attraction, the Lakshmi Devi temple, was built by the Hoysalas in the year 1114 CE during the rule of king Vishnuvardhana. The temple is situated amidst pristine coconut plantations and has a lake at its rear which adds to the scenic beauty.

Lakshmi Devi Temple

It is one of the earliest known temples built in Hoysala style and is built with Chloritic schist or Soapstone. The temple does not stand on a *jagati* (platform) which became popular in later Hoysala temples. The temple is said to have been built by a merchant called Kullahana Rahuta and his wife Sahaja Devi. The temple is a *chatuskuta* construction (four towers) built inside 7 ft tall stone enclosure with the entrance through a porch which is supported by circular lathe turned pillars. Three of the *vimanas* (shrines) have a common square *mantapa* (hall) with 9 bays. The fourth *vimana* is connected to the *mantapa* via an oblong extension consisting of 2 bays. The extension also has two lateral entrances into the temple. All the *vimana* have their original tower (superstructure) intact.

The towers are in Kadamba *nagara* style. Each *vimana* has a vestibule connecting it to the central *mantapa*. On top of the vestibule is its own tower called *sukanasi* (or nose which looks like low extension of the main tower over the shrine). The *sukanasi* is a tier lower than the main tower over the shrine. All the four *sukanasi* are intact and so are the *kalasa* of the main towers. The *sukanasi* holds the Hoysala emblem of Sala fighting the tiger. Of the four towers, three are undecorated and they look stepped pyramidal with a pile of dented horizontal mouldings with the *kalasa* on top. The fourth tower is very well decorated which is typical of Hoysala designs and is the tower of the main shrine that houses the Lakshmi Devi image.

The *mantapa* is open and square. The reason for the square plan is the presence of shrines on all four sides of the *mantapa* with no side open for staggering. There is a separate fifth shrine of Bhairava, an avatar of Lord Shiva. The shrine is complete with its own *vimana* and tower with a *kalasa* on top, a nose and Hoysala emblem on the it. Another unusual feature of the temple is the existence of four more shrines at each corner of the temple complex with two sides of each shrine attached to the courtyard wall. Each of these minor shrines has its own tower, *kalasa* and Hoysala emblem. On the whole the temple complex has nine towers which is unusual for a Hoysala temple.

Overall the temple has the older Hoysala style where there is only one eaves running round the temple where the main towers meet the wall of the shrine. At the base of the wall of the shrines are 5 mouldings and between the mouldings and the eaves, the usual panels of Hoysala sculptures depicting Hindu gods, goddesses and their attendants is missing. Instead, the whole space is taken up by decorative miniature towers on pilasters. The ceiling of the main hall is supported by 18 lathe turned pillars. Inside there are two sculptures of large demonic living corpses called *betala*. The main shrine facing east has a 3 ft tall image of goddess Lakshmi with an attendant on either side. In her four hands, the image holds a conch in the upper right hand, a *chakra* (discuss) in the upper left, a rosary in the lower right and a mace in the lower left. In the shrines facing north, south and west are the idols of Kali, Vishnu, and *Boothanatha* Linga (the universal symbol of Shiva). A sculpture of *Tandaveswara* (dancing Shiva) exists in the circular panel at the center of the ceiling of the *mantapa*. Other important sculptures are those of *Gajalakshmi* (form of Lakshmi), *Thandaveshwara* and *Yoganarasimha* (form of Vishnu) found on the doorway of the temple.

Veera Narayana Temple, Belavadi

The Veera Narayana temple is located in Belavadi, also known as Ekachakranagara, a village in Chikmagalur district of Karnataka state, India. The temple was built by the Hoysala Empire. Belavadi is located 29 km southeast of Chikmagalur town on the Chikmagalur-Javagal highway and 10 km north of Halebidu. It is located at a very convenient distance from the famous temple towns of Belur and Halebidu and a visit to this quiet town is a rewarding experience.

Veeranarayana Temple

This ornate *trikuta* (three toweres) temple was built in 1200 CE by Hoysala Veera Ballala II. The material used is Chloritic schist. Each of the shrines has a complete superstructure (tower on top of shrine) and is one of the largest examples of Hoysala architecture. While the famous temples at Belur and Halebidu are known for their intricate sculptures, this temple is known for its architecture.

The plan of this temple is unique in that two of the shrines face each other on either side of a wide and spacious open *mantapa* (hall) containing 37 bays. There is also an older shrine containing a closed *mantapa* with 13 bays and a closed *mantapa* with 9 bays at the end of which is a central shrine. This third shrine is an older construction and exhibits a perfect Hoysala architectural idiom containing all the basic elements of Hoysala temple. The inner walls of the older shrine are plain but its roof is well decorated. In all, the temple has 59 bays, indicating the use of many pillars, most of which are lathe turned and hence bell shaped while others have carvings on them. The outer wall of the temple shows the older Hoysala style where there is one eaves running around the temple where the superstructure meets the wall of the shrine and below this are decorative towers on pilasters. A panel of Hindu deities and their attendants are below these miniature towers followed by a set of five different mouldings forming the base of the wall.

The newer structure containing the two symmetrical shrines have different plans. One shrine is square while the other is star shaped. The tower of the shrine below the *kalasa* consists of three tiers of decorated miniature roofs. They also have different shaped *Sukanasi* which consist of two tiers of decorated miniature roofs. In all other aspects the two shrines are identical. All shrines have well sculptured decoration on the towers and the sculptures on the walls are bold and look good from a distance. The important sculptures with fine finish are that of Lord Krishna dancing on the head of *Kalia* the serpent and *Garuda* (eagle). This is a Vaishnava temple and all three shrines have images of Lord Vishnu in different forms. The central shrine (older shrine) has an 8 ft (2.4 m) tall image of *Narayana* with four hands which is considered one of the best examples of Hoysala art. It is well elaborated with ornamentation standing on a *padmasana* (lotus seat), the southern shrine has an 8 ft (2.4 m) tall image of *Venugopala* including a *garuda* pedestal (Krishna with flute) and the northern shrine has a 7 ft (2.1 m) tall image of *Yoganarasimha,* sitting in a yoga posture. *Kirtimukhas* (demon faces) are used to make the *vimana* (prayer hall) towers ornate along with other sculptures.

Architectural Elements

Mantapa

The *mantapa* is the hall where groups of people gather during prayers. The entrance to the *mantapa* normally has a highly ornate overhead lintel called a *makaratorana* (*makara* is an imaginary beast and *torana* is an overhead decoration). The open *mantapa* which serves the purpose of an outer hall (outer *mantapa*) is a regular feature in larger Hoysala temples leading to an inner small closed *mantapa* and the shrine(s). The open *mantapas* have seating areas made of stone with the *mantapa's* parapet wall acting as a back rest. The seats may follow the same staggered square shape of the parapet wall. The open *mantapa* is the largest part of the temple and is the place supporting larger congregations of people. The ceiling here is supported by numerous pillars that create many bays. The shape of the open *mantapa* is best described as staggered-square and is the style used in most Hoysala temples. Even the smallest open *mantapa* has 13 bays. The walls have parapets that have half pillars supporting the outer ends of the roof which allow plenty of light making all the sculptural details visible. The *mantapa* ceiling is generally ornate with sculptures, both mythological and floral. The ceiling consists of deep and domical surfaces and contains sculptural depictions of banana bud motifs and other such decorations. The Amruteswara temple in Chikmagalur district has forty-eight domes in the *mahamantapa* ("great open hall").

If the temple is small it will consist of only a closed *mantapa* (enclosed with walls extending all the way to the ceiling) and the shrine. The closed *mantapa*, well decorated inside and out, is larger than the vestibule connecting the shrine and the *mantapa* and has four lathe-turned pillars to support the ceiling, which may be deeply domed. The four pillars divide the hall into nine bays. The nine bays result in nine finely decorated ceilings.. Pierced stone latticework screens placed between pillars to filter the light is a characteristic Hoysala stylistic element.

A porch adorns the entrance to a closed *mantapa*, consisting of an awning supported by two half-pillars (engaged columns) and two parapets, all richly decorated. The closed *mantapa* is connected to the shrine(s) by a vestibule, a square area that also connects the shrines. Its outer walls are finely decorated, but as the size the vestibule is not large, this may not be a conspicuous part of the temple. The vestibule also has a short tower called the *sukanasi* or "nose" upon which is mounted the Hoysala emblem. In Belur and Halebidu, these sculptures are quite large and are placed at all doorways.

The outer and inner *mantapa* (open and closed) have circular lathe-turned pillars having four brackets at the top. Over each bracket stands sculptured figure(s) called *salabhanjika* or *madanika*. The pillars may also exhibit fine ornamental carvings on the surface and no two pillars are alike. This is how Hoysala art differs from the work of their early overlords, the Western Chalukyas, who added sculptural details to the circular pillar base and left the top plain. The lathe-turned pillars are 16, 32, or 64-pointed; some are bell-shaped and have properties that reflect light. The Parsvanatha Basadi at Halebidu is a good example. The shaft of the pillar is a monolith with the base left as a square and with well-sculpted figures adorning the top.

Vimana

The *vimana,* also called the cella, contains the most sacred shrine wherein resides the image of the presiding deity. The *vimana* is often topped by a tower which is quite different on the outside than on the inside. Inside, the vimana is plain and square, whereas outside it is profusely decorated and can be either stellate ("star-shaped") or shaped as a staggered square, or feature a combination of these designs, giving it many projections and recesses that seem to multiply as the light falls on it. Each projection and recess has a complete decorative articulation that is rhythmic and repetitive and composed of blocks and mouldings, obscuring the tower profile. Depending on the number of shrines (and hence on the number of towers), the temples are classified as *ekakuta* (one), *dvikuta* (two), *trikuta* (three), *chatushkuta* (four) and *panchakuta* (five). Most Hoysala temples are *ekakuta, dvikuta* or *trikuta.* In temples with multiple shrines, all essential parts are duplicated for symmetry and balance. A temple's minor shrine usually has its own tower. There are cases where a temple is *trikuta* but has only one tower over the main shrine (in the middle). So the terminology *trikuta* may not be literally accurate. Smaller shrines attached to the outer walls and facing outward from a larger *vimana* are a common feature.

The highest point of the temple (*kalasa*) has the shape of a beautiful water pot and stands on top of the tower. This portion of the *vimana* is often lost due to age and has been replaced with a metallic pinnacle. Below the *kalasa* is a large, highly-sculptured structure resembling a dome which is made from large stones and looks like a helmet. It may be 2 m by 2 m in size and follows the shape of the shrine. Below this structure are domed roofs in a square plan, all of them much smaller and crowned with small *kalasas.* They are mixed with other small roofs of different shapes and are ornately decorated. The tower of the shrine usually has three or four tiers of rows of decorative roofs while the tower on top of the *sukanasi* has one less tier, making the tower look like an extension of the main tower (the "nose"). One decorated roof tier runs on top of the wall of a closed *mantapa* above the heavy eaves of an open *mantapa* and above the porches.

Below the superstructure of the *vimana* are temple "eaves" projecting half a meter from the wall. Below the eaves two different decorative schemes may be found, depending on whether a temple was built in the early or the later period of the empire. In the early temples built prior to the 13th century, there is one eave and below this are decorative miniature towers. A panel of Hindu deities and their attendants are below these towers, followed by a set of five different mouldings forming the base of the wall. In the later temples there is a second eave running about a metre below the upper eaves with decorative miniature towers placed between them. The wall images of gods are below the lower eaves, followed by six different mouldings of equal size. This is broadly termed "horizontal treatment".

The six mouldings at the base are divided in two sections. Going from the very base of the wall, the first horizontal layer contains a procession of elephants, above which are horsemen and then a band of foliage. The second horizontal section has depictions of the Hindu epics and *Puranic* scenes executed with detail. Above this are two friezes of *yallis* or *makaras* (imaginary beasts) and *hamsas* (swans). The *vimana* (tower) is divided into three horizontal sections and is even more ornate than the walls.

Sculpture

Hoysala artists are famous for their sculptural detail, be it in the depiction of the Hindu epics, *yallis,* deities, *kirthimukha* (gargoyles), eroticism or aspects of daily life. Their medium, the soft chlorite schist, enabled a virtuoso carving style. Their workmanship shows an attention paid to precise detail. Every aspect down to a fingernail or toenail is perfected.

Kirthimukha

Kirtimukha (Face-of-Glory) is a Sanskrit word for a fierce demon face with horns, huge fangs, and gaping mouth often used as a decorative motif in Indian and Southeast Asian temple architecture. It is generally placed above openings such as gates, windows and archways.

The monstrous face with bulging eyes sits over the lintel of the gate to the sanctum sanctorum in many Indian temples.

The word *mukha* in Sanskrit means face or mask, and the word *kirti*means glory. The *kirtimukha* is used as a decorative element placed over doors and windows for protection.

Salabhanjika

Salabhanjika refers to the sculpture of a woman, displaying stylized feminine features, standing near a tree and grasping a branch. The name of these figures comes from the Sanskrit *úâlabañjika* meaning 'breaking a branch of a sala tree'. They are also known as *madanakai, madanika* or *shilabalika.*

Artistic Tradition

The salabhanjika is a standard decorative element of Indian sculpture, a graceful stone sculpture representing a young female under a stylized tree in various poses, such as dancing, grooming herself or playing a musical instrument. The salabhanjika's female features, like breasts and hips, are often exaggerated. Frequently these sculpted figures display complex hairdos and an abundance of jewelry.Dr.udai narain roy pointed out that originally salabhanjika referred to a kind of udyana-krida popular among women.

The salabhanjika concept stems from ancient symbolism linking a chaste maiden with the sala tree or the asoka tree through the ritual called *dohada,* or the fertilisation of plants through contact with a young woman. The symbolism changed over the course of time and the salabhanjika became figures used as ornamental carvings, usually located in the area where worshipers engage in circumambulation, near the garbhagriha of many Hindu temples. Placed at an angle, salabhanjika figures also were used in temple architecture as a bracket figures.

Salabhanjikas are also often mentioned in ancient and modern Indian poetry, like in the Malayalam verses:

Salabanjikakal kaikalil kusumathala menthi varavelkkum.

Locations

Some of the most renowned salabanjika sculptures are to be found in the Hoysala temples of Belur, Halebidu and Somanathapura, in south-central Karnataka.

Another less-known location famous for its outstanding salabanjikas is a Chalukya period temple in Jalasangvi, Homnabad Taluk on the Gulbarga-Bidar state highway, at the northern end of Karnataka. Its well-endowed Madanika figures in seductive *tribhanga* poses are *"...moon breasted, swan-waisted and elephant-*

hipped", according to the Indian artistic canons. These older feminine sculptures were the source of inspiration for the later Hoysala bracket-figures.

The *sthamba buttalikas* are pillar images that show traces of Chola art in the Chalukyan touches. Some of the artists working for the Hoysalas may have been from Chola country, a result of the expansion of the empire into Tamil-speaking regions of Southern India. The image of *mohini* on one of the pillars in the *mantapa* (closed hall) of the Chennakeshava temple is a fine example of Chola art.

General life themes are portrayed on wall panels such as the way horses were reined, the type of stirrup used, the depiction of dancers, musicians, instrumentalists, and rows of animals such as lions and elephants (where no two animals are identical). Perhaps no other temple in the country depicts the Ramayana and Mahabharata epics more effectively than the Hoysaleshwara temple at Halebidu.

Erotica was a subject the Hoysala artist handled with discretion. There is no exhibitionism in this, and erotic themes were carved into recesses and niches, generally miniature in form, making them inconspicuous. These erotic representations are associated with the *Shakta* practice. The temple doorway is heavily engraved with ornamentation called *Makaratorana* (*makara* being an imaginary beast) and each side of the doorway exhibits sculptured *Salabhanjika* (maidens).

Apart from these sculptures, entire sequences from the Hindu epics (commonly the Ramayana and the Mahabharata) have been sculpted in a clockwise direction starting at the main entrance. The right to left sequence is the same direction taken by the devotees in their ritual circumambulation as they wind inward toward the inner sanctum. Depictions from mythology such as the epic hero Arjuna shooting fish, the elephant-headed god Ganesha, the Sun god Surya, the weather and war god Indra, and Brahma with Sarasvati are common. Also frequently seen in these temples is Durga, with several arms holding weapons given to her by other gods, in the act of killing a buffalo (a demon in a buffalo's form) and Harihara (a fusion of Shiva and Vishnu) holding a conch, wheel and trident. Many of these friezes were signed by the artisans, the first known instance of signed artwork in India.

Research

Surveys in modern times have indicated that 1000–1500 structures were built by the Hoysalas, of which about a hundred temples have survived to date.

The Hoysala style is an offshoot of the Western Chalukya style, which was popular in the 10th and 11th centuries. It is distinctively Dravidian, and owing to its unique features, Hoysala architecture qualifies as an independent style. While the Hoysalas introduced innovative features into their architecture, they also borrowed features from the earlier great builders of *Karnata* like the Kadambas, Western Chalukyas. These features were the use of chloritic schist or soapstone as a basic building material, pierced stone window screens which were very popular in Hoysala temples, and the *vimana* which follows a stellate pattern. All these features were popular with their early overlords, the Western Chalukyas.

Other features were the stepped style of *vimana* tower called the *Kadamba shikhara,* which was inherited from the Kadambas. Engrained in the craftsmanship of Hoysala sculptors was their knowledge of the effect of light and shade on carved walls, which they used to maximum effect in their sculptures in the numerous projections and recesses. The Hoysala sculpture in all its richness is said to be a challenge to photography. The artistry of the Hoysalas in stone has been compared to the finesse of an ivory worker or a goldsmith. The abundance of jewelry worn by the sculpted figures and the variety of hairstyles and headdresses depicted give a fair idea of the lifestyles of the Hoysala times.

Notable Craftsmen

While the Hoysalas had the services of great architects and sculptors, some names stand out in their history. While medieval Indian artisans preferred to remain anonymous, Hoysala artisans signed their works, which has given researchers fascinating details about their lives, families, guilds, etc. Apart from the architects and sculptors, people of other guilds such as goldsmiths, ivory carvers, carpenters, and silversmiths also contributed to the completion of temples. The artisans were from diverse geographical backgrounds and included famous locals. Prolific architects included Amarashilpi Jakanachari, a native of Kaidala in Tumkur district, who also built temples for the Western Chalukyas. Ruvari

Malithamma built the Kesava Temple at Somanathapura and worked on forty other monuments, including the Amruteshwara temple at Amruthapura.

Malithamma specialised in ornamentation, and his works span six decades. His sculptures were typically signed in shorthand as *Malli* or simply *Ma*. Dasoja and his son Chavana from Balligavi were the architects of Chennakesava Temple at Belur; Kedaroja was the chief architect of the Hoysaleswara Temple at Halebidu. Their influence is seen in other temples built by the Hoysalas as well. Names of other locals found in inscriptions are Maridamma, Baicoja, Caudaya, Nanjaya and Bama, Malloja, Nadoja, Siddoja, Masanithamma, Chameya and Rameya. Artists from Tamil country included Pallavachari and Cholavachari.

Notable Temples

Some famous temples built by the Hoysalas are shown in the table.

Famous Hoysala Temples in Karnataka (1113–1268)

Deity	*Location*	*Year*	*King*
Amruteshwara	Amruthapura	1196	Veera Ballala II
Chennakesava	Aralaguppe	1250	Vira Someshwara
Ishvara	Arsikere	1220	Veera Ballala II
Mallikarjuna	Basaralu	1234	Vira Narasimha II
Chennakesava	Belur	1117	Vishnuvardhana
Viranarayana	Belavadi	1200	Veera Ballala II
Lakshmidevi	Doddagaddavalli	1113	Vishnuvardhana
Hoysaleswara	Halebidu	1120	Vishnuvardhana
Someshvara	Haranhalli	1235	Vira Someshwara
Lakshminarasimha	Haranhalli	1235	Vira Someshwara
Lakshminarayana	Hosaholalu	1250	Vira Someshwara
Lakshminarasimha	Javagallu	1250	Vira Someshwara
Bucheshvara	Koravangala	1173	Veera Ballala II
Nageshvara	Mosale	1200	Veera Ballala II
Chennakesava	Mosale	1200	Veera Ballala II
Lakshminarasimha	Nuggehalli	1246	Vira Someshwara
Kesava	Somanathapura	1268	Narasimha III

Language

The support of the Hoysala rulers for the Kannada language was strong, and this is seen even in their epigraphs, often written in polished and poetic language, rather than prose, with illustrations of floral designs in the margins. According to historian Sheldon Pollock, the Hoysala era saw the complete displacement of Sanskrit, with Kannada dominating as the courtly language. Temples served as local schools where learned Brahmins taught in Sanskrit, while Jain and Buddhist monasteries educated novice monks. Schools of higher learning were called *Ghatikas*. The local Kannada language was widely used in the rising number of devotional movements to express the ecstatic experience of closeness to the deity (*vachanas* and *devaranama*).

Literary works were written in it on palm leaves which were tied together. While in past centuries Jain works had dominated Kannada literature, Shaiva and early Brahminical works became popular during the Hoysala reign. Writings in Sanskrit included poetry, grammar, lexicon, manuals, rhetoric, commentaries on older works, prose fiction and drama. Inscriptions on stone (*Shilashasana*) and copper plates (*Tamarashasana*) were written mostly in Kannada but some were in Sanskrit or were bilingual. The sections of bilingual inscriptions stating the title, genealogy, origin myths of the king and benedictions were generally done in Sanskrit. Kannada was used to state terms of the grants, including information on the land, its boundaries, the participation of local authorities, rights and obligations of the grantee, taxes and dues, and witnesses. This ensured the content was clearly understood by the local people without ambiguity.

10

Pandyan Dynasty

The Pandyan Empire was an ancient Tamil state in South India. The Pandyas, Chola, Chera and Pallava Dynasties are the four Dravidian Tamil Dynasties which ruled South India til the 15th century CE. They initially ruled from Korkai, a seaport on the Southernmost tip of the Indian Peninsula, and in later times moved to Madurai. *Pandyan* was well known since the ancient period, with contacts, even diplomatic, reaching the Roman Empire; during the 13th century AD, Marco Polo mentioned it as the richest empire in existence.

The Pandyan Empire was home to temples including Meenakshi Amman Temple in Madurai, and Nellaiappar Temple built on the bank of the river Thamirabarani in Tirunelveli.

The Pandyas of Southern India are believed to have been founded around five to six centuries before the Christian Era. Their recorded existence and mention are found in records dating to as early as 550 BC. Emperor Augustus of Rome at Antioch knew of the Pandyan of Dramira and received a Pandyan ambassador with letters and gifts from this ancient Tamil Kingdom. Strabo described an ambassador to emperor Augustus Caesar from a South Indian King called Pandyan. The country of the Pandyas, Pandi Mandala, was described as *Pandyan Mediterranea* by *Periplus* and *Modura Regia Pandyan* by Ptolemy.

The early Pandyan Dynasty of the Sangam Literature faded into obscurity upon the invasion of the Kalabhras. The dynasty revived under Kadungon in the early 6th century, pushed the Kalabhras out of the Tamil country and ruled from Madurai. They again went into decline with the rise of the Cholas in the 9th century and were in constant conflict with them. The Pandyas allied themselves with the Sinhalese and the Cheras in harassing the Chola empire until they found an opportunity for reviving their fortunes during the late 13th century.

The Later Pandyas (1150-1350) entered their golden age under Maravman Sundara Pandiyan and Jatavarman Sundara Pandyan (c. 1251), who expanded the empire into Telugu country, conquered Kalinga (Orissa) and invaded and conquered Sri Lanka. They also had extensive trade links with the Southeast Asian maritime empires of Srivijaya and their successors. During their history, the Pandyas were repeatedly in conflict with the Pallavas, Cholas, Hoysalas and finally the Muslim invaders from the Delhi Sultanate. The Pandyan Kingdom finally became extinct after the establishment of the Madurai Sultanate in the 16th century.

The Pandyas excelled in both trade and literature before the Christian Era. They controlled the pearl fisheries along the South Indian coast, between Sri Lanka and India, which produced some of the finest pearls in the known ancient world. Tradition holds that the legendary Sangams were held in Madurai under their patronage, and that some of the Pandya Kings were poets themselves.

Etymology

In Sangam Tamil lexicon the word Pandya means *old country* in contrast with Chola meaning *new country*, Chera meaning *hill country* and Pallava meaning *branch* in Sanskrit. The Chera, Chola and Pandya are the traditional Tamil siblings and together with the Pallavas are the major Kings that ruled ancient Tamilakkam.

Historians have used several sources to identify the origins of the early Pandyan dynasty with the pre-Christian Era and also to piece together the names of the Pandyan kings. Pandyas were the longest ruling dynasty of Indian history. Unfortunately, the exact genealogy of these kings has not been authoritatively established yet.

Sources

Sangam Literature

Various Pandya kings find mention in a number of poems in the Sangam Literature. Among them Nedunjeliyan, 'the victor of

Talaiyalanganam', and Mudukudimi Peruvaludi 'of several sacrifices' deserve special mention. Beside several short poems found in the *Akananuru* and the *Purananuru* collections, there are two major works — *Mathuraikkanci* and the *Netunalvatai* (in the collection of *Pattupattu*) — which give a glimpse into the society and commercial activities in the Pandyan kingdom during the Sangam age.

It is difficult to estimate the exact dates of these Sangam age Pandyas. The period covered by the extant literature of the Sangam is unfortunately not easy to determine with any measure of certainty. Except the longer epics *Silapathikaram* and *Monometallic,* which by common consent belong to an age later than the Sangam age, the poems have reached us in the forms of systematic anthologies. Each individual poem has generally attached to it a colophon on the authorship and subject matter of the poem. The name of the king or chieftain to whom the poem relates and the occasion which called forth the eulogy are also found.

It is from these colophons, and rarely from the texts of the poems themselves, that we gather the names of many kings and chieftains and the poets and poetesses patronized by them. The task of reducing these names to an ordered scheme in which the different generations of contemporaries can be marked off one another has not been easy. To add to the confusions, some historians have even denounced these colophons as later additions and untrustworthy as historical documents.

Any attempt at extracting a systematic chronology from these poems should take into consideration the casual nature of these poems and the wide differences between the purposes of the anthologist who collected these poems and the historian's attempts to arrive at a continuous history. Pandyas are also mentioned by Greek Megesthenes where he writes about southern kingdom being ruled by women. Huien tsang also mentions about it citing his Buddhist friend at Kanchi and calls it Malakutta or Malakotta but the capital city is not mentioned.

Epigraphy

The earliest Pandya to be found in epigraph is Nedunjeliyan, figuring in the *Minakshipuram* record assigned from the second to the first centuries BCE. The record documents a gift of rock-cut beds, to a Jain ascetic. Punch marked coins in the Pandya country dating from around the same time have also been found. Pandyas are also mentioned in the Pillars of Ashoka (inscribed 273-232 BCE). In his inscriptions Asoka refers to the peoples of south India— the Cholas, Cheras, Pandyas and Satiyaputras — as recipients of his Buddhist proselytism. These kingdoms, although not part of the Mauryan Empire, were on friendly terms with Asoka:

"The conquest by Dharma has been won here, on the borders, and even six hundred yojanas (5,400–9,600 km) away, where the Greek king Antiochos rules, beyond there where the four kings named Ptolemy, Antigonos, Magas and Alexander rule, likewise in the south among the Cholas, the Pandyas, and as far as Tamraparni (Sri Lanka)."

Kharavela, the Kalinga king who ruled during the second century BCE, in his Hathigumpha inscription, claims to have destroyed a confederacy of Tamil states ("Tamiradesasanghatam") which had lasted 132 years, and to have acquired a large quantity of pearls from the Pandyas.

Foreign Sources

According to the Mahavamsa-a historical poem written in the Pali language, of the kings of Sri Lanka-King Vijaya (543 BC-505 BC) married a Pandyan Princess. Along with Vijaya, all the men in his crew got married to Madurai girls and arrived Srilanka with a great celebration.

Megasthenes knew of the Pandyan kingdom around 300 BC. He described it in *Indika* as *occupying the portion of India which lies southward and extends to the sea.* According to his account, it had 365 villages, each of which was expected to meet the needs of the royal household for one day in the year. He described the Pandyan queen at the time, *Pandaia* as a daughter of Heracles.

The Periplus of the Erythraean Sea (c. 60-100 CE) describes the riches of a 'Pandian Kingdom':

...Nelcynda is distant from Muziris by river and sea about five hundred stadia, and is of another Kingdom, the Pandian. This place also is situated on a river, about one hundred and twenty stadia from the sea....

According to Hiuen-Tsang, the Pandya country was a depot for sea pearls, its people were harsh and of different religions.

They were very good at trade. The Chinese historian Yu Huan in his 3rd century text, the *Weilüe*, mentions The Kingdom of Panyue:

...The kingdom of Panyue is also called Hanyuewang. *It is several thousand li to the southeast of Tianzhu (Northern India)...The inhabitants are small; they are the same height as the Chinese...*

The Roman emperor Julian received an embassy from a Pandya about 361. A Roman trading centre was located on the Pandyan coast at the mouth of the Vaigai river, southeast of Madurai).

Pandyas also had trade contacts with Ptolemaic Egypt and, through Egypt, with Rome by the first century, and with China by the 3rd century. The 1st century Greek historian Nicolaus of Damascus met, at Damascus, the ambassador sent by a king from Dramira "named Pandyan or, according to others, Porus" to Caesar Augustus around 13 CE (Strabo XV.1-4, and Strabo XV.1-73).

In 1288 and again in 1293 the Venetian traveler Marco Polo visited the Pandyan kingdom and left a vivid description of the land and its people. Polo exclaimed that:

"The darkest man is here the most highly esteemed and considered better than the others who are not so dark. Let me add that in very truth these people portray and depict their gods and their idols black and their devils white as snow. For they say that God and all the saints are black and the devils are all white. That is why they portray them as I have described."

History

The earliest Tamil literary works, such as the Kalittokai, mention a continent called Kumari Nadu or Kumari Kandam, which was believed to have been located to the South of the present-day Kanyakumari tens of thousands of years ago, between the then Kumari and Pahruli rivers. Pandyan kings such as Chenkon, and the Cheras supposedly ruled this country, tens of thousands of years ago. They fought and defeated the Nagas, who might have been a non-Dravidian people, or another species of living beings (the word Naga also means a snake). Kalittokai again mentions a war between the combined forces of Villavars (Cheras) and the Meenavars (Pandyas), who fought a fierce war against the Nagas, their arch-enemies but eventually losing the war and subsequently the Central India to the Nagas. Bhil Meena of North India could be the equivalent rulers in North India.

Also, the Pandyas, along with the Cheras and the Cholas, find mention as one of the three ruling dynasties of the Southern region of the then Bharatavarsha, in the very ancient [Hindu] epic of the Ramayana. They are also mentioned in the Aitareya Aranyaka, and the Mahabharata, where they are (along with the Cheras and the Cholas) believed to have been on the side of the Pandavas in the Great War.

Although there are many instances of the Pandyan Empire being referred to in surviving ancient Hindu texts including the Mahabharata, we currently have no way of determining a cogent genealogy of these ancient kings. In order to maintain verifiability of this article, the names of these early Pandya Kings have been omitted. We have a connected history of the Pandyas from the fall of Kalabhras during the middle of the 6th century. Kalittokai mentions that many ethnically different non Tamil Naga tribes such as Maravar, Eyinar, Oliar, Oviar, Aruvalur and Parathavar migrated to the Pandyan kingdom and started living there in the Third Tamil Sangam period 2000 years ago.. The Pandyan kings had the title Maran.

The following lists of the Pandya kings are based on the authoritative *A History of South India from the Early Times to the Fall of Vijayanagar* by K.A.N. Sastri, Oxford U Press, New Delhi (Reprinted 1998).

Early Pandyas

The following is a partial list of Pandyan emperors who ruled during the Sangam age:

- Nedunj Cheliyan I (Aariyap Padai Kadantha Nedunj Cheliyan)
- Pudappandiyan
- Mudukudumi Paruvaludhi
- Nedunj Cheliyan II
- Nan Maran
- Nedunj Cheliyan III (Talaiyaalanganathu Seruvendra Nedunj Cheliyan)
- Maran Valudi
- Musiri Mutriya Cheliyan
- Ukkirap Peruvaludi.

First Empire

After the close of the Sangam age, the first Pandyan empire was established by Kadungon in the 6th century by defeating the Kalabhras. The following chronological list of the Pandya emperors is based on an inscription found on the Vaigai riverbeds.

- Kadungon 560-590 A.D.

Kadungon was a Pandya king who revived the Pandya rule in South India in the 7th century CE. Along with the Pallava king Simhavishnu, he is credited with ending the Kalabhra rule, marking the beginning of a new era in the Tamil speaking region. Most historians, including R. C. Majumdar, state the period of Kadungon rule as 590-620 CE.

The Sangam literature mentions early Pandya dynasty, which is believed to have gone into obscurity during the Kalabhra interregnum. The dynasty was revived by Kadungon, who is considered as the first important Pandya ruler.

Not much is known about Kadungon. Most of the knowledge about him comes from the Velvikudi (or Velvikkud) inscription of the Pandya king Parantaka Nedunchadaiyan (also Nedunjadaiyan or Nedunchezhiyan). According to this inscription, Kadungon defeated several petty chieftains and destroyed "the bright cities of unbending foes". It describes him as the one who liberated the Pandya country from the Kalabhras and emerged as a "resplendent sun from the dark clouds of the Kalabhras". His defeat of Kalabhras (considered Jains or Buddhists) was hailed as the triumph of Brahminism.

Kadungon's title was "Pandyadhiraja", and his capital was Madurai. He was succeeded by his son Maravarman Avanisulamani.

- Maravarman Avani Culamani 590-620 A.D
- Cezhiyan Cendan 620-640 A.D
- Arikesari Maravarman Nindraseer Nedumaaran 670-710 A.D.

Arikesari Maravarman was a Pandyan king who ruled the ancient Tamil kingdom between 670 and 710 A.D. He was the successor of Jayantavarman(640-670A.D.). Arikesari was succeeded by his son Kochadaiyan Ranadhiran.

Conquests

He is credited with having defeated the Chera king in multiple battles. He also subjugated the recalcitrant Parathavar of the coastal areas and the inhabitants of the Kurunadu.

- Kochadaiyan Ranadhiran 710-735 A.D.

Kochadaiyan Ranadhiran (710-735 A.D.) was a Pandyan king. He was the son and successor of Arikesari Maravarman.

Conquests

He asserted his superiority over the Cheras and Cholas and subdued the Marathas in the city of Mangalapuram, the modern day Mangalore. He also started the hostilities with the Chalukyas of Badami and the Gangas. He also undertook a campaign against the Ay chieftains. He defeated them in Kurunadu in south Travancore and this earned him the allegiance of the Ay chief.

Arikesari Parankusa Maravarman Rajasimha I 735-765 A.DMaravarman Rajasimha I was an one of early Pandyan kings. He was the son and successor of Kochadaiyan Ranadhiran. He ruled over the Pandyan kingdom aggressively and gained territory by forging an alliance with Chitramaya against the Pallava king, Nandivarman Pallavamalla.

Wars and Conquests

Kongu Nadu

He defeated the ruler of Kongu Nadu and crossed the Cauvery to bring about the subjugation of Malakongam, which was situated between Trichy and Thanjavur districts. The Malava chieftain who suffered defeat gave up his daughter in marriage to Rajasimha.

Chalukya and Sripurusha

Rajasimha continued the onslaught into the Ganga kingdom of Sripurusha, beyond Pandikodumudi. Sripurusha sought the help of the Chalukya king Kirtivarman II. Both of them suffered defeats at the hands of this powerful invader from the south in 750 A.D. The Chalukya king then gave his daughter to Jatila Parantaka, the son of Rajasimha I.

- Parantaka Nedunjadaiyan 765-790 A.D
- Rasasingan II 790-800 A.D

- Varagunan I 800-830 A.D
- Sirmara Srivallabha 830-862 A.D.

Varagunavarman II 862-880 A.D Varagunavarman II was a Pandyan king who ruled the Tamil kingdom from 862-880 A.D..

Death

Varagunavarman tried to assert his independence but suffered defeat at the handsof Apaajita, the son of Pallava king Nripatunga at Sri Purambiyam near Kumbhakonam. He died shortly after and was succeeded by his younger brother Parantaka Viranarayan Sadaiyan in 880 A.D.

Parantaka Viranarayana 880-900 A.D

Maravarman Rajasimha II 900-920 A.D Maravarman Rajasimha II was the last Pandyan king of the first Pandyan empire. He was the son and successor of Parantaka Viranarayana. He ruled the Pandyan kingdom from 900 to 920 A.D.

Conquests

He opposed the Chola king of Thanjavur at Kodumbalur and plundered the Chera capital at Vanchi in Kongu Nadu.

Defeats

In 910 A.D he suffered defeat at the hands of Parantaka Chola I, the son of Aditya Chola. Parantaka totally invaded the Pandyan kingdom and earned the title *Maduraikonda*(the one who captured Madurai). Rajasimha appealed to Kassapa V, the king of Ceylon for assistance. But even the combined forces of the Pandyas and the Sinhalese suffered could not keep the Cholas at bay and they suffered a huge defeat in Vellur near Madurai.

After the successive defeats, Rajasimha II fled to Ceylon but then unable to secure refuge, he went to Kerala, as he himself had descended in part from a chera king where he spent the rest of his days keeping a low profile.

After the defeat of the Kalabhras, the Pandya kingdom grew steadily in power and territory. With the Cholas in obscurity, the Tamil country was divided between the Pallavas and the Pandyas, the river Kaveri being the frontier between them.

After Vijayalaya Chola conquered Thanjavur by defeating the Muttarayar chieftains around 850, the Pandyas went into a period of decline. They were constantly harassing their Chola overlords by occupying their territories. Parantaka I invaded the Pandya territories and defeated Rajasimha III. However, the Pandyas did not wholly submit to the Cholas despite loss of power, territory and prestige. They tried to forge various alliances with the Cheras and the Kings of Lanka and tried to engage the Cholas in war in order to free themselves from Chola supremacy. But right from the times of Parantaka I to the early 12th century up to the times of Kulottunga Chola I the Pandyas could not overpower the Cholas who right from AD 880-1210 remained the most powerful empire spread over South India, Deccan and the Eastern and Western Coast of India during this period.

Under the Cholas

The Chola domination of the Tamil country began in earnest during the reign of Parantaka Chola II. Chola armies led by Aditya Karikala, son of Parantaka Chola II defeated Vira Pandya in battle. The Pandyas were assisted by the Sinhalese forces of Mahinda IV. Pandyas were driven out of their territories and had to seek refuge on the island of Sri Lanka. This was the start of the long exile of the Pandyas. They were replaced by a series of Chola viceroys with the title *Chola Pandyas* who ruled from Madurai from c. 1020.

The following list gives the names of the Pandya kings who were active during the 10th century and the first half of 11th century. It is difficult to give their dates of accession and the duration of their rule. Nevertheless, their presence in the southern country requires recognition.

- Sundara Pandya I
- Vira Pandya I
- Vira Pandya II
- Amarabhujanga Tivrakopa
- Jatavarman Sundara Chola Pandya
- Maravarman Vikrama Chola Pandya
- Maravarman Parakrama Chola Pandya
- Jatavarman Chola Pandya
- Srivallabha Manakulachala (1101-1124)
- Maaravaramban Seervallaban (1132-1161)
- Parakrama Pandiyan (1161-1162)

- Kulasekara Pandyan III
- Vira Pandyan III
- Jatavarman Srivallaban (1175-1180)
- Jatavarman Kulasekaran I (1190-1216).

Jatavarman Kulasekaran I

Jatavarman Kulasekaran I. was a Pandyan king, who ruled regions of South India between 1190-1216 CE.

Accession and Background

Kulasekaran acceded to the Pandyan throne after his father Vikkirama Pandyan in 1190 CE. Vikkirama Pandyan had gained the throne of Madurai with the help of Kulothunga Chola III. Kulothunga had defeated the rebellion of Vira Pandyan and his Sri Lankan allies and awarded the throne to Vikkirama Pandyan. Vikkiraman's son Kulasekaran became the ruler in 1190.. He was a brother-in-law of the Chera prince Kothai Ravivarman.

War and Defeat

Kulasekaran was a vassal of the Chola empire. When Kulothunga was warring with Hoysalas in the north, he refused to pay tribute to the Cholas. This led to a Chola invasion in retribution. In 1205 CE, the Chola armies defeated the Pandyan army and sacked Madurai.

The ancient coronation hall of Pandyan kings was destroyed, the remains plowed with asses and sowed with weeds. Inscriptions found at Kudimiyanmalai and Cheranur give graphic descriptions of the invasion and the sacking of Madurai. Kulasekaran and his younger brothers fled Madurai to the *Palai* (desert wastes) lands. The invaders looted Madurai and distributed the wealth to the destitute.

Kulothunga performed a *Virabhishekam* (tribute of bravery) and crowned himself as *Thiribhuvana veeran* (Lord of Three Worlds). Kulasekaran surrendered to Kulothunga with his wife and son. Kulothunga acknowledged the surrender and gave his kingdom back. Madurai remained under Chola dominance till 1216 CE. These excesses of Kulothunga directly led to the later Pandyan reprisal under Kulasekaran's younger brother and successor Maravarman Sundara Pandyan I.

Distinction from other Kulasekarans

There are records of at least three later Pandyan kings bearing the same name *Jatavarman Kulasekaran*. This king is identified and distinguished using his *meikeerthi* which starts with the words *poovin kizhathi*. He is the Kulasekaran who donated the village *"Rajaghambeeera Chathurvedi Mangalaam"* to 1080 Brahmins in 1214 CE

Pandya Revival

The 13th century is the greatest period in the history of the Pandyan Empire. Their power reached its zenith under Jatavarman Sundara Pandyan in the middle of the 13th century. The foundation for such a great empire was laid by Maravarman Sundara Pandyan early in the 13th century.

Maravarman Sundara Pandyan (1216-1238)

Maravarman Sundara Pandyan I was a Pandyan king, who ruled regions of South India between 1216–1238 CE. He laid the foundation for the Pandya revival, after being dominated by the Cholas for several centuries.

Accession

Sundara Pandyan came to power in 1216 CE after his elder brother Jatavarman Kulasekara Pandyan. Kulasekara Pandyan was a vassal of the Chola King Kulothunga Chola III. He had opposed and been defeated by Kulothunga Chola III in 1205 CE, when the victorious Chola armies burned down the ancient Pandyan coronation hall in Madurai. This sowed the seed for revenge when Sundara Pandyan took power.

War against the Cholas

To avenge his brother's humiliation in the hands of the Kulothunga Chola III, Sundara Pandyan invaded the Chola kingdom soon after his accession. Kulothunga Chola III was nearing the end of his long 40 year reign and was hampered by old age and the swiftness of the Pandyan invasion. Sundara Pandyan sacked the Chola cities of Thanjavur and Uraiyur and drove both the Chola king and his crown prince Rajaraja Chola III into exile. To celebrate his victory he performed a *virabisheka* (lit. anointment of heroes) in the coronation hall of Cholas (*mudikondasolapuram*) at

Ayirattali in Thanjavur district. Later he marched his armies up to Chidambaram and camped at Pon Amaravathi. He commemorated his victories over the Cholas by conducting a *Thulabaram*-a form of Hindu worship where the devotee offers tribute in equal measure to his weight-at the Chidambaram temple.

Kulothunga Chola III appealed for aid to his son-in-law, the Hoysala monarch Veera Ballala II. Ballala sent an army under his son, the crown prince Vira Narasimha II. Buckling under the Hoysala threat Sundara Pandyan agreed to restore the Chola kingdom to Kulothunga, but only after the Cholas acknowledged his suzerainty. Sundara Pandyan's victories over Cholas are described in the *Thirukkolur* (in present day Tirunelveli district) inscriptions.

Second Pandyan Empire

Kulothunga made his formal submission to Pandyan rule in 1217 CE at Pon Amaravathi, ending nearly three centuries of Chola dominion over Tamil Nadu. This was the beginning of the Pandyan revival and the second Pandyan empire was born.. Kulothunga died the following year in 1218 CE and his successor Rajaraja Chola III was an incompetent ruler under whose rule the Chola kingdom finally crumbled.

In 1225 CE Sundara Pandyan defeated and drove away a company of Odda (Oriya) Soldiers who had invaded the Chola heartland and occupied Srirangam.. He allied himself with the kadava chieftain Kopperunchinga I against the Cholas and Hoysalas.

After the defeat and capture of Rajaraja Chola III at Tellaru in 1231 CE by Kopperunchinga, Vira Narasimha II intervened decisively against the Kadava-Pandiyan alliance by sending an army under his generals Appanna and Goppayya. Kopperunchinga was defeated and Raja Raja was restored to Chola throne in 1231 CE. While his generals were moving against Kopperrunchinga, Narasimha himself defeated Sundara Pandiyan at Mahendramangalam on the banks of Kaveri in 1231 CE.

Sundara Pandyan had to acquiese in the restoration of Raja Raja.. After Mahendramangalam, peace was made between the warring Chola, Hoysala, Kadava and Pandyan kingdoms and sealed by dynastic marriages.

Legacy and Titles

Under Sundara Pandyan, the Pandyan revival began and the second Pandyan empire rose. Before him, the Pandyas were the vassals of the Cholas and he laid the strong foundations for Pandyan dominance in the later parts of the 13th century. According to the Thiruvandipuram inscriptions he awarded himself the titles of *Kaliyugaraman* and *Adisayapandiyadevan*. The coins issued by him also bear the title of *sonadugondan* (Conquerer of Chola Country).

His meikeerthi begins with the words:

- Sundaravaramban Kulasekaran II (1238-1240)
- Maravarman Sundara Pandyan II (1238-1251)
- Jatavarman Sundara Pandyan (1251-1268)
- Maaravaramban Kulasekara Pandyan I (1268-1308)
- Sundara Pandyan IV (1309-1327)
- Vira Pandyan IV (1309-1345).

Bibliography

Adikaram, E. W.: *Early History of Buddhism in Ceylon,* D. S. Puswella, Migoda, 1946.

Agrawala, V. S.: *Shiva Mahadeva: The Great God,* Veda Academy, Varanasi, 1966.

Ahmad, Imtiaz: *State and Foreign Policy: India's Role in South Asia,* Vikas, New Delhi, 1993.

Ahmad, Jamil-ud-din: *Some Recent Speeches and Writings of Mr. Jinnah,* Lahore, Ashraf, 1952.

Aiyar, R. Krishnaswami: *Outlines of Vedaanta,* Chetana, Bombay, 1978.

Archer, W. G.: *The Kama Sutra,* Unwin Hyman, London, 1990.

Ashton, S.R. : *British Policy Towards the Indian States, 1905-1939,* London, Curzon, 1982.

Aurobindo, Sri: *Vyasa and Valmiki,* Acharya Press, Pondicherry, 1956.

Avalon, Arthur and Ellen: *Hymns to the Goddess,* Ganesh and Co., Madras, 1964.

Aziz, Ashraf: *Light of the Universe: Essays on Hindustani Film Music,* Three Essays Collective, New Delhi, 2003.

Bagchi, P. C.: *Studies in Dharmashastra,* University of Calcutta Press, Calcutta, 1939.

Bahadur, K.P.: *The Wisdom of Vedaanta,* Sterling Publishers Private Limited, New Delhi, 1996.

Banerjea, J. N.: *Pauranic and Vedanta Religion,* University of Calcutta, Calcutta, 1996.

Bankimchandra, C.: *Essentials of Dharma,* Sanskrit Book Depot, Calcutta 1979.

Basu, Manoranjan: *Dharmashastra: A General Study,* Shrimati Mira Basu, Calcutta, 1976.

Beaumont, Roger : *Sword of the Raj: The British Army in India, 1747-1947*, Indianapolis, Bobbs-Merrill, 1977.

Benjamin, Joseph : *Scheduled Castes in Indian Politics and Society*, New Delhi, Ess Ess Publications, 1989.

Bhattacharyya, B.: *Nispannayogavali of Mahapandita Abhyakara Gupta*, Oriental Institute, Baroda, 1949.

Borchert, Bruno: *Mysticism: Its History and Challenge*, Samuel Wiser, York Beach, 1994.

Bose, D. N.: *Dharmashastra: Their Philosophy and Occult Secrets*, Kali Press, Calcutta, 1965.

Bowle, John: *The Imperial Achievement: The Rise and Transformation of the British Empire*, Little, Brown, 1974.

Brockington, J. L.: *Righteous Rama: The Evolution of an Epic*, Oxford, London, 1984.

Bromley, D.: *Krishna Consciousness in the West*, Bucknell University Press, Lewisburg, 1989.

Brooks, E.: *The Original Analects: Sayings of Confucius and His Successors*. Columbia University Press, New York, 1988.

Bruhn, Klaus: *The Jina-Images of Deogarh*, MacMillan, Leiden, 1969.

Burke, Mary Louise: *Swami Vivekananda in America: New Discoveries*, Advaita Ashrama, Calcutta, 1966.

Chaudhary, M.: *Partition and the Curse of Rehabilitation*, Calcutta, Bengal Rehabilitation Organization, 1964.

Chaudhuri, Nirad: *Thy Hand, Great Anarch! India: 1921-1952*, London, Chatto & Windus, 1987.

Coomeraswamy, Ananda K.: *Buddha and the Gospel of Buddhism*, MacMillan, London, 1928.

Crawford, Cromwell S.: *Ram Mohan Roy: His Era and Ethics*, Acharya Press, New Delhi, 1984.

Dalton, Dennis : *Gandhi's Power : Nonviolence in Action*, New Delhi, OUP, 2001.

Danielou, Alain: *The Complete Kama Sutra*, Park Street Press, Rochester, 2000.

Dasgupta, Shahana: *Rani Lakshmibai: The Indian Heroine*, Rupa & Company, Calcutta, 2002.

Datta, V.N.: *Sati: Widow Burning in India*, Manohar, New Delhi, 1990.

David, M. D.: *John Wilson and his Institutions*, Mumbai, 1957.

De Bary: *Self and Society in Ming Thought*, Columbia University Press, New York, 1970.

De, Sushil Kumar: *Ancient Indian Erotics and Erotic Literature*, Firma K. L. Mukhopadhyay, Calcutta, 1959.

Deak, Istvan: *The Lawful Revolution: Louis Kossuth and the Hungarians 1848-1849*, Columbia University Press, 1979.

Dhar, Niranjan: *Vedanta and Bengal Renaissance*, Minerva Associates, Calcutta, 1977.

Dikshit, D.P. *Political History of the Chalukyas of Badami*. New Delhi: Abhinav, 1980.

Donat, K.: *Meditate the Tantric Yoga Way*, George Allen and Unwin, London, 1973.

Doniger, W.: *The Rig Veda: An Anthology*, Penguin, New York, 1981.

Duboi, Abbe: *Hindu Manners, Customs and Ceremonies*, Fifth Indian Impression, CUP, 1985.

Dwivedi, M.: *The Principal Upanishads*, Adyar Library, Madras, 1931.

Eaton, Richard M.: *Sufis of Bijapur, 1300-1700: Social Roles of Sufis in Medieval India*, Princeton University Press, Princeton, 1978.

Edwardes, Michael: *Battles of the Indian Mutiny*, London; B. T. Batsford Ltd., 1963.

Erickson, Erik H.: *Gandhi's Truth: On the Origins of Militant Nonviolence*, Norton, New York, 1970.

Farquhar, J.N.: *Modern Religious Movements in India*, Munshiram, New Delhi, 1967.

Fay, Peter Ward: *The Opium War, 1840-42*, University of North Carolina Press, 1975.

Fisher, Michael H.: *The Politics of British Annexation of India - 1757-1857*, Oxford, 1996.

Frauwallner, E..: *History of Indian Philosophy*, Motilal, Delhi, 1973.

Gambhirananda, S.: *Brahma Sutra Shamkar Bhasya*, Adavita Ashrama, Calcutta, 1977.

Gambhirananda, Swami: *Brahma Sutra Shamkar Bhasya*, Adavita Ashrama, Calcutta, 1977.

Gandhi, M. K.: *The Story of My Experiment With Trust*, Washington, Public Affairs Press, 1948.

Garbe, R.: *The Philosophy of Ancient India*, Chicago University Press, Chicago, 1899.

Goradia, Nayana: *Lord Curzon: The Last of the British Moghuls*, New Delhi, Oxford University Press, 1993.

Goudriaan, T.: *Ritual and Speculation in Early Tantrism*, State University of New York Press, New York, 1992.

Gough, A.E.: *The Philosophy of the Upanisads and Ancient Indian Metaphysics*, MacMillan, London, 1882.

Grant, G. P.: *Philosophy in the Mass Age*, Copp Clark, Toronto, 1959.

Grisenold, H.D.: *Insights into Modern Hinduism*, Oxford, New York, 1934.

Growse, F. S.: *The Ramayana of Tulasidasa*, Motilal Banarsidass, Delhi, 1995.

Gurumurthy, S. : *Hindu Heritage, Assimilative, Not Divisive*, Vigil, Madras 1993.

Haich, E.: *Sexual Energy and Yoga*, Aurora Fress, New York, 1982.

Hasan, Murhirul: *Legacy of a Divided Nation: India's Muslims Since Independence*, New Delhi, Oxford, 1997.

Hasan, Mushirul: *India's Partition: Process, Strategy and Mobilization*, New Delhi, Oxford UP, 1993.

Heifetz, Hank: *The Origin of the Young God: Kalidasa's Kumara-sambhava*, University of California Press, Berkeley, 1985.

Heimann, Betty: *Facets of Indian Thought*, Geroge Allen & Unwin, London, 1964.

Heinsath, Charles: *Indian Nationalism and Hindu Social Reform*, Princeton University Press, Princeton, 1964.

Heschel, J.: *God in Search of Man: A Philosophy of Judaism*, Noonday Press, New York, 1997.

Hirschman, Edwin: *White Mutiny: The Ilbert Bill Crisis in India and the Genesis of the Indian National Congress*, New Delhi, Heritage, 1980.

Hixon, L.: *Mother of the Universe: Visions of the Goddess, Tantric Hymns of Enlightenment*, Quest Books, Wheaton, 1994.

Hopkins, J.: *Kalachakra Tantra Rite of Initiation*, Wisdom Publications, Boston, 1982.

Hopkirk, Peter: *The Great Game: The Struggle for Empire in Central Asia*, Kodansha, 1992.

Hume, R.E.: *The Thirteen Principle Upanishads*, Oxford University Press, London, 1971.

Hutchins, Francis: *Spontaneous Revolution: The Quit India Movement*, New Delhi, Manohar, 1971.

Irene, S.: *Vedic Heritage Teaching Program*. Arsha Vidya Gurukulam, Coimbatore, 1994.

Iyar, K.: *Vedanta: The Science of Reality*, Ganesh and Co., Mardas, 1930.

Iyengar, B.K.S.: *Light on the Yoga Sutras of Patanjali*, Aquarian Press, London 1993.

Jacob, K.: *Religion and Ethics in Advaita*, C.M.S. Press, Kottayam, 1982.

Jafar, Malik Muhammad: *Jinnah as a Parliamentarian*, Lahore, Afzar Publications, 1977.

Jain, Kailash Chand, *Lord Mahavira and His Times*, Saraswati Press, Delhi, 1974.

James, Lawrence: *The Rise and Fall of the British Empire*, St. Martin's, 1997.

James, Robert Rhodes: *The British Revolution, 1880-1939*, New York, Knopf, 1976.

Jean, M.: *Tantrik Yoga*, The Aquarian Press, Wellingborough, 1970.

John, B.: *Mantras: Sacred Words of Power*, George Allen and Unwin, London, 1977.

John, Elsner: *Pilgrimage: Past and Present in the World Religions*, Harvard University Press, Cambridge, 1995.

John, K.: *The Origin and Development of the State Cult of Confucius*, Paragon Book, New York, 1966.

Karmarkar, D.: *Sankara's Advaita*, Karnatak University, Dharwar, 1976.

Kaushik, Asha : *Globalization, Democracy and Culture : Situating Gandhian Alternatives*, Jaipur, Pointer, 2002.

Kaviraj, G.: *Aspects of Indian Thought*, University of Burdwan, Calcutta, 1966.

Kavlekar, K.K. : *Non-Brahmin Movement in Southern India, 1873-1949*, Kolhapur, Shivaji University, 19790

Keith, A.B. : *Rigveda Brahmanas*, Harvard University Press, Cambridge, 1920.

Keith, Arthur Berriedale: *The Religion and Philosophy of the Veda and Upanishads*, MacMillan, Delhi, 1925.

Kishwar, Madhu : *Religion at the Service of Nationalism, and Other Essays*, OUP, Delhi, 1998.

Klaus, K.: *A Survey of Hinduism,* State University of New York Press, Albany, 1989.

Knipe, M.: *Hinduism: Experiments in the Sacred,* Harper, San Francisco, 1991.

Knott, K.: *Hinduism, A Very Short Introduction,* Oxford University Press, New York, 1998.

Kosambi, D. D. : *The Culture and Civilisation of Ancient India in Historical Outline,* London, Routledge and Kegan Paul, 1956.

Kottackal, Jacob: *Religion and Ethics in Advaita,* C.M.S. Press, Kottayam, 1982.

Kuiper, F.B.J. : *Aryans in the Rigveda,* Rodopi, Amsterdam, 1991.

Kuppuswamy, Sastri S.: *Compromises in the History of Advaitic Thought,* Kalyani Press, Madras, 1940.

Louis, Fischer: *Essential Gandhi: An Anthology of His Writings,* Vintage, New York, 1983.

Low, D. A. and Brasted, Howard: *Freedom, Trauma, Continuities: Northern India and Independence,* New Delhi, Sage Publications, 1998.

Maheshwari, Shriram: *Rural Development in India: A Public Policy Approach,* New Delhi, Sage, 1995.

Makhan, L.: *The Ramayana of Valmiki,* Munshiram Manoharlal, New Delhi, 1978.

Mathew, Arnold: *Culture and Anarchy,* The University Press, Cambridge, 1935.

Mayer, A. : *Caste in an Indian Village: Change and Continuity 1954-1992,* Delhi, OUF, 1996.

Mazumder, Sukhendu : *Politico-Economic Ideas of Mahatma Gandhi: Their Relevance in the Present Day,* New Delhi, Concept Pub., 2004.

Mearns, David J.: *Shiva's Other Children: Religion and Social Identity amongst Overseas Indians,* Sage, Walnut Creek, 1995.

Mearns, J.: *Shiva's Other Children: Religion and Social Identity amongst Overseas Indians,* Sage, Walnut Creek, 1995.

Mehra, Parshotam: *A Dictionary of Modern Indian History, 1707-1947*, New Delhi, Oxford University Press, 1985.

Metcalf, Thomas R.: *The Aftermath of the Revolt: India, 1857-1870*, Princeton, Princeton University, 1964.

Mohan, K.: *The Mahabharata*, Munshiram Manoharlal, Delhi 1997.

Mookerjee, Ajit: *Kali The Feminine Force*, Thames and Hudson, London, 1988.

Mookerji, Satkari: *Modern Polity and Vedanta*, Sanskrit College, Calcutta, 1972.

Moon, Penderel: *The British Conquest and Dominion of India*, London, Duckworth, 1989.

Morris-Jones, W.H.: *The Government and Politics of India*, London, Hutchinson, 1971.

Nanda, B. R. : *Gandhi and His Critics*, Oxford University Press, Delhi, 1993.

Neale, Walter C.: *Economic Change in Rural India: Land Tenure and Reform in the United Provinces, 1800-1955*, New Haven, 1962.

Nevile, P.: *Lahore: A Sentimental Journey*, New Delhi, Penguin, 1993.

Oddie, G.A. : *Hindu and Christian in South-East India*, London, Curzon Press, 1991.

Pathak, Dr S.P.: *Jhansi during the British Rule*, Ramanand Vidya Bhawan, Delhi, 1987.

Preston, Diana: *The Boxer Rebellion*, Berkley Books, 2000.

Raimundo Panikkar: *The Vedic Experience: Mantramanjari*, Longman Todd, London, 1977.

Raja, C. Kunhan : *The Taittiriya Sarvanukramani of Yaska*, Madras, 1931.

Ramamurti, A.: *Advaitic Mysticism of Sankara*, Visvabharati, Santiniketan, 1974.

Ranajit Guha: *A Construction of Humanism in Colonial India*, CASA, Amsterdam, 1993.

Renou, Louis: *The Nature of Dharmashastra*, Walker and Co., New York, 1997.

Robson, Brian: *Sir Hugh Rose and the Central India Campaign*, Sutton Publishing Ltd for the Army Records Society, UK, 2000.

Satyapal Verma: *Role of Reason in Sankara Vedanta*, Parimal Publication, Delhi, 1992.

Savarkar, Vinayak Damodar : *The Indian War of Independence* 1857 Rajdhani Granthagar, Delhi, 1988.

Scheftelowitz, Isidor : *Die Kasmirische Rezension von Katyayanas Sarvanukramani,* Zeitschrift fur Indologie und Iranistik, 1922.

Shukla, D. N.: *Vastu-Shastra,* Motilal Banarsidass, Delhi, 1966.

Singh, Birendra Kumar: *Early Chalukyas of Vatapi, circa A.D. 500 to 757*, Delhi, Eastern Book Linkers, 1991.

Smith, Col. J. T. : *Silver and the India Exchanges,* Effingham Wilson, London, 1876.

Strauss, L.: *Political Philosophy,* The Bobbs Merrill Co., New York, 1975.

Swami Vishnu Tirtha: *Devatma Shakti,* Swami Shivom Tirth, Rishikesh, 1962.

Talageri, Shrikant : *Aryan Invasion Theory and Indian Nationalism,* Voice of India, Delhi, 1993.

Tejomayananda, Swami: *Hindu Culture: An Introduction,* Chinmaya Publications, Piercy, 1993.

Thapar, Romila : *Ashoka and the Decline of the Mauryas,* London, Oxford University Press, 1961.

Thompson, Edward: *The Making of the Indian Princes,* Oxford University Press, London, 1943.

Trautmann, Thomas R.: *Kautilya and the Arthasastra: A Statistical Study,* Leiden, Brill, 1971.

Trimingham, J.: *Sufi Orders in Islam,* Oxford University Press, New York, 1998.

Utpat, V.N.: *Riddles of Buddha and Ambedkar,* Itihas Patrika Prakashan, Thane 1988.

Vable, D.: *The Arya Samaj. Hindu without Hinduism.* Vikas Publ., Delhi, 1983.

Vedalankar, Pandit Nardev : *Basic Teachings of Hinduism,* Veda Niketan, Durban, 1978.

Visvantha, K.: *Essentials of Hinduism,* Narosa Pub. House, New Delhi, 1989.

Wendy Doniger: *Siva: The Erotic Ascetic,* Oxford University Press, Delhi, 1998.

Zaidi, A. Moin: *Evolution of Muslim political Thought in India,* New Delhi: S. Chand, 1975.

Index

E

F

G

H

I

J

K

L

M

N

O

P

R

□□□